READING

- Comprehension - Spelling - Grammar - Review

5

Contents

Week 1
- Day 1 **Comprehension** Compare and contrast 2
- Day 2 **Comprehension** Compare and contrast 3
- Day 3 **Spelling** Vowel exceptions 4
- Day 4 **Spelling** Vowel exceptions 5
- Day 5 **Grammar** Types of nouns 6

Week 2
- Day 1 **Comprehension** Analyzing character actions 7
- Day 2 **Comprehension** Analyzing character actions 8
- Day 3 **Spelling** Endings: rse, rce 9
- Day 4 **Spelling** Endings: rse, rce 10
- Day 5 **Grammar** Demonstrative pronouns 11

Week 3
- Day 1 **Comprehension** Compare and contrast 12
- Day 2 **Comprehension** Compare and contrast 13
- Day 3 **Spelling** Endings: ent, ant 14
- Day 4 **Spelling** Endings: ent, ant 15
- Day 5 **Grammar** Commas in places and dates 16

Week 4
- Day 1 **Comprehension** Sequencing events 17
- Day 2 **Comprehension** Sequencing events 18
- Day 3 **Spelling** Endings: and, end, ond 19
- Day 4 **Spelling** Endings: and, end, ond 20
- Day 5 **Grammar** Verb phrases 21

Week 5
- Day 1 **Comprehension** Visualization 22
- Day 2 **Comprehension** Visualization 23
- Day 3 **Spelling** Suffix: fy 24
- Day 4 **Spelling** Suffix: fy 25
- Day 5 **Grammar** Punctuating abbreviations 26

Week 6
- Day 1 **Comprehension** Making inferences 27
- Day 2 **Comprehension** Making inferences 28
- Day 3 **Spelling** Homophones 29
- Day 4 **Spelling** Homophones 30
- Day 5 **Grammar** Verbal adjectives 31

Week 7
- Day 1 **Comprehension** Finding facts and information 32
- Day 2 **Comprehension** Finding facts and information 33
- Day 3 **Spelling** Endings: or, ure 34
- Day 4 **Spelling** Endings: or, ure 35
- Day 5 **Grammar** Punctuating dialogue 36

Week 8
- Day 1 **Comprehension** Word study 37
- Day 2 **Comprehension** Word study 38
- Day 3 **Spelling** Suffix: ic 39
- Day 4 **Spelling** Suffix: ic 40
- Day 5 **Grammar** Indefinite pronouns 41

Week 9
- Day 1 **Comprehension** Making inferences 42
- Day 2 **Comprehension** Making inferences 43
- Day 3 **Spelling** Silent letters 44
- Day 4 **Spelling** Silent letters 45
- Day 5 **Grammar** Modal adverbs 46

REVIEW 1
- Spelling 47
- Grammar 48
- Comprehension 50

Week 10
- Day 1 **Comprehension** Word study 52
- Day 2 **Comprehension** Word study 53
- Day 3 **Spelling** Suffix: ity 54
- Day 4 **Spelling** Suffix: ity 55
- Day 5 **Grammar** Interjections 56

Week 11
- Day 1 **Comprehension** Point of view 57
- Day 2 **Comprehension** Point of view 58
- Day 3 **Spelling** Compound words 59
- Day 4 **Spelling** Compound words 60
- Day 5 **Grammar** Commas before conjunctions 61

Week 12
- Day 1 **Comprehension** Analyzing character actions 62
- Day 2 **Comprehension** Analyzing character actions 63
- Day 3 **Spelling** Latin origins 64
- Day 4 **Spelling** Latin origins 65
- Day 5 **Grammar** Present and past perfect tense 66

Week 13
- Day 1 **Comprehension** Figurative language 67
- Day 2 **Comprehension** Figurative language 68
- Day 3 **Spelling** Suffix: ive 69
- Day 4 **Spelling** Suffix: ive 70
- Day 5 **Grammar** Commas and tag questions 71

Week 14
- Day 1 **Comprehension** Drawing conclusions 72
- Day 2 **Comprehension** Drawing conclusions 73
- Day 3 **Spelling** Ending: ish 74
- Day 4 **Spelling** Ending: ish 75
- Day 5 **Grammar** Using exclamation points 76

Week 15
- Day 1 **Comprehension** Cause and effect 77
- Day 2 **Comprehension** Cause and effect 78
- Day 3 **Spelling** Prefixes: un, dis, mis 79
- Day 4 **Spelling** Prefixes: un, dis, mis 80
- Day 5 **Grammar** Commas for direct address 81

Week 16
- Day 1 **Comprehension** Drawing conclusions 82
- Day 2 **Comprehension** Drawing conclusions 83
- Day 3 **Spelling** Plurals 84
- Day 4 **Spelling** Plurals 85
- Day 5 **Grammar** Avoiding shifts in tense 86

Week 17
- Day 1 **Comprehension** Main idea and details 87
- Day 2 **Comprehension** Main idea and details 88
- Day 3 **Spelling** Suffix: ist 89
- Day 4 **Spelling** Suffix: ist 90
- Day 5 **Grammar** Relative and interrogative pronouns 91

Week 18
- Day 1 **Comprehension** Summarizing 92
- Day 2 **Comprehension** Summarizing 93
- Day 3 **Spelling** Palindromes and portmanteaus 94
- Day 4 **Spelling** Palindromes and portmanteaus 95
- Day 5 **Grammar** Adverbs of degree 96

REVIEW 2
- Spelling 97
- Grammar 98
- Comprehension 100

Week 19
Day 1 **Comprehension** Cause and effect 102
Day 2 **Comprehension** Cause and effect 103
Day 3 **Spelling** Suffix: ous 104
Day 4 **Spelling** Suffix: ous 105
Day 5 **Grammar** Commas to separate parts of sentences 106

Week 20
Day 1 **Comprehension** Making connections 107
Day 2 **Comprehension** Making connections 108
Day 3 **Spelling** Plurals: s, ies 109
Day 4 **Spelling** Plurals: s, ies 110
Day 5 **Grammar** Adverbials of time 111

Week 21
Day 1 **Comprehension** Making predictions 112
Day 2 **Comprehension** Making predictions 113
Day 3 **Spelling** Adding to fer 114
Day 4 **Spelling** Adding to fer 115
Day 5 **Grammar** Future perfect tense 116

Week 22
Day 1 **Comprehension** Figurative language 117
Day 2 **Comprehension** Figurative language 118
Day 3 **Spelling** Endings: age, idge 119
Day 4 **Spelling** Endings: age, idge 120
Day 5 **Grammar** Commas to avoid misunderstanding 121

Week 23
Day 1 **Comprehension** Reading diagrams 122
Day 2 **Comprehension** Reading diagrams 123
Day 3 **Spelling** Suffixes: ment, ship, hood, dom 124
Day 4 **Spelling** Suffixes: ment, ship, hood, dom 125
Day 5 **Grammar** Sequence adverbs 126

Week 24
Day 1 **Comprehension** Fact or opinion? 127
Day 2 **Comprehension** Fact or opinion? 128
Day 3 **Spelling** Vowel sounds 129
Day 4 **Spelling** Vowel sounds 130
Day 5 **Grammar** Prepositions 131

Week 25
Day 1 **Comprehension** Audience and purpose 132
Day 2 **Comprehension** Audience and purpose 133
Day 3 **Spelling** Suffixes: ion, ian 134
Day 4 **Spelling** Suffixes: ion, ian 135
Day 5 **Grammar** Colons to introduce new information 136

Week 26
Day 1 **Comprehension** Reading diagrams 137
Day 2 **Comprehension** Reading diagrams 138
Day 3 **Spelling** Digraph: ch 139
Day 4 **Spelling** Digraph: ch 140
Day 5 **Grammar** Commas and dashes 141

Week 27
Day 1 **Comprehension** Audience and purpose 142
Day 2 **Comprehension** Audience and purpose 143
Day 3 **Spelling** Tricky words 144
Day 4 **Spelling** Tricky words 145
Day 5 **Grammar** Correlative conjunctions 146

REVIEW 3
Spelling 147
Grammar 148
Comprehension 150

Week 28
Day 1 **Comprehension** Main idea and details ... 152
Day 2 **Comprehension** Main idea and details ... 153
Day 3 **Spelling** Digraphs: oo, ou ... 154
Day 4 **Spelling** Digraphs: oo, ou ... 155
Day 5 **Grammar** Relative clauses ... 156

Week 29
Day 1 **Comprehension** Cause and effect ... 157
Day 2 **Comprehension** Cause and effect ... 158
Day 3 **Spelling** Digraphs: wh, ph, gh ... 159
Day 4 **Spelling** Digraphs: wh, ph, gh ... 160
Day 5 **Grammar** Capital letters in titles ... 161

Week 30
Day 1 **Comprehension** Making inferences ... 162
Day 2 **Comprehension** Making inferences ... 163
Day 3 **Spelling** Suffixes: ence, ance ... 164
Day 4 **Spelling** Suffixes: ence, ance ... 165
Day 5 **Grammar** Compound and complex sentences ... 166

Week 31
Day 1 **Comprehension** Figurative language ... 167
Day 2 **Comprehension** Figurative language ... 168
Day 3 **Spelling** Eponyms ... 169
Day 4 **Spelling** Eponyms ... 170
Day 5 **Grammar** Commas and parentheses ... 171

Week 32
Day 1 **Comprehension** Making connections ... 172
Day 2 **Comprehension** Making connections ... 173
Day 3 **Spelling** Suffix: ly ... 174
Day 4 **Spelling** Suffix: ly ... 175
Day 5 **Grammar** Adverbs and prepositions ... 176

Week 33
Day 1 **Comprehension** Fact or opinion? ... 177
Day 2 **Comprehension** Fact or opinion? ... 178
Day 3 **Spelling** que ... 179
Day 4 **Spelling** que ... 180
Day 5 **Grammar** Sentences: subject, verb, object ... 181

Week 34
Day 1 **Comprehension** Making connections ... 182
Day 2 **Comprehension** Making connections ... 183
Day 3 **Spelling** Word building ... 184
Day 4 **Spelling** Word building ... 185
Day 5 **Grammar** Active and passive voice ... 186

Week 35
Day 1 **Comprehension** Audience and purpose ... 187
Day 2 **Comprehension** Audience and purpose ... 188
Day 3 **Spelling** Loan words ... 189
Day 4 **Spelling** Loan words ... 190
Day 5 **Grammar** Sentence fragments ... 191

Week 36
Day 1 **Comprehension** Word study ... 192
Day 2 **Comprehension** Word study ... 193
Day 3 **Spelling** Prefixes: anti, circum, extra, semi ... 194
Day 4 **Spelling** Prefixes: anti, circum, extra, semi ... 195
Day 5 **Grammar** Punctuating sentences ... 196

REVIEW 4
Spelling ... 197
Grammar ... 198
Comprehension ... 200

ANSWERS ... 202

Year Planner

	Week 1	Week 2	Week 3	Week 4	Week 5	Week 6	Week 7	Week 8	Week 9
Comprehension	Compare and contrast	Analyzing character actions	Compare and contrast	Sequencing events	Visualization	Making inferences	Finding facts and information	Word study	Making inferences
Spelling	Vowel exceptions	Endings: rse, rce	Endings: ent, ant	Endings: and, end, ond	Suffix: fy	Homophones	Endings: or, ure	Suffix: ic	Silent letters
Grammar	Types of nouns	Demonstrative pronouns	Commas in places and dates	Verb phrases	Punctuating abbreviations	Verbal adjectives	Punctuating dialogue	Indefinite pronouns	Modal adverbs
Review	Spelling			Grammar			Comprehension		

	Week 10	Week 11	Week 12	Week 13	Week 14	Week 15	Week 16	Week 17	Week 18
Comprehension	Word study	Point of view	Analyzing character actions	Figurative language	Drawing conclusions	Cause and effect	Drawing conclusions	Main idea and details	Summarizing
Spelling	Suffix: ity	Compound words	Latin origins	Suffix: ive	Ending: ish	Prefixes: un, dis, mis	Plurals	Suffix: ist	Palindromes and portmanteaus
Grammar	Interjections	Commas before conjunctions	Present and past perfect tense	Commas and tag questions	Using exclamation points	Commas for direct address	Avoiding shifts in verb tense	Relative and interrogative pronouns	Adverbs of degree
Review	Spelling			Grammar			Comprehension		

	Week 19	Week 20	Week 21	Week 22	Week 23	Week 24	Week 25	Week 26	Week 27
Comprehension	Cause and effect	Making connections	Making predictions	Figurative language	Reading diagrams	Fact or opinion?	Audience and purpose	Reading diagrams	Audience and purpose
Spelling	Suffix: ous	Plurals: s, ies	Adding to fer	Endings: age, idge	Suffixes: ment, ship, hood, dom	Vowel sounds	Suffixes: ion, ian	Digraph: ch	Tricky words
Grammar	Commas to separate parts of sentences	Adverbials of time	Future perfect tense	Commas to avoid misunderstanding	Sequence adverbs	Prepositions	Colons to introduce information	Commas and dashes	Correlative conjunctions
Review	Spelling			Grammar			Comprehension		

	Week 28	Week 29	Week 30	Week 31	Week 32	Week 33	Week 34	Week 35	Week 36
Comprehension	Main idea and details	Cause and effect	Making inferences	Figurative language	Making connections	Fact or opinion?	Making connections	Audience and purpose	Word study
Spelling	Digraphs: oo, ou	Digraphs: wh, ph, gh	Suffixes: ence, ance	Eponyms	Suffix: ly	que	Word building	Loan words	Prefixes: anti, circum, extra, semi
Grammar	Relative clauses	Capital letters in titles	Compound and complex sentences	Commas and parentheses	Adverbs and prepositions	Sentences: subject, verb, object	Active and passive voice	Sentence fragments	Punctuating sentences
Review	Spelling			Grammar			Comprehension		

Week 1 Day 1 Comprehension

Above and Below

> **Compare and contrast**
> To compare and contrast information, look for the similarities and differences between details in the text.

Read the passage.

Put a box around the word that tells where the tunnels were.

Circle the nouns that tell what Jakob and Tibalt would have seen in the cave.

Highlight the word that tells in which part of the cave the stalactites were.

Jakob led Tibalt through the tunnels. There were guards all the way along. There wasn't much need for guards in this peaceful underground city, but they added to Zelig's power.

Jakob and Tibalt arrived at the crystal gardens. The huge cave was filled with beautiful limestone formations. The strange, pale shapes glittered in the light from the firefly lanterns. Long, thin stalactites hung from the roof, and chunky stalagmites rose up from the floor.

Color the adjectives that describe the stalactites.

Color the adjective that describes the stalagmites.

Highlight the word that tells in which part of the cave the stalagmites were.

Circle the correct answer.

1 How are stalactites and stalagmites **similar**?
- a Both form underwater.
- b Both form in limestone caves.
- c Both form on trees.
- d Both form on forest floors.

Color the correct answer in each of the following pairs.

2 Stalactites and stalagmites …
- a ○ are the same shape.   ○ are different shapes.
- b ○ grow in different directions.   ○ grow in the same direction.
- c ○ grow on the same part of the cave.   ○ grow on different parts of the cave.

RL.5.3 Compare and contrast two or more characters, settings, or events in a story or drama, drawing on specific details in the text.

Week 1 Day 2 Comprehension

Above and Below

Read the passage.

Circle the word that shows Jakob's home is underground.

Color what Jakob's family ate for supper.

Underline where Felda lived.

Below world

Jakob walked slowly home. From the tunnel, he could smell supper cooking on the fire. He opened the door to his dark, damp home chamber.

Della, Jakob's mother, was pouring mushroom stew into three bowls. "Supper will be ruined if we don't eat it now."

Above world

Felda lived in a large cottage in a small village. Her father, Baldric, was the village chief.

Jakob and Tibalt sat down with the villagers. They ate food with the most amazing tastes. Bread was mixed with herbs, and the fruits were sweet and juicy.

Highlight two adjectives that describe Jakob's home.

Put a box around the word that shows the relationship between Jakob and Della.

Circle the word that shows the relationship between Felda and Baldric.

Read the whole story

1. List at least one **similarity** between Jakob and Felda's lives.

_____

_____

2. How is Felda's home **different** from Jakob's?

_____

_____

_____

3. How is the food in the above world **different** from the food in the below world?

_____

_____

_____

RL.5.3 Compare and contrast two or more characters, settings, or events in a story or drama, drawing on specific details in the text.

Week 1 　Day 3 　Spelling

Vowel exceptions

Usually the letters **ea** make the long vowel sound **ee**; e.g., t**ea**m. Sometimes they make a **different sound**; e.g., br**ea**k. Usually the letters **ai** make the long vowel sound **ay**; e.g., p**ai**nt. Sometimes they make a **different sound**; e.g., s**ai**d. Usually the letters **ou** make the long vowel sounds **oo** or **ow**; e.g., w**ou**ld, b**ou**nce. Sometimes they make a **different sound**; e.g., c**ou**sin.

List

deaf
head
said
idea
meant
four
bread
bargain
thread
great
famous
wealth
cousin
nourish
really
break
curtain
dread
already
heavy

1 **Write the word.**

2 **Sort the words.**

　a Words with *ea*

　b Words with *ou*

　c Words with *ai*

3 **Fill in the missing letters.**

　a __ eal____　　**b** br_____d
　c m_____nt　　**d** co___s__n
　e __r__ak　　　**f** n____r__sh
　g f__m____s　　**h** d____f
　i a__re____y　　**j** g____t

4 **Name.**

　a 　**b** 　**c** 　**d**

Week 1 Day 4 Spelling

Vowel exceptions

1 Revise your spelling list from page 4. Underline the mistake. Write the word correctly.

a The audience applauded as the curtein fell. _____
b The chocolate mud cake was very hevy to eat. _____
c Our pet dog was old and def. _____
d Watching movies was a great ideea. _____
e There were fore cupcakes left over. _____
f Throughout his life he had saved all of his welth. _____
g He sed he would be home for dinner. _____
h Dad patted me on the hed as he walked past. _____
i We got a real bargein at the Venice Beach market. _____

Challenge words

2 Write the word.

deadly _____
dreamed _____
knead _____
meadow _____
couple _____
aisle _____
haiku _____
captain _____
trouble _____
boulder _____

3 Word clues. Which challenge word matches?

a open field of grass _____
b Japanese poem _____
c leader _____
d source of difficulty _____
e fatal _____
f large rock _____
g imagined _____
h corridor _____
i two people _____
j fold and stretch dough _____

4 Another way to say it. Which challenge word could replace the underlined word/s?

a The spider's bite is <u>lethal</u>. _____
b He walked hurriedly down the supermarket <u>lane</u> looking for rice. _____
c They lifted the <u>large rock</u> with a crane. _____
d She <u>fantasized</u> about a beach vacation, as the weather was cold. _____

Week 1 Day 5 Grammar

Types of nouns

Nouns that refer to general people, places, and things are called **common nouns**; e.g., girl, sheep, table. Nouns that name thoughts, qualities, and feelings are called **abstract nouns**; e.g., anger, kindness, patience. Nouns that refer to specific people, places, things, days, and months are called **proper nouns**; e.g., Sean, Paris, Washington Monument.

1 **Identify the type of noun.**

Shade the common nouns **red**, the abstract nouns **blue**, and the proper nouns **green**.

puzzlement Canadian Rosh confusion ears hair

2 **Complete each sentence with an abstract noun.**

A mature person shows _maturity_.

a A wise person shows _____.

b A successful person has _____.

c An angry person shows _____.

d A poor person lives in _____.

3 **Complete the sentences.**

a Someone from America is an _____.

b Someone from _____ speaks Italian.

c Someone from _____ speaks Portuguese.

d Someone from Russia speaks _____.

4 **Find the common nouns. Use the first letter of each word to make an abstract noun.**

a What do you wear on your head? _____

b What do we get from hens? _____

c What is a red or green fruit that grows on trees? _____

d What is a baby sheep called? _____

e What is a drink that is made from leaves? _____

f What is an empty space in the ground called? _____

The abstract noun is _ _ _ _ _ _.

Week 2 Day 1 Comprehension

Just Call Me Jungle Boy

Interpreting character behavior, feelings, and motivation
To interpret a character's feelings and what motivates them to behave in a certain way, look for clues in the text. The clues are usually in the words and punctuation.

Read the passage.

Highlight a group of words that shows how Oscar feels about his new home.

Circle the verb that shows how Mom feels about her new home.

Put a **box** around the adjective that describes how Georgia is feeling.

No way! Can't be! Please tell me this isn't happening. Help me someone! I look at my dad. His smile is so wide it covers his whole face. Mom is crying. My sister, Georgia, seems pretty upset too. Her mouth hangs open. Her eyes are bulging.

"Welcome to your new home," announces Dad. "What do you think, Oscar?"

"I … I … I don't know what to say," I stammer.

Underline the sentence that shows how Dad is feeling.

Circle the punctuation that emphasizes Oscar's feelings.

Color the verb that describes the way Oscar answers Dad.

Circle the correct answers.

1 How does Oscar **feel** about the family's new home? He …
   a loves it.   b thinks it is alright.   c doesn't like it.   d thinks it is haunted.

2 Which sentence from the text is the best **clue** to question 1's answer?
   a Her eyes are bulging.   b Please tell me this isn't happening.
   c Her mouth hangs open.   d What do you think Oscar?

3 Which punctuation emphasises Oscar's feelings?
   a .   b ,   c "   d !

4 Which adjective best describes how Dad **feels** about their new home?
   a enthusiastic   b disappointed   c curious   d upset

5 Which sentence is the best **clue** to question 4's answer?
   a Help me someone!   b His smile is so wide it covers his whole face.
   c Mom is crying.   d I look at my dad.

RL.5.1 Quote accurately from a text when explaining what the text says explicitly and when drawing inferences from the text.

Week 2 Day 2 Comprehension

Just Call Me Jungle Boy

Read the whole story

Read the passage.

Underline the words that show the narrator's opinion of Georgia's novel.

Highlight the words that show how Georgia feels about Nell's grandson.

We've been in our new home in the jungle for about two months now. It seems like forever though.

Georgia has discovered writing and writes great long letters to Tania. She's even started a novel—well she calls it a novel. Georgia doesn't care about Richard anymore. Not since she discovered Nell's earthy grandson. He's the same age as Georgia and she thinks he's gorgeous. Mom and Dad are pretty happy too. Dad's veggie garden is thriving and Mom's really into cooking.

Color the words that show how Georgia's feelings toward Richard have changed.

Underline the clue to how Mom feels about living in the jungle.

1 What is the narrator's **opinion** of Georgia's novel? Support your answer with evidence from the text.

_____
_____
_____

2 Explain why Georgia no longer cares about Richard.

_____
_____
_____

3 How can we tell that Mom now feels more positive about living in the jungle?

_____
_____
_____
_____

RL.5.1 Quote accurately from a text when explaining what the text says explicitly and when drawing inferences from the text.

Week 2 | Day 3 | Spelling

Endings: rse, rce

> Words that end in **rse** and **rce** have the same end sound; e.g., ho**rse**, fie**rce**.

List

horse
worse
purse
verse
force
scarce
fierce
reverse
sparse
adverse
course
diverse
source
converse
immerse
averse
terse
divorce
resource
pierce

1 Write the word.

_____

2 Sort the words.

a Words that end in *rse*

_____ _____
_____ _____
_____ _____
_____ _____
_____ _____
_____ _____

b Words that end in *rce*

_____ _____
_____ _____
_____ _____

3 Complete these words with *rse* or *rce*.

a reve_____   b divo_____
c dive_____   d sou_____
e imme_____   f spa_____
g pu_____   h fie_____
i resou_____   j ve_____

4 Complete each sentence with a list word.

a She rode her _____ daily on the farm.
b The shark looked _____ with its toothy grin.
c I read my favorite _____ from a poem before bed.
d The rain had been _____, so the crops were struggling.
e I like to _____ with my friends on the phone.
f My dad has an _____ reaction to peanuts.
g I will _____ myself to get up earlier tomorrow morning.
h The mess in my room is _____ today than it was yesterday.

L.5.2.E Spell grade-appropriate words correctly, consulting references as needed.

Week 2 Day 4 Spelling

Endings: rse, rce

1 **Revise your spelling list from page 9.** Which list word means?

a Where something begins _____
b To prick or break _____
c In short supply _____
d Strength or effort _____
e To completely cover in liquid _____
f Of different kinds or sorts _____

Challenge words

2 **Write the word.**

coarse _____
rehearse _____
traverse _____
reimburse _____
intersperse _____
coerce _____
disperse _____
commerce _____
enforce _____
reinforce _____

3 **Word clues.** Which challenge word matches?

a cover or cross _____
b scatter _____
c rough _____
d persuade _____
e trade _____
f add strength _____

4 **Hidden words.** Find the challenge word.

a herrehearseqreh _____
b foreenenforcecefo _____
c reimreimburseurse _____
d erserreinforceres _____

5 **Another way to say it.** Which challenge word could replace the underlined word/s?

a Dad bought me the skateboard and I will <u>pay</u> him later. _____
b Sophie and her friends will <u>practice</u> the play tonight. _____
c The fabric was <u>rough</u> and scratchy on her skin. _____
d Her brother would <u>bully</u> her into doing his chores for him. _____
e They will <u>scatter</u> the seeds over the soil. _____
f They <u>impose</u> the rules to keep the community safe. _____
g The ship had to <u>cross</u> the rough seas. _____
h Dad used more posts to <u>strengthen</u> the fence. _____

Week 2 Day 5 Grammar

Demonstrative pronouns

A **demonstrative pronoun** points out or "demonstrates" a particular person or thing; e.g., I want to do **that**. The demonstrative pronouns are **this**, **that**, **these**, and **those**.

1 Which pronoun correctly completes the sentence?

a (This, These) _____ is the one I want.
b I think (that, these) _____ are tastier.
c Was (these, that) _____ Maria I was talking to?
d (Those, This) _____ is the one I want, thank you.
e (That, Those) _____ are definitely his shoes.

2 Does the underlined pronoun refer to a person, or a thing?

a I don't want these oranges; I want <u>those</u>. _____
b Is <u>that</u> what you bought yesterday? _____
c Are <u>these</u> the cheapest you could find? _____
d Who is <u>that</u> walking down the road? _____
e <u>This</u> is the artist I was telling you about. _____

3 Circle the pronouns that correctly complete the sentences.

a (This/These) is for Harry, and (that/those) is for Sarah.
a (These/This) are mine, and (that/those) are his.

4 In the following sentences, underline the demonstrative pronouns.

a Who will help us set it up? Would you be prepared to do that?
b What kind of books does he like to read? Do you think he'd read this?
c Which should I choose? I like the color of these, but I prefer the shape of those.

L.5.1 Demonstrate command of the conventions of standard English grammar and usage when writing or speaking.

Week 3 Day 1 Comprehension

Hitler's Daughter

Compare and contrast
To compare and contrast information, look for the similarities and differences between details in the text.

Read the passage.

(Circle) where the children live.

Put a box around what Ben thinks of Anna's choice.

Highlight Mark's reaction to Anna's choice.

The novel is set against a backdrop of muddy roads and mournful cows in modern-day, rural Australia. The story of Hitler's daughter is told by Anna, one of four children who wait at the same bus shelter every morning. One of the children usually chooses a character and Anna makes up a story about the character. But one morning Anna decides that she will choose the character. The other children are surprised when she announces who the subject of her story will be. Ben thinks it's a "cool" choice; Mark protests that Hitler did not have a daughter; and little Tracey does not know who Hitler is.

Underline who usually gets to choose the character.

Color who chooses the character for the new story.

Circle the correct answers.

1. What **similar** experiences do Anna and Mark share? Choose two answers.
   a They catch the same bus to school.   b They are both good storytellers.
   c They both live in rural Australia.   d They both know about Hitler's daughter.

2. How is Anna's latest story **different** from her previous ones? This time she ...
   a is not choosing the character.   b is choosing the character.
   c is reading it from a book.   d is acting it out.

3. How is Ben's reaction to Anna's announcement **different** from Mark's? Ben is ...
   a less enthusiastic than Mark.   b more surprised than Mark.
   c more upset than Mark.   d more enthusiastic than Mark.

4. Which word is the **clue** to question 3's answer?
   a protests   b surprised   c cool   d know

Week 3 Day 2 Comprehension

Hitler's Daughter

Read the passage.

Underline words that show how the reviewer thinks readers will respond to the story.

Highlight Mark's fear.

Put a box around two characters in Jackie French's story.

Circle the character in Anna's story.

The story unfolds over a series of gray, wet mornings, and like the children at the bus stop, the reader can't wait to hear what happens next. French explores the effect that Anna's story has on Mark, a naturally curious boy. Anna's story gets him thinking, and he begins to take a greater interest in news bulletins about suffering in some faraway country. He fears that, like Hitler's daughter, he could be part of something evil without realizing it.

But the character who is really at the center of this novel is Heidi, Hitler's daughter. Heidi is a young girl who loves her father, even though he publicly rejects her.

1. According to the reviewer, how will the reader's response to Anna's story be **similar** to the children's?

_____

_____

2. How does Mark believe that his situation might be **similar** to Hitler's daughter's?

_____

_____

_____

3. Describe a **difference** between Mark and Heidi.

_____

_____

_____

RL.5.3 Compare and contrast two or more characters, settings, or events in a story or drama, drawing on specific details in the text.

Week 3 Day 3 Spelling

Endings: ent, ant

> Many words that end in **ent** and **ant** have the same end sound; e.g., tal**ent**, eleph**ant**.

List

tenant
rodent
instant
urgent
pendant
tyrant
fluent
entrant
violent
evident
assistant
serpent
elegant
applicant
ancient
significant
magnificent
radiant
apparent
opponent

1 Write the word.

2 Sort the words.

a ent

b ant

3 Complete these words with *ent* or *ant*.

a eleg_____
b urg_____
c radi_____
d tyr_____
e magnific_____
f entr_____
g viol_____
h evid_____
i ten_____
j serp_____
k applic_____
l signific_____

4 Underline the spelling mistake. Write the word correctly.

a The serpant slithered over the hot ground. _____
b The aincient ruins were being preserved for future generations. _____
c Guinea pigs are a type of rodant. _____
d My mom's assistent answered her phone when I rang. _____
e She wore a pretty silver pendent. _____
f I didn't like the movie as it was very vilent. _____
g My brother was my opponant in the tennis tournament. _____

L.5.2.E Spell grade-appropriate words correctly, consulting references as needed.

Week 3 Day 4 Spelling

Endings: ent, ant

1 Revise your spelling list from page 14. Which list word means?

a A bully
b Brutal
c Bright and shining
d Enemy
e Obvious
f A snake
g Very old
h Helper
i Grand
j Able to speak easily
k Important
l A small mammal

Challenge words

2 Write the word.

warrant
turbulent
inhabitant
instrument
participant
equivalent
persistent
extravagant
nutrient
adamant

3 Word clues. Which challenge word matches?

a resident
b determined
c equal to
d excessive
e rough
f player

4 Hidden words. Find the challenge word.

a prohwarrantent
b qtinstrumentmant
c extrnutrientant
d nuextravagantent

5 Complete the sentence.

a Bananas are a good source of the _____ potassium.
b Sam will be a _____ in the running race.
c The ocean was _____ due to the rough wind.
d The policeman had a _____ for his arrest.
e Her _____ parents spoiled her with a new camera.
f My favorite musical _____ is the flute.
g He is an _____ of South Carolina.
h She was _____ in her swimming training.

Week 3 Day 5 Grammar

Commas in places and dates

When writing the names of places and dates, use **commas** to separate:
- the name of the street, city, and state; e.g., 4441 Jackson Street, Dallas, Texas
- the name of the day, month, and year; e.g., Friday, January 22, 2018.

1 **Fill in the commas in the following sentences.**

a Our plane landed in Phoenix Arizona.

b My grandparents live in an old house on Woodrow Drive Richmond Virginia.

c Their business address is 112 Madison Avenue Santa Monica California.

d We are leaving for Europe on Saturday February 3.

e My sister was born on May 14 2010.

f The incident occurred on Tuesday October 6 1998.

2 **Circle the punctuation errors in the following sentences.**

a My friend lives at 2387, Beach Road, Tampa.

b The Rio Olympics started on August, 5, 2016.

c On Tuesday, September, 27, 2016, they moved to Raleigh, North Carolina.

d The American Civil War started on April, 12, 1861, and ended on May, 13, 1865.

e They have been living at 6396, Lincoln Avenue since April 21, 2015.

3 **Answer the following questions, using the correct punctuation.**

a When were you born?
I was born on _____

b What is your address?
My address is _____

c When will you turn twelve?
I'll turn twelve on _____

L.5.2 Demonstrate command of the conventions of standard English capitalization, punctuation, and spelling when writing.

Week 4 Day 1 Comprehension

The Wolf and the Seven Kids

Sequencing events
To identify the sequence of events in a text, look at numbers and words that give clues to the order in which things happen.

Read the passage.

Circle where the mother goat was.

Underline what the wolf said to the kids.

Put a box around why the kids wouldn't open the door.

Highlight what the wolf did after he left the goats' cottage.

Color what the wolf did after he chewed on the chalk.

One day when the mother goat was out, her kids heard a gruff voice outside.

"Open the door," said the gruff voice. "Your mother is home with food." The little kids were hungry, but they remembered their mother's warning.

"You are not our mother," they bleated. "Your voice is too gruff!"

The wolf went away and chewed on a lump of chalk to make his voice softer. Then he returned to the goats' cottage.

1 Write numbers next to the following sentences to show the order in which the events happened.

a ☐ The wolf said he was the kids' mother.
b ☐ The mother goat went out and left her kids at home.
c ☐ The kids said the wolf's voice was too gruff.
d ☐ The wolf left the cottage.
e ☐ The kids would not let the wolf in.
f ☐ The wolf returned to the goats' cottage.
g ☐ The wolf came to the goats' cottage.
h ☐ The wolf made his voice softer.

RL.5.1 Quote accurately from a text when explaining what the text says explicitly and when drawing inferences from the text.

Week 4 | Day 2 | Comprehension

The Wolf and the Seven Kids

Read the passage.

Underline the first thing the wolf did.

Highlight what the wolf did after rubbing chalk on his feet.

Put a box around what the kids did when they thought the wolf was their mother.

The wolf went away and rubbed chalk on his feet. He returned to the cottage a third time.

"My little treasures, it's your mother with yummy treats."

The kids saw the white feet, heard the soft voice, and flung the door open. The wolf chased the terrified kids, catching them one by one and putting them in a sack. When he caught the sixth kid, he threw the sack over his shoulder and made for his lair. The seventh, smallest kid remained hidden.

When the mother goat returned, she found the frightened kid and left at once to find the others.

Underline what the wolf did with the kids when he caught them.

Circle where the wolf went after he had caught the kids.

Color what happened when the mother goat returned.

1 Rewrite the following paragraph so that the events are in the correct order.

> He caught six of them and put them in a sack. The kids let the wolf in. The seventh kid, who had remained hidden, told his mother what had happened. He came back to the cottage a third time. The wolf then threw the sack over his shoulder and made for his lair. The wolf rubbed chalk on his feet. The wolf chased the terrified kids.

RL.5.1 Quote accurately from a text when explaining what the text says explicitly and when drawing inferences from the text.

Week 4 · **Day 3** · **Spelling**

Endings: and, end, ond

> Some words that end in the letters **and**, **end**, and **ond** have the same end sound; e.g., thous**and**, leg**end**, alm**ond**. There are **exceptions** to this rule; e.g., dem**and**, pret**end**, bey**ond**.

List

1 Write the word.

- second _____
- legend _____
- husband _____
- depend _____
- intend _____
- beyond _____
- pretend _____
- defend _____
- island _____
- thousand _____
- garland _____
- amend _____
- almond _____
- diamond _____
- suspend _____
- descend _____
- command _____
- attend _____
- offend _____
- demand _____

2 Sort the words.

a and
_____   _____
_____   _____
_____   _____

b end
_____   _____
_____   _____
_____   _____
_____   _____
_____   _____

c ond
_____   _____
_____   _____

3 Complete the words with *and*, *end*, or *ond*.

a sec_____   b garl_____
c husb_____ d alm_____
e int_____   f susp_____
g pret_____ h comm_____
i dem_____   j off_____

4 Word clues. Which list word matches?

a a precious jewel
_____

b a type of nut
_____

c the man a woman is married to
_____

d to move downwards
_____

e to make-believe
_____

f to protect from harm
_____

g land surrounded by water
_____

h chain or wreath made of flowers
_____

L.5.2.E Spell grade-appropriate words correctly, consulting references as needed.

Week 4 Day 4 Spelling

Endings: and, end, ond

1 **Revise your spelling list from page 19.** Which list word means?
  a. Number equal to ten times one hundred
  b. To act falsely so as to trick
  c. To be present at
  d. To hang from a higher position
  e. To trust or rely on
  f. To tell forcefully or to order

Challenge words

2 **Write the word.**

errand
reprimand
reverend
reprehend
Holland
correspond
commend
comprehend
apprehend
vagabond

3 **Hidden words.** Find the challenge word.
  a. auiderrandiyub
  b. iaydcommenduajb
  c. ausbvagabondoiyn
  d. asccorrespondaois
  e. asinreverendopaih
  f. asdjcomprehendo

4 **Word clues.** Which challenge word matches?
  a. scold
  b. capture
  c. communicate

5 **Another way to say it.** Which challenge word could replace the underlined word/s?
  a. The policewoman will <u>capture</u> the criminal.
  b. I will teach my dog to <u>understand</u> sit, beg, and roll.
  c. Mom will <u>tell me off</u> for being late.
  d. My brother received a <u>scolding</u> for his messy room.
  e. Amsterdam is a city in <u>the Netherlands</u>.
  f. Everyone will <u>compliment</u> his brilliant recital.
  g. His story will <u>match</u> with hers.
  h. The <u>vagrant</u> slept in the park at night.

Week 4 Day 5 Grammar

Verb phrases

A **verb phrase** is a **group of words** that is **built around a main verb**. Most verb phrases are formed by placing one or more **auxiliary verbs before** the **main verb**; e.g., The children **have been** **playing** outside.
Verb phrases are also formed by placing **to** in front of the **main verb**. These verb phrases only make sense in a sentence when they are used with other verbs; e.g., I **am going** **to** **eat** this pizza.

1 Highlight the main verb in the following verb phrases.

- a is ironing
- b is hoping to catch
- c will dance
- d can trust
- e could see
- f might slip
- g will be sleeping
- h have been swimming
- i was trying to work

2 Complete the sentences with a verb phrase from Question 1. Use each phrase once.

- a You _____ him as he is very honest.
- b We _____ a herd of antelope in the distance.
- c The girl _____ her shirt to remove any creases.
- d He asked them to be quiet because he _____.
- e If we put on some music, the children _____.
- f The children _____ by the time we arrive.
- g Be careful going down the slope as you _____.
- h They _____ in their new pool.
- i My dad _____ the biggest fish.

3 Complete the verb phrases in the following sentences with an auxiliary verb from the box. Use each verb once.

- a You really _____ have finished that by now.
- b I _____ going to call him on my cell phone.
- c She _____ been to Europe many times before.
- d We _____ hoping you would be able to help us.
- e The parrots _____ squawking in the trees.
- f The eggs _____ break if you drop the carton.

| were |
| are |
| should |
| am |
| might |
| has |

L.5.1 Demonstrate command of the conventions of standard English grammar and usage when writing or speaking.

Week 5 Day 1 Comprehension

Gregory Blaxland's Journal

Visualization

Visualizing the people, places, things, and events you read about helps build better understanding of the text. Looking for key words in the text helps create the images.

Read the passage.

Highlight the words and phrases that helped you visualize the exploration party as they set out from Mr. Blaxland's farm.

Color the words and phrases that helped you visualize the exploration party setting up camp.

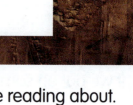

Underline the words and phrases that helped you visualize the crossing of the Nepean River.

On Tuesday, May 11, 1813, Mr. Gregory Blaxland, Mr. William Wentworth, and Lieutenant Lawson, attended by four servants, with five dogs, and four horses laden with provisions, ammunition, and other necessaries, left Mr. Blaxland's farm at the South Creek, for the purpose of endeavoring to effect a passage over the Blue Mountains, between the Western River, and the River Grose.

They crossed the Nepean, or Hawkesbury River, at the ford, on to Emu Island, at four o'clock p.m., and having proceeded through forest land and good pasture, encamped at five o'clock at the foot of the first ridge.

1 Read the passage again. As you do so, visualize what you are reading about. Draw a picture of the images you create.

Setting out from Mr. Blaxland's farm

RI.5.1 Quote accurately from a text when explaining what the text says explicitly and when drawing inferences from the text.

Week 5 Day 2 Comprehension

Gregory Blaxland's Journal

Read the passage.

Underline the words and phrases that helped you visualize the exploration party traveling towards Grose Head.

On the following morning (May 12), as soon as the heavy dew was off, which was about nine o'clock, the exploration party proceeded to ascend the ridge at the foot of which they had camped the preceding evening. Here they found a large lagoon of good water, full of very coarse rushes.

The high land of Grose Head appeared before them at about seven miles distance, bearing north by east. They proceeded this day about three miles and a quarter, in a direction varying from south-west to west-north-west, but, for a third of the way, due west. The land was covered with scrubby brush-wood, very thick in places, with some trees of ordinary timber, which much incommoded (inconvenienced) the horses.

Highlight the words and phrases that helped you visualize the exploration party reaching the top of the ridge.

1 Read the passage again. As you do so, visualize what you are reading about. Draw a picture of the images you create.

Heading towards Grose Head	Reaching the top of the ridge

RI.5.1 Quote accurately from a text when explaining what the text says explicitly and when drawing inferences from the text.

Week 5 · Day 3 · Spelling

Suffix: fy

> Many verbs end in the suffix **fy**, which means to make or do something; e.g., to make liquid → lique**fy**.

List ① **Write the word.**

- verify _____
- amplify _____
- satisfy _____
- glorify _____
- gratify _____
- justify _____
- qualify _____
- notify _____
- signify _____
- modify _____
- classify _____
- horrify _____
- simplify _____
- mystify _____
- terrify _____
- magnify _____
- identify _____
- beautify _____
- certify _____
- liquefy _____

② **Complete these list words.**

- a sim_____
- b gra_____
- c cla_____
- d jus_____
- e amp_____
- f sig_____
- g liq_____
- h bea_____
- i ide_____
- j mys_____

③ **Rewrite the syllables in the correct order.**

- a fy/sa/tis _____
- b ue/liq/fy _____
- c fy/i/mod _____
- d ri/fy/ter _____
- e mys/fy/ti _____
- f pli/fy/sim _____
- g ni/sig/fy _____
- h i/grat/fy _____
- i ti/fy/jus _____
- j fy/no/ti _____
- k ni/mag/fy _____
- l ti/cer/fy _____

④ **Underline the spelling mistake. Write the word correctly.**

- a The speakers will amplifie the sound in the auditorium. _____
- b We will magnyfy the ant to see it better. _____
- c We had to notefy everyone of the new starting time. _____
- d The mess in my room will horify my mother! _____
- e We added some fresh flowers to bewtify the room. _____
- f We could identifie the food by the delicious smell. _____
- g I like to classifie my stamps by colors. _____
- h I tried to justifie why I should be allowed to stay up later. _____

Week 5 Day 4 Spelling

Suffix: fy

1 **Revise your spelling list from page 24.** Which list word means?

a To recognize
b To make sure something is true
c To tell about
d To praise, honor, or worship
e To make something appear larger
f To endorse or guarantee

Challenge words

2 **Write the word.**

specify
pacify
unify
crucify
rectify
intensify
dignify
personify
electrify
diversify

3 **Word Clues.** Which challenge word matches?

a to give honor or prestige
b to shock
c to indicate explicitly
d to bring together
e give human characteristics to something

4 **Hidden words.** Find the challenge word.

a cruscrucifyaosu
b sifydiversifyasug
c divepacifypac
d aiysrectifysiyu

5 **Complete the sentence.**

a We will _____ the flowers in our creative writing.
b The fake lightning will _____ the stage.
c The pacifier worked to _____ the baby.
d I will _____ the situation by explaining the mistake.
e The business will _____ into luxury yachts.
f I will _____ the color jumper I would like.
g The hard times would _____ the family.
h I will not _____ your accusation with a response!

L.5.2.E Spell grade-appropriate words correctly, consulting references as needed.

Week 5 Day 5 Grammar
Punctuating abbreviations

An **abbreviation** is a shortened form of a word or phrase. It is usually followed by a period; e.g., Mister = Mr., Street = St., Nevada = Nev.

1 Draw lines to match the words or phrases to their abbreviations.

a Monday — R.I.
b Montana — mi.
c for example — M.D.
d Road — fwy.
e Rhode Island — Mon.
f medical doctor — Mont.
g Maryland — Miss.
h mile — e.g.
i Mississippi — Rd.
j freeway — Md.

2 Fill in the periods in the following sentences.

a Our friends' address is 16 George Washington Dr , Miami, Fla
b Philadelphia, Pa Is where you can see the famous Liberty Bell
c I added 6 oz butter and 1 tsp vanilla essence to the mixture
d The invitation was addressed to Dr and Mrs Butler
e The special offer is available between Jan and Apr next year
f Washington, D C is the capital city of the U S
g The sign on the door said Prof J S Wright

3 In each sentence, circle the word that has the wrong punctuation. Write it correctly.

a My aunt and uncle live in Los Angeles, calif _____
b The pilot's name was capt Maria Ashworth. _____
c Martin Luther King, jr was born in Atlanta. _____

Week 6 Day 1 Comprehension

Gold

Making inferences
Use clues in the text to make inferences (form opinions). The clues help you find the answers that are hiding in the text.

Read the passage.

Highlight the words that tell what James Marshall was doing when he discovered gold.

Circle the word that suggests that America experienced more than one gold rush.

On January 24, 1848, James Marshall found flakes of gold while building a timber mill at Coloma in California. News of the find soon spread, and there followed the first and biggest gold rush in America.

After Marshall's discovery, about 400,000 people traveled to California in search of gold. Before the gold rush, San Francisco was a small town. It quickly became a city. People built roads, churches, and schools. They also built new steamships and railroads.

Underline the words that show that California's population increased after 1848.

Put a **box** around two words that describe San Francisco before and after the gold rush.

Circle the correct answers.

1 Which is the best **inference**? James Marshall …
  a did not know he had found gold.
  b was searching for gold.
  c discovered gold by accident.
  d hid his gold in a timber mill.

2 Which group of words is the **clue** to question 1's answer?
  a On January 24, 1848
  b while building a timber mill
  c at Coloma in California
  d After Marshall's discovery

3 Which is the best **inference**?
  a America experienced more than one gold rush.
  b There had been several gold rushes in America before 1848.
  c There had been one gold rush in America before 1848.

4 Which word is the **clue** to question 3's answer?
  a Before   b After   c biggest   d first

RI.5.1 Quote accurately from a text when explaining what the text says explicitly and when drawing inferences from the text.

Week 6 | Day 2 | Comprehension

Gold

Read the passage.

Circle the key word that tells why gold can be easily shaped.

Color the word that shows how gold alloy is different from pure gold.

Put a **box** around the metals that are added to gold to make rose gold.

Gold is a useful decorative metal. It does not tarnish or corrode. It is extremely malleable, so artists can easily shape it. Other metals, such as iron, are not very malleable.

People measure the purity of gold in carats. Pure gold is 24 carats.

Gold in jewelry is usually gold alloy, which is harder than pure gold. The three most popular gold alloys are white gold, yellow gold, and rose gold. White gold is gold mixed with silver, nickel, or palladium. Yellow gold is gold mixed with copper and silver. Rose gold is gold mixed with yellow gold and 25% copper.

Underline the type of gold that results from adding copper and silver to gold.

Highlight three metals that can be added to gold to make white gold.

1. We can **infer** that gold is a good metal to use in jewelry-making. What are the **clues**?

_____
_____
_____
_____

2. We can **infer** that the gold used to make jewelry does not always look the same. What **evidence** is there in the text to support this statement?

_____
_____
_____
_____
_____

RI.5.1 Quote accurately from a text when explaining what the text says explicitly and when drawing inferences from the text.

Week 6 Day 3 Spelling

Homophones

Homophones are words that sound the same but are **spelled differently** and have **different meanings**; e.g., where, we're, wear.

List

peace _____
piece _____
guest _____
guessed _____
past _____
passed _____
you _____
ewe _____
horde _____
hoard _____
sweet _____
suite _____
wary _____
weary _____
steal _____
steel _____
bridle _____
bridal _____
patients _____
patience _____

1 Write the word.

2 Fill in the correct list words.

a The _____ had correctly _____ where his bedroom was. (guessed, guest)

b The chocolates in the hotel _____ are _____ and delicious. (sweet, suite)

c We halved the _____ of cake to keep the _____ between the two siblings. (peace, piece)

d There was a _____ of people trying to find the _____ of old coins. (hoard, horde)

3 Unscramble these list words.

a oyu _____ b dohre _____
c iepce _____ d eltsa _____
e spadse _____ f etius _____
g rwya _____ h rdibla _____
i intspate _____ j uesdegs _____

4 Underline the mistake. Write the word correctly.

a My grandparents horde old newspapers dating back to 1975. _____
b We walked right passed the store. _____
c The horse whinnied as his bridal was too tight. _____
d The guessed arrived at the hotel too early to check in. _____
e The group was working toward world piece. _____
f The you bleated loudly as we walked through the field. _____
g The chocolate brownie was suite and moist. _____
h We were wary after our long hike in the wilderness. _____

L.5.2.E Spell grade-appropriate words correctly, consulting references as needed.

Week 6 Day 4 Spelling

Homophones

1 Revise your spelling list from page 29.

Write the missing syllable.

a _____/tience
b wea/_____
c _____/dle
d _____/dal
e wa/_____

2 Name.

a
b
c

Challenge words

3 Write the word.

morning _____
mourning _____
principle _____
principal _____
weather _____
whether _____
compliment _____
complement _____
stationary _____
stationery _____

4 Word Clues. Which challenge word matches?

a to praise _____
b climate _____
c dawn _____
d static _____
e a belief _____
f pen and paper _____

5 Hidden words. Find the challenge word.

a ourmorningingn _____
b whewhethermou _____
c cipaprincipalprin _____
d ompcomplimente _____

6 Complete the sentences using challenge words.

a We are unsure _____ the _____ will be sunny tomorrow.
b The customer gave the chef a _____ on his ability to _____ his meal with tasty sides.
c We didn't know that in the _____ we would be _____ the loss of our pet.
d The _____ cupboard was always _____ in the office.

30 L.5.2.E Spell grade-appropriate words correctly, consulting references as needed.

Week 6 Day 5 Grammar

Verbal adjectives

> Some verbs that end in **ing** and **ed** can be used as adjectives; e.g., a **boring** story, a **bored** child.

1 In the following sentences, highlight the adjectives.

a   We saw a flashing light up ahead.
b   The kitten made mewling sounds.
c   I poured chilled soda into the glass.
d   She had a worried look on her face.

2 Turn the verbs in parentheses into adjectives.

a   She said she didn't want to become a (laugh) _____-stock.
b   The comedian told us an (amuse) _____ story.
c   He turned around with a (surprise) _____ look on his face.
d   The fire fighter rescued the dog from the (burn) _____ building.

3 Sort the phrases. Are the underlined words being used as verbs, or adjectives?

> a <u>changing</u> situation   has been <u>changing</u>   was <u>damaged</u>   <u>damaged</u> goods
> to <u>confuse</u>   a <u>confusing</u> story   a <u>completed</u> task   has been <u>completed</u>

Verbs	Adjectives

4 In the following sentences, turn the relative clause into an adjective. Write the new sentence.

The girl, <u>who was blushing</u>, apologized.   *The <u>blushing</u> girl apologized.*

a   The tree, <u>which was flowering</u>, made a beautiful sight.
_____

b   The spoons, <u>which had been damaged</u>, are in the packet.
_____

L.5.1 Demonstrate command of the conventions of standard English grammar and usage when writing or speaking.

Week 7 | Day 1 | Comprehension

Fitness

Finding facts and information
To find facts and information in a text, ask the questions **Who? What? Where?** or **When?** The answers can be clearly seen in the text.

Read the passage.

Circle the longest race in athletics.

Highlight the place where the first Olympic marathon was held.

Put a box around the Greek soldier who ran from Marathon to Athens.

The marathon is the longest running race in athletics.

The first Olympic marathon was held in Athens in 1896. It was based on the legend of Pheidippides, a Greek soldier who ran approximately 25 miles carrying a message from the town of Marathon to Athens in 490 BC.

At the 1908 Olympic Games, the distance was set at 26.2 miles, which was the distance from Windsor Castle to the stadium in London.

Circle the year in which the first Olympic marathon was run.

Underline the distance an Olympic marathon runner must cover.

Color the place from which the marathon started in 1908.

Circle the correct answers.

1 **Where** was the first Olympic marathon held?
 a London b Windsor c Athens d Rio de Janeiro

2 **When** did Pheidippides run from Marathon to Athens?
 a 1908 b 490 BC c 1896 d 409 BC

3 **Who** was Pheidippides? Pheidippides was a Greek …
 a athlete. b wrestler. c sailor. d soldier.

4 **How long** is an Olympic marathon?
 a 26.2 miles b 20.2 miles c 22.6 miles d 25 miles

5 Between **which** two places was the 1908 Olympic marathon run?
 a Marathon and Athens b Windsor Castle and London
 c London and Oxford d Lincoln Castle and London

RI.5.1 Quote accurately from a text when explaining what the text says explicitly and when drawing inferences from the text.

Week 7 Day 2 Comprehension

Fitness

Read the passage.

Highlight which drugs are illegal.

Color the words that tell which drugs are legal.

Circle the word that describes the taking of illegal drugs.

Some athletes take performance-enhancing drugs to gain an advantage over their competitors. This is illegal.

Some drugs are legal for athletes, such as those for treating injuries. Others are banned because they improve performance and are dangerous to an athlete's health. Taking these drugs is called doping—it is a way of cheating.

The World Anti-Doping Agency promotes the fight against doping in sport. National anti-doping agencies regularly test athletes to find out if they are taking banned drugs.

Put a box around the organization that helps to fight against the taking of illegal drugs in sport.

<u>Underline</u> how anti-doping agencies make sure athletes are not taking banned drugs.

① **Which** drugs that athletes sometimes take are illegal?

② **Which** drugs are athletes allowed to take?

③ **Which** organisation helps to fight against doping in sport?

④ **How** do anti-doping agencies make sure athletes are not taking banned drugs?

RI.5.1 Quote accurately from a text when explaining what the text says explicitly and when drawing inferences from the text.

Week 7 Day 3 Spelling

Endings: or, ure

The letters **or** and **ure** at the **end of a word** often make the sound **er**; e.g., flav**or**, cult**ure**.

List ① **Write the word.**

vapor
culture
armor
flavor
pasture
clamor
texture
future
lecture
figure
valor
nurture
rigor
furniture
sculpture
leisure
tumor
moisture
creature
torture

② **Sort the words.**

a Words that end in *or*

b Words that end in *ure*

③ **Fill in the missing letters.**

a fur___it___ ___ ___
b l___ ___s___re
c ar___ ___r
d t___mo___
e p___ ___tu ___
f ___a___o___
g m___ ___st___ ___e
h ___ ___rtu___ ___

④ **Name.**

a

b

c

d

34 L.5.2.E Spell grade-appropriate words correctly, consulting references as needed.

Week 7 Day 4 Spelling

Endings: or, ure

1 **Revise your spelling list from page 34.** Complete each sentence with a list word.
   a The _____ of the rock was rough and scratchy.
   b The _____ on the ground showed that it had been raining.
   c Reading was her favorite _____ activity.
   d She saved money so that in the _____ she could buy a computer.
   e Strawberry is his favorite _____ of milkshake.
   f My dad received a medal of _____ for his bravery in the war.
   g They enforced the new law with great _____.
   h They are carving a _____ of a bear out of stone.
   i The _____ skaters practiced their routine daily.
   j For a tiny _____, the cicada certainly makes a lot of noise!

Challenge words

2 **Write the word.**
   departure _____
   signature _____
   fervor _____
   neighbor _____
   composure _____
   rupture _____
   exposure _____
   temperature _____
   agriculture _____
   miniature _____

3 **Word clues.** Which challenge word matches?
   a autograph _____
   b fever _____
   c farming _____
   d leaving _____
   e tiny _____
   f person next door _____

4 **Hidden words.** Find the challenge words.
   a sureexposureexp _____
   b vorffervorvofe _____
   c surocomposureco _____
   d rapprruptureure _____

5 **Another way to say it.** Which challenge word could replace the underlined word?
   a The <u>break</u> in the dam wall caused a flood. _____
   b Diana kept her <u>self-control</u> during the angry fight. _____
   c The reporter was working on a story about the <u>unveiling</u> of underworld crime. _____

Week 7 Day 5 Grammar

Punctuating dialogue

Dialogue is a **conversation** between two or more people. **Quotation marks (" ")** are placed around the speaker's words, including any punctuation; e.g., Alex said**, "I**s the ride over yet, Sarah?**"** Also remember that:
- A speaker's **first word** always begins with a **capital letter**, even if it comes after a comma
- A **new speaker** needs a **new paragraph**.

1 Fill in the quotation marks in the following dialogue.
a What are you doing with that spade? I asked.
b I'm going to dig for treasure, replied my little brother.
c Oh, yes, I said, and where do you think it's buried?
d In the vegetable patch, said Marco, under the cabbages.

2 Fill in the missing punctuation in the following dialogue.
a "Where's Marco " asked Mom.
b "In the garden " I said "digging for treasure "
c "Not in my vegetable patch, I hope " said Mom.

3 Punctuate the following dialogue.
a What do you think you're doing   yelled Mom
b Digging for treasure replied Marco, innocently
c My beautiful cabbages   wailed Mom You've destroyed them
d But they were in the way said Marco I had to dig them up to find the treasure

Week 8 Day 1 Comprehension

Have You Misplaced Half a Million Dollars?

Word study
You can work out the meaning of words using clues in the text.

Read the passage.

In the first sentence, circle two words that are similar in meaning.

Is there a chance you could have misplaced more than $550,000 from lost bank accounts or life insurance policies? That's how much is waiting to be claimed by three Americans who are living or who have lived in Jefferson County, Texas, and we want to reunite these people with their money.

Underline the amount of money waiting to be claimed.

Highlight the prefix in the words reunite and reunited.

The total unclaimed money pool has risen to a record $610 million with 20,000 new additions to the database in the past year. So even if you have searched before, now is the time to search again and be reunited with your lost money.

Circle the correct answers.

1. In paragraph 1, which word helps us understand what "misplaced" means?
   - a chance
   - b lost
   - c areas
   - d bank

2. In paragraph 2, what is meant by the term "money pool"?
   - a a place where money is washed
   - b a machine that counts money
   - c a pond with money floating on it
   - d a collection of money

3. Which group of words is the best clue to question 2's answer?
   - a a record $610 million
   - b the database
   - c 20,000 new additions
   - d the past year

4. In paragraph 2, how does the prefix "re-" change the meaning of the word "united"? It means the people will ...
   - a never be united with their money.
   - b be parted from their money.
   - c be united with their money again.
   - d have to wait for their money.

L.5.4.A Use context as a clue to the meaning of a word or phrase.

Week 8 | Day 2 | Comprehension

Have You Misplaced Half a Million Dollars?

Read the passage.

Highlight the words that describe Ms. Rickard's job.

In paragraph 1, put a box around the word that is similar in meaning to often.

Ms. Delia Rickard, a Chairwoman at the Federal Reserve Bank of Dallas, said, "If you've changed addresses frequently, or had a number of bank accounts or life insurance policies, there might be money waiting to be claimed by you."

"There might also be money to be claimed by you under the deceased estate of somebody who has died and left you money."

"Searching for the lost money is quick and easy, and you could soon find money that you had long forgotten about," Ms. Rickard said.

Underline the words that help to explain what a deceased estate is.

Color the phrase that is similar in meaning to looking for.

1. Which words tell us that Ms. Rickard has a high position at the Federal Reserve Bank?
   _____

2. What does the word "frequently" mean?
   _____

3. What does it mean if someone is "deceased"?
   _____

4. Which words in the text helped you work out the meaning of the word "deceased"?
   _____
   _____

L.5.4.A Use context as a clue to the meaning of a word or phrase.

Week 8 Day 3 Spelling

Suffix: ic

> A **suffix** is added to the end of a word to make a new word with a slightly different meaning. Some words can be **turned into adjectives** by adding the suffix **ic**; e.g., hero → hero**ic**. The suffix **ic** is often in nouns and adjectives that come from **Greek**, **Latin**, or **French**; e.g., hero**ic**.

List

music
poetic
tragic
topic
plastic
basic
artistic
public
tonic
magnetic
heroic
romantic
dramatic
angelic
specific
symbolic
historic
fantastic
academic
horrific

1 Write the word.

2 Complete the sentence with a list word.

a She plays beautiful _____ on the piano.
b If it's not private, it's _____.
c The old building is of _____ importance.
d My photos aren't that good as my camera is pretty _____.
e Something that has the power to attract things is _____.
f A dove is _____ of peace.
g He chose an interesting _____ for his speech.
h The juice is in a _____ bottle.

3 Fill in the missing syllables.

a po/et/_____
b hor/rif/_____
c _____/a/dem/_____
d ar/_____/_____
e an/_____/ic
f ton/_____
g _____/tas/tic
h ro/_____/tic
i trag/_____
j he/_____/_____

4 Write the list words in alphabetical order.

L.5.2.E Spell grade-appropriate words correctly, consulting references as needed.

Week 8 Day 4 Spelling

Suffix: ic

1 **Revise your spelling list from page 39.** Which list word means?

a Noble and courageous _____

b Having to do with education _____

c Sound with tones and rhythms that can be listened to and enjoyed _____

d A medicine that brings back one's strength _____

e Out of the ordinary and exciting _____

f Showing skill in creating _____

Challenge words

2 **Write the word.**

realistic _____
mechanic _____
strategic _____
optimistic _____
automatic _____
enthusiastic _____
scientific _____
sympathetic _____
democratic _____
photographic _____

3 **Hidden words.** Find the challenge word.

a tomioptimisticoa _____
b phophotographica _____
c thenthusiasticasn _____
d asunsympatheticy _____
e istirealisticreal _____
f ficscientificscui _____
g cratdemocraticde _____
h memmechanicme _____
i matautomaticauto _____
j egicstrategicstrat _____

4 **Complete the sentence.** Which challenge word matches?

a The _____ experiment taught them how plants grew.

b It was a _____ move to keep their best swimmer until last.

c The _____ doors opened when a bug flew in front of the sensor.

d He brought his camera and other _____ equipment.

e The _____ repaired our car.

f She was very _____ about her chances.

g He was kind and _____ to his sad friend.

h Mom was _____ about my sporting abilities.

Week 8 Day 5 Grammar

Indefinite pronouns

Indefinite pronouns refer to people and things in a **general way**. This is usually because the people or things have already been named or don't need to be; e.g., Either **everyone** goes, or **no one** goes. When an indefinite pronoun comes before a noun, it does the work of a determiner; e.g., **Both dogs** are at the vet.

1 Complete each sentence with an indefinite pronoun from the box. Use each pronoun once.

> something   most   none   some

a These strawberries are delicious, but _____ are sweeter than others.
b I quickly had _____ to eat before I went to basketball practice.
c I looked in the box for a chocolate, but there were _____ left.
d By the next morning, _____ of the ice had melted.

2 Circle the verb that correctly completes the sentence.

a Nobody (dance, dances) as gracefully as Alexi.
b Some of them (has, have) ordered pasta for lunch.
c Many of the children (want, wants) to play basketball.
d Each of them (was, were) hoping to win the main prize.

3 Complete the puzzle with indefinite pronouns.

> nobody both one everybody
> any none many anybody each

Across:
2. Yes! That's the ____!
4. I looked, but there were ____ left.
7. Has ____ seen my pencil?
8. Are there ____ in the cupboard?

Down:
1. I hope ____ comes to my party.
3. There was ____ in the shop.
5. They ____ have their own room.
6. I ate not one, but ____ cupcakes.

L.5.1 Demonstrate command of the conventions of standard English grammar and usage when writing or speaking.

Week 9 Day 1 Comprehension

Modern Wonders

Making inferences
Use clues in the text to make inferences (form opinions). The clues help you find the answers that are hiding in the text.

Read the passage.

Circle what the tallest buildings in the world are called.

Underline what made it possible to build very tall structures.

Modern skyscrapers are the tallest buildings in the world. Modern building materials make it possible to build such tall structures.

Developers built the first modern skyscrapers in New York City during the 1800s. The population in the city was growing rapidly, but because it sat on an island, there wasn't much space for new buildings. The only way to make room was to build taller buildings.

Put a box around where New York City is situated.

Color when the first skyscrapers in New York City were built.

Circle the correct answers.

1. Which is the best **inference**? In ancient times there were no …
   a buildings.   b skyscrapers.   c tall structures.   d cities.

2. Which sentence is the best **clue** to question 1's answer?
   a Modern building materials make it possible to build such tall structures.
   b Modern skyscrapers are the tallest buildings in the world.
   c The only way to make room was to build taller buildings.

3. Which is the best **inference**? New York City is surrounded by …
   a mountains.   b forests.   c water.   d farmland.

4. Which word is the **clue** to question 3's answer?
   a skyscrapers   b structures   c materials   d island

5. Which is the best **inference**? There have been skyscrapers in New York City for …
   a about 100 years.   b about 150 years.   c exactly 100 years.   d five centuries.

Week 9 Day 2 Comprehension

Modern Wonders

Read the passage.

Burj Dubai is a modern skyscraper in the United Arab Emirates. It is the tallest human made structure in the world.

Burj Dubai is 2,683 feet tall. The tower contains apartments, hotels, shops, swimming pools, and offices. It has an observation deck on level 124. More than 7,000 people, mainly from India, Pakistan, Bangladesh, China, and the Philippines, worked to build Burj Dubai.

The architects invented a new structural system to build the tower. They had to consider differences between ground level and the building's final height—the temperature can vary up to 46°F, humidity can differ by 30%, and the air can be 10% thinner.

Circle the word that suggests that people live in Burj Dubai.

Highlight the word that shows that people can buy things in Burj Dubai.

Underline where the people who built Burj Dubai came from.

Color the difference in temperature between ground level and Burj Dubai's final height.

1 We can **infer** that people live in Burj Dubai. Which word is the **clue**?

_____

2 What can we **infer** about the people who worked to build Burj Dubai? Support your answer by quoting from the text.

_____
_____
_____

3 What **evidence** is there to **suggest** that the height of Burj Dubai caused problems for the architects?

_____
_____
_____

RI.5.1 Quote accurately from a text when explaining what the text says explicitly and when drawing inferences from the text.

Week 9 Day 3 Spelling
Silent consonants

> A **silent consonant** is a letter that is **not pronounced** in a word; e.g., lam**b**, solem**n**, this**t**le.

List
- debt
- doubt
- lamb
- sandwich
- glisten
- solemn
- column
- soften
- answer
- whose
- subtle
- succumb
- muscle
- fascinate
- crescent
- Wednesday
- rhyme
- thistle
- whistle
- moisten

1 Write the word.

2 Underline the silent consonants in each word.
- a sandwich
- b solemn
- c subtle
- d fascinate
- e debt
- f whistle
- g whose
- h rhyme
- i moisten
- j thistle
- k glisten
- l column
- m lamb
- n muscle
- o answer
- p Wednesday
- q doubt
- r crescent
- s soften
- t succumb

3 Unscramble these list words.
- a ensmol
- b utbdo
- c sletiht
- d sctrcnee
- e csbmucu
- f netsiom
- g ftsnoe
- h ebtd
- i hsowe
- j euslbt
- k wdanscih
- l tewshil
- m rewsna
- n elcsum

4 Underline the spelling mistake. Write the word correctly.
- a Wenesday is in the middle of the week.
- b My right leg musle hurt after I finished running.
- c I made a chicken and cheese sanwich for my lunch.
- d She saw the water glissen in the sunlight.
- e Thomas likes to wistle as he walks to the skate park.
- f No words ryme with orange and silver.
- g I read a funny colum in the magazine.
- h The stories about the ancient pharaohs fasinate me.

L.5.2.E Spell grade-appropriate words correctly, consulting references as needed.

Week 9 Day 4 Spelling

Silent consonants

1 Revise your spelling list from page 44. Which list word means?
- a To give in to; yield
- b To make slightly wet
- c To not know for sure
- d To attract and hold the interest of
- e Serious in appearance or mood
- f A plant with purple flowers

Challenge words

2 Write the word.
- abscess
- assignment
- campaign
- foreign
- government
- psychology
- pneumonia
- receipt
- raspberry
- mortgage

3 Hidden words. Find the challenge word.
- a aiccampaignasihc
- b supnpneumoniai
- c fgovgovernmenta
- d aiusgtreceiptaosu
- e mortmortgagega
- f aseaassignmenta

4 Word clues. Which challenge word matches?
- a task
- b people in authority
- c ulcer
- d from overseas

5 Complete the sentence.
- a The reporter's _____ is to interview the politician.
- b English was a _____ language to our new French neighbor.
- c The T-shirt she wore was the color of a _____.
- d He was interested in _____ because he wanted to know how the mind worked.
- e The shop assistant handed me a _____ after I purchased new clothes.
- f The dentist told me the pain was caused by an _____.

L.5.2.E Spell grade-appropriate words correctly, consulting references as needed.

Week 9 Day 5 Grammar

Modal adverbs

Adverbs add meaning to verbs, adjectives, and other adverbs. **Modal adverbs** show **possibility**, or how certain we are about something. This is called modality; e.g., I will **definitely** be going! (certain), I will **probably** be going (uncertain).

1 Circle the modal adverb in each sentence.

a They obviously want us to enter the competition.
b Those are possibly the tallest giraffes I've ever seen.
c You surely don't mean to stay in your pajamas all day!
d She was clearly surprised to see us there.
e That is undoubtedly the best route to take.
f He evidently does not wish to speak to you.

2 How certain is it that the following events will take place? Write certain or uncertain in the spaces.

a He will definitely be playing in the grand final. _____
b Perhaps they will let us go home early today. _____
c I will certainly be watching that program again. _____
d We will probably go to the zoo tomorrow. _____
e Clearly, this is going to take a long time to complete. _____

3 Circle the phrase that best describes an apple.

a probably a healthy snack   b definitely a healthy snack   c possibly a healthy snack

4 Complete the following sentences. Include the modal adverb in parentheses in your sentence.

a Wearing a hat when you're in the sun _____
_____ (definitely)

b Doing your cello practice before dinner _____
_____ (probably)

L.5.1 Demonstrate command of the conventions of standard English grammar and usage when writing or speaking.

REVIEW 1: Spelling

Spelling

> Use this review to test your knowledge. It has three parts—**Spelling**, **Grammar**, and **Comprehension**. If you're unsure of an answer, go back and read the rules and generalizations in the blue boxes.

You have learned about:
- vowel exceptions
- endings: and, end, ond
- endings: or, ure
- endings: rse, rce
- suffix: fy
- suffix: ic
- endings: ent, ant
- homophones
- silent letters

1 In each sentence, the spelling error has been underlined. Write the correct spelling. 2 marks

  a "First, I want to see the <u>fierse</u> lion," I announced. _____

  b The Pyramid of Kukulkan is an <u>anciant</u> temple and the center of Chichen Itza. _____

  c This year, our family will <u>attand</u> the Circleville Pumpkin Show in Ohio. _____

  d Tourists like to learn about the <u>cultor</u> and traditions of the countries they visit. _____

2 Which word correctly completes this sentence? 1 mark

The _____ wait in the lobby to see the well-known pediatrician.

  a patience   b patient   c patients   d patient's

3 This sentence has one word that is incorrect. Write the correct spelling. 1 mark

My mother is a famos computer engineer who works at MIT. _____

4 Write the vowel digraphs to correctly complete these words. 2 marks

  a s___d   b c___sin   c h___vy   d thr___d

5 Circle the correct word to complete each sentence. 3 marks

  a The artist was very (specify/specific) about how to set up for the exhibition.

  b We dressed up as truly (horrify/horrific) characters for Halloween.

  c Our microscope is able to (magnify/magnetic) tiny objects for us to examine.

6 This sentence has one word that is incorrect. Write the correct spelling. 1 mark

Salar de Uyuni continues to fasinate visitors.

_____

Your score ☐ 10

REVIEW 1: Grammar

Grammar

You have learned about:

- nouns
- verb phrases
- punctuating dialogue
- demonstrative pronouns
- abbreviations
- indefinite pronouns
- commas
- adjectives
- modal adverbs

1 In each sentence, circle the abstract noun and underline the proper noun. 2 marks

a She asked Ava to show more maturity.

b My father spent his childhood in Chicago.

c I first had the idea last Friday while I was waiting for the bus.

d The artist, Michelangelo, was a man of great talent.

2 Complete each sentence with the correct word in parentheses. 2 marks

a _____ is the book I chose. (This, These)

b I thought _____ were the best. (this, these)

c _____ is my favorite restaurant. (That, Those)

d Are _____ the pencils I gave you? (that, those)

3 Fill in the commas in the following sentences. 2 marks

a The ski resort is near Denver Colorado.

b We last went skiing in December 2017.

c Our new address is 2817 Jackson Avenue Atlanta Georgia.

d We moved into our new house on Tuesday September 27 2016.

4 Complete each sentence so that it makes sense. 2 marks

a The children _____ making decorations for the party.

b This time tomorrow, we _____ be enjoying ourselves at Disney World.

c We _____ baked three cakes for the fundraiser.

d I had _____ waiting for 30 minutes before the bus arrived.

REVIEW 1: Grammar

Grammar

5 **In each sentence, circle the word that has the wrong punctuation. Write it correctly.** 1 mark

   a I often see mrs Kowalski when I go to the shops. _____

   b I have an appointment with dr Jackson tomorrow. _____

6 **In each sentence, turn the verb in parentheses into an adjective.** 3 marks

   a This is the most (bore) _____ book I've ever read.

   b Last year the region was hit by a (devastate) _____ earthquake.

   c Some of the tasks were very (challenge) _____ .

   d We had an (amaze) _____ view from our balcony.

   e The toy airplane had a (damage) _____ wing.

   f I had a (boil) _____ egg for breakfast.

7 **Fill in the missing punctuation in the following sentences.** 4 marks

   a What would you like for dinner   asked Mom

   b Fold your clothes said Margie, and then put them in the drawer

8 **Complete the following sentence with TWO pronouns from the list:** *everything, something, nothing, everybody, somebody, nobody.* 2 marks

I asked **a** _____ , but **b** _____ was willing to help me.

9 **Complete the second sentence in each pair with a modal adverb from the box. The two sentences should be similar in meaning. Use each word once.** 2 marks

| definitely | undoubtedly | probably | perhaps |

   a I might buy a driverless car. _____ I'll buy a driverless car.

   b I've decided to buy the car. I will _____ buy the car.

   c There's a chance I'll buy the car. I will _____ buy the car.

   d It is without doubt the fastest car. It is _____ the fastest car.

Your score ☐ / 20

REVIEW 1: Comprehension

Summer Camp

Read the passage and then use the comprehension skills you have learned to answer the questions.

"Come on, Tash!" Leah called. "It's a four-hour drive back, in case you've forgotten!"

I looked up apprehensively, and gave a sigh of relief when I saw the smile on Leah's face. After the way I'd acted, I was lucky she was even talking to me.

Leah had always been my best friend. We were almost like sisters.

This year, we had both been excited about going on our first summer camp together. But I didn't count on how much trouble I would cause between us in those three days!

It all started the evening we arrived. Leah was telling the girls in our cabin about her plans for her birthday party—she wanted to have a pool party with a clown act. I thought that was pretty lame and without thinking, I blurted out, "Clown acts are for babies!"

The others started laughing and I joined in, even though I noticed that Leah's face had turned the color of a beetroot.

I should have apologized then, but I didn't. Instead, spurred on by the reactions of the other campers, I would whisper "Bozo" every time I saw Leah. In the end, she was so upset she went to see our camp leader, Ling.

"Tash, we need to talk," Ling announced gravely that night.

She told me that my teasing had made Leah very unhappy. I was overcome with shame when I realized that the only reason I had carried on with the teasing was because of the laughs I got from other campers. Leah was my best friend and I hadn't taken her feelings into consideration at all. I had let her down badly.

I immediately went to find Leah to tell her how sorry I was. Luckily, she is a great person and after we'd talked it through, she forgave me.

Although I will always regret the way I treated Leah at camp, it taught me a valuable lesson: friends should always support each other, even when they have lame ideas.

1 Who is telling the story? 1 mark   **LITERAL**
    a Ling   **b** Leah
    c Tash   **d** Leah's sister

REVIEW 1: Comprehension

Summer Camp

2 When does this story start? It starts when ... 1 mark **LITERAL**
  a they arrive at summer camp.
  b Tash teases Leah.
  b Leah talks to Ling.
  d they are about to leave camp.

3 Tash looked at Leah apprehensively. This means she looked at her ... 1 mark **VOCABULARY**
  a quickly.
  b nervously.
  c secretly.
  d angrily.

4 Leah's face had turned the color of a beetroot. This suggests that Leah was ... 1 mark
  a furious.
  b scared. **INFERENTIAL**
  c disappointed.
  d embarrassed.

5 What is the most likely reason Tash continued teasing Leah? She ... 1 mark **INFERENTIAL**
  a thought Leah wouldn't mind.
  b enjoyed the reaction of their friends.
  c was angry with Leah.
  d thought she was being clever.

6 Why did Tash whisper "Bozo" when she saw Leah? "Bozo" is ... 1 mark
  a a common name for a clown.
  b Leah's nickname. **INFERENTIAL**
  c a private joke between Tash and Leah.
  d a secret code.

7 Why did Ling want to talk to Tash? Ling wanted to ... 1 mark **LITERAL**
  a warn Tash about Leah's behavior.
  b find out why Leah was upset.
  c tell Tash why Leah was upset.
  d tell Tash that Leah was going home.

8 Which word best describes Tash's behavior? 1 mark **INFERENTIAL**
  a wise
  b brave
  c enthusiastic
  d selfish

9 Which group of words is the best clue to question 8's answer? 1 mark **INFERENTIAL**

_____

_____

10 Do you think Tash will tease Leah if she does have a clown act at her party? Give a reason for your answer. 1 mark **INFERENTIAL**

Your score ☐ / 10

Your Review 1 Scores

Spelling	Grammar	Comprehension	Total
☐ +	☐ +	☐ =	☐
10	20	10	40

Week 10 Day 1 Comprehension

Runaway

Word study
To identify the descriptive verbs in a text, look for the verbs that tell exactly how an action is performed; e.g., 'raced' instead of 'ran.' Descriptive verbs help you visualize actions.

Read the passage.

Circle the verb that shows how Shane freed himself.

Put a box around the verb that helps us see how Tony walked away from Shane.

Shane shook himself free. Had Tony eaten mush for breakfast? It must have gone straight to his brain. "What do you mean, she's not hurting anyone? First she stole my hamburger and then she took my towel."

"Right," snapped Tony. "You ask her but leave me out of it." He stomped off. Sand sprayed everywhere as he kicked at clumps of grass.

Highlight the verb that shows that Tony spoke in a nasty way.

Underline the verb that helps us visualize what the sand looked like when Tony kicked at the clumps of grass.

Circle the correct answers.

1. Which verb in the passage could be replaced with "said"?
   a. stomped   b. shook   c. stole   d. snapped

2. Why is the verb you chose in question 1 more effective than "said"?
   It shows that Tony was …
   a. annoyed.   b. pleased.   c. impressed.   d. confused.

3. Which verb in the passage could be replaced with "walked"?
   a. gone   b. kicked   c. stomped   d. took

4. Why is the verb you chose in question 3 more effective than "walked"?
   It shows how …
   a. clumsy Tony was.   b. angry Tony was.   c. happy Tony was.   d. silly Tony was.

5. In the final sentence, why is sprayed a more effective verb than "went"?
   a. It imitates the sound of the sand.
   b. It helps us imagine what the sand felt like.
   c. It creates an image of what the sand looked like.

L.5.5 Demonstrate understanding of figurative language, word relationships, and nuances in word meanings.

Week 10 Day 2 Comprehension

Runaway

Read the passage.

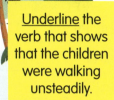

Read the whole story

Circle the verb that is similar in meaning to "was crying."

Highlight the verb that shows that Shane was struggling to breathe as he spoke.

The girl hugged Ruby, who was sobbing. "Are you OK?" the girl asked him.

Shane wasn't sure, but he nodded. "Is she... she OK?" he spluttered, pointing to Ruby.

"Yeah, she's just in shock. She thought you were dead."

Ruby wouldn't look at Shane. She had no breath for talking anyway. The three of them staggered back to shore and collapsed onto the sand.

Underline the verb that shows that the children were walking unsteadily.

Put a box around the verb that helps us visualize how the children fell down.

1 What does the verb "was sobbing" suggest about the way Ruby was crying?

_____
_____

2 What does the verb "spluttered" tell us about the way Shane asked the question?

_____
_____

3 What picture does the verb "staggered" give us of the way the children moved?

_____
_____

4 In the final sentence, why is the verb "collapsed" more effective than "fell down"?

_____
_____
_____

L.5.5 Demonstrate understanding of figurative language, word relationships, and nuances in word meanings.

Week 10 | Day 3 | Spelling

Suffix: ity

> A **suffix** is added to the end of a word to make a new word with a slightly different meaning. Some words can be turned into **nouns** by adding the suffix **ity**; e.g., major → major**ity**.
> If a word ends in **e**, **drop the e** before adding **ity**; e.g., pur**e** → pur**ity**. If a word ends in **le**, change **le to il** before adding **ity**; e.g., responsib**le** → responsib**ility**.

List

1 Write the word.

- electricity _____
- reality _____
- curiosity _____
- publicity _____
- ability _____
- equality _____
- clarity _____
- intensity _____
- normality _____
- hostility _____
- minority _____
- security _____
- identity _____
- majority _____
- mobility _____
- continuity _____
- brutality _____
- prosperity _____
- personality _____
- maturity _____

2 Write the list words in alphabetical order.

_____ _____
_____ _____
_____ _____
_____ _____
_____ _____
_____ _____
_____ _____
_____ _____
_____ _____
_____ _____

3 Fill in the missing letters.

a m___b___li___ ___
b h___sti___ ___ ___ ___
c conti___ ___i___ ___
d ___i___orit___
e ___ros___ ___r___ ___ ___
f pu___l___cit___
g ___lar___ ___ ___

4 Complete each sentence with a list word.

a His swimming _____ has improved.
b The _____ of the workout made me sweaty and tired.
c Thomas Edison created _____ in 1879.
d We lock our front door for _____ when we aren't at home.
e The _____ of our family eat cereal for breakfast.
f She had a kind and happy _____.
g He watched the older children playing, and then _____ got the better of him.

Week 10 Day 4 Spelling

Suffix: ity

1 **Revise your spelling list from page 54.** Which list word means?

a Having ease and flexibility of motion _____

b The power to do something _____

c The condition of being very cruel _____

d The true situation _____

e The state or condition of being pure or clear _____

f The attention someone gets from the media _____

g A stong desire to know or learn something _____

Challenge words

2 **Write the word.**

possibility _____
opportunity _____
community _____
simplicity _____
necessity _____
productivity _____
uniformity _____
sensitivity _____
flexibility _____
responsibility _____

3 **Hidden words.** Find the challenge word.

a proproductivityeti _____

b filflexibilityexib _____

c sennecessityess _____

d niuuniformitytiy _____

e sinsimplicityitie _____

f popopportunityun _____

g enssensitivityive _____

4 **Word clues.** Which challenge word matches?

a a group of people _____

b all the same _____

c a chance _____

5 **Complete the sentence.**

a Looking after a pet is a big _____.

b The weather forecast told us that rain was a _____ for tomorrow.

c Dancers do exercises to improve their _____.

d His room looked neat because of its _____.

e Food and water are a _____ to human beings.

f She has a _____ to grass that makes her very itchy.

g He had an _____ to be on television.

L.5.2.E Spell grade-appropriate words correctly, consulting references as needed.

Week 10 Day 5 Grammar

Interjections

Interjections are informal words or phrases that are usually used to express **feelings**. They are often followed by an exclamation point; e.g., Ouch**!** Yippee**!**

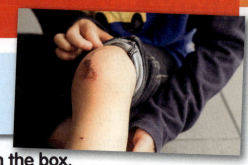

1 Complete each sentence with an interjection from the box.

a _____! How disgusting!
b _____! Where did you get that?
c _____! We won!
d _____, I've made the same mistake again.
e _____! This watermelon is delicious!
f _____! What a relief!

Oh, no	Phew
Hooray	Wow
Ugh	Yum

2 Match the interjections to the sentences. Write the answers in the spaces.

Hello! Huh? Awesome! Sure Boo! Yay! Shhh! Whoa!

a You must be quiet now, children. _____
b Did I scare you? _____
c It's good to see you again. _____
d You're driving too fast! _____
e You may definitely have another slice of cake. _____
f I've found the ring! _____
g What did you say? _____
h You've done very well! _____

3 Write sentences to match the following interjections.

a Brrr! _____

b Hmmm! _____

c Uh-oh! _____

Week 11 Day 1 Comprehension

Chatroom Trap

Point of view
To identify point of view, look at the way characters behave and feel. The clues are in the way they express their opinions and views about a subject.

Read the passage.

Underline the words that show that Sally is sure she will succeed.

Highlight the sentence that shows that Faisal is worried.

Circle the adjective that describes Corinne's reaction to Sally's question.

Color the words that show what Sally's opinion of the Internet is.

Put a box around the words that show how Sally feels about chatrooms.

The tingling sensation at the back of Sally's head was intense. "Don't worry, Faisal. I'll find out who Venny is."

Faisal shuddered, "You're my only hope."

Sally and Corinne walked to their first class. Corinne was one of the seven students on the list.

"Are you a member of a chatroom?" Sally asked.

Corinne was surprised. "Why? You think the Internet's a waste of time!"

"Well, I do, but that doesn't answer my question."

Corinne shrugged. "Sure I am."

"You know chatrooms aren't safe," Sally warned.

Circle the correct answers.

1 How does Sally **view** the challenge of finding out Venny's identity?
 a She is worried she won't succeed.   b She is confident she will succeed.
 c She has a few doubts.   d She thinks it is a hopeless task.

2 Which sentence is the best **clue** to question 1's answer?
 a "Sure I am."   b Faisal shuddered, "You're my only hope."
 c "I'll find out who Venny is."   d Corinne was surprised.

3 What do Faisal's words suggest about his **feelings**? They suggest he is …
 a desperate.   b hopeful.   c optimistic.   d enthusiastic.

4 How does Sally **feel** about chatrooms? Sally thinks chatrooms are …
 a fun.   b harmless.   c boring.   d dangerous.

5 Which phrase is the best **clue** to question 4's answer?
 a a waste of time   b aren't safe   c tingling sensation   d only hope

RL.5.1 Quote accurately from a text when explaining what the text says explicitly and when drawing inferences from the text.

Week 11 | Day 2 | Comprehension

Chatroom Trap

Read the passage.

Underline the first reason Sally thinks people will find out Faisal's secret.

Circle the word that shows that Faisal is not sure if he should tell people his secret.

Sally said, "People will find out your secret one day. You'll go somewhere high and ... you'll faint. Then everyone will know."

"Maybe." Faisal didn't want to think about that.

"Faisal, you'll have to tell people for your own safety. No matter what you do, Julian could still tell someone at any time," Sally said.

Faisal scowled.

"You can tell people in your own way, in your own time. But you have to do it," Sally concluded.

Faisal kicked the ground. "I can't. It's just too embarrassing."

Highlight a second reason Sally believes Faisal should tell people his secret.

Put a box around the verb that shows that Faisal is unhappy about revealing his secret.

Color Faisal's reason for not telling people his secret.

1. From Sally's **point of view**, what is the best thing Faisal can do?

_____

_____

2. What reasons does Sally give to support her **point of view**?

_____

_____

_____

_____

3. How does Faisal **feel** about telling people his secret? Support your answer with quotes from the passage.

_____

_____

_____

Week 11 Day 3 Spelling

Compound words are two or more words that make one word; e.g., daybreak.

Compound words

List
- deadline
- daybreak
- teammate
- highway
- goodbye
- warehouse
- background
- eyesight
- textbook
- watermelon
- cartwheel
- newsstand
- bookcase
- spacewalk
- headache
- butterfingers
- timetable
- weeknight
- tablespoon
- skyscraper

1 Write the word.

2 Fill in the missing part.
- a cart_____
- b _____walk
- c time_____
- d _____stand
- e good_____
- f _____way
- g butter_____
- h _____line
- i sky_____
- j ware_____
- k _____spoon
- l water_____
- m eye_____
- n back_____
- o _____mate
- p _____book
- q head_____
- r _____case
- s day_____
- t week_____

3 Fill in the missing syllables.
- a time/ta/_____
- b _____/ache
- c sky/_____/per
- d but/_____/fin/gers
- e wa/_____/mel/_____
- f ta/_____/spoon
- g text/_____
- h book/_____

4 Word clues. Which list word matches?
- a something an astronaut would do
- b a pain in the head
- c the ability to see
- d a space to store your books on
- e after dark from Monday to Friday
- f saying farewell
- g a member of your group
- h the date by which something must be done

L.5.2.E Spell grade-appropriate words correctly, consulting references as needed.

Week 11 Day 4 Spelling

Compound words

1 **Revise your spelling list from page 59.** Name.

a

b

c

d

Challenge words

2 Write the word.

wastepaper
superhuman
blindfold
courthouse
earthbound
undercurrent
thunderbolt
bodyguard
candlelight
earthworm

3 **Hidden words.** Find the challenge word.

a asrbodyguardaish
b snugroublindfolda
c ghcandlelightcani
d efsuperhumanah
e ththunderboltasin
f pewastepaperza
g sdundercurrentas
h eaearthwormasih
i urtcourthousech
j ouearthboundea

4 **Another way to say it.** Which challenge word could replace the underlined word/s?

a The judge delivered the sentence in the <u>law court</u>.
b The man amazed everyone with his <u>extraordinary</u> strength.
c We could sense the <u>feeling</u> of hostility in the room.
d The celebrity's <u>escort</u> made sure that she arrived safely.
e The <u>little animal</u> buried itself in the dirt.
f I couldn't see where I was going because of the <u>mask</u>.
g The plane remained <u>grounded</u> because of a technical fault.

Week 11 Day 5 Grammar

Commas before conjunctions

When joining **two main** clauses, always use a **comma** before the **conjunction**; e.g.; I tripped on the wet floor**,** **but** I didn't hurt myself.

1 **Fill in the commas in the following sentences.**
   a I made myself a sandwich and then I ate it.
   b He has tried many times yet he can't get it right.
   c You can read a book or you can watch a movie.
   d I bought tickets for the show but now I can't go.
   e It started to rain so we put up our umbrella.

2 **Join each pair of sentences with the conjunction in parentheses. Remember the commas.**
   a I enjoy science fiction movies. I don't like horror movies. (but)
   _____
   _____

   b Our water bottles were empty. We filled them at the next camp. (so)
   _____
   _____

   c We have packed the car. We are ready to go. (and)
   _____
   _____

   d You can have a chocolate milkshake. You can try the new caramel flavor. (or)
   _____
   _____

   e I have asked the children to be quiet. They continue to make a noise. (yet)
   _____
   _____

3 **Complete the following sentence.**
   Our train has arrived, but _____
   _____

L.5.2 Demonstrate command of the conventions of standard English capitalization, punctuation, and spelling when writing.

Week 12 Day 1 Comprehension

Racing for the Birdman

Interpreting character behavior, feelings, and motivation
To interpret a character's feelings and what motivates them to behave in a certain way, look for clues in the text. The clues are usually in the words and punctuation.

Read the passage.

"The islanders are very worried about what is causing the red rain. They think it will damage the Moai," whispered Uncle Earl.

"Mo... what?" Flynn tried to say the word.

"MOW-I." Mia sounded the word out slowly for Flynn. "The famous statues of Easter Island. Don't tell me you've never heard of them?"

Flynn shrugged. Mia pulled a book out of her bag and showed Flynn the photograph on the back cover. It was of a long, stone face with a pointed nose, wearing a kind of crown, attached to a short, stone body.

"So this is how you know about all of this?" asked Flynn. He wasn't surprised. No matter how little warning they had, Mia still managed to fit in some research.

Underline the sentence that shows that Flynn does not know who the Moai are.

Highlight the question Mia asks Flynn.

Put a box around Flynn's reaction to Mia's question.

Color why Flynn is not surprised that Mia knows about the Moai.

Circle the correct answers.

1 How does Mia **react** when Flynn shows that he does not know what the Moai are? She is ...

   a angry.   **b** astonished.   **c** pleased.   **d** amused.

2 Which sentence is the **clue** to question 1's answer?

   a Flynn tried to say the word.   **b** Mia sounded the word out slowly for Flynn.
   c Mia says, "Don't tell me you've never heard of them?"

3 What information does the passage give us about Mia? Mia ...

   a has a curious mind.   **b** does not like to read.
   c only reads nonfiction books.   **d** likes books about famous monuments.

4 What **evidence** is there in the passage to support question 3's answer? Mia has ...

   a a book in her bag.   **b** done research on the Moai.
   c a photograph of the Moai.   **d** been on many expeditions.

RL.5.1 Quote accurately from a text when explaining what the text says explicitly and when drawing inferences from the text.

Week 12 Day 2 Comprehension

Racing for the Birdman

Read the passage.

Underline two sentences that show what Makemake wants Flynn to do.

Circle the word that shows that Flynn is shocked.

Highlight the phrase that shows Flynn's reaction when he sees the burn.

Color the sentence that shows that Flynn is worried about helping the true Birdman.

The woman nodded as though she understood it all. She looked at Flynn very seriously. "Makemake has chosen you to protect the treasured egg."

"WHAT?" cried Flynn, jumping to his feet.

The woman took her hand away from his arm. Flynn's mouth gaped when he saw the burn there. A deep red outline formed the shape of a bird.

The woman pointed to a mask on the wall. Flynn thought he looked just like a god of thunder.

"He is the one making the red rain," said the woman. "He is trying to warn us of danger. Makemake wants Flynn to make sure that the true Birdman finds the sooty tern's first egg of the season."

"Danger?" croaked Flynn.

1 How does Flynn **feel** when the woman tells him that Makemake has chosen him to protect the treasured egg? Support your answer with quotes from the passage.

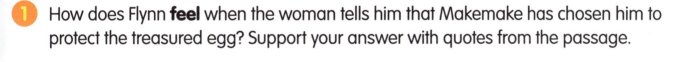

2 How does Flynn **react** when he sees the burn on his arm? Support your answer with **evidence** from the passage.

3 What **evidence** is there to suggest that Flynn is worried about carrying out the task Makemake has set him?

Week 12 Day 3 Spelling

Latin origins

Many English words have their origins in **Latin** words; e.g., **litera** means *letter* and from litera we form the words, **litera**l, **litera**cy, **litera**te.

List

- literacy
- habitat
- benefit
- inhabit
- dome
- literate
- domestic
- alien
- domain
- literal
- aquatic
- aquarium
- habitable
- habitation
- inhabitant
- aquaplane
- feral
- benign
- aquanaut
- literary

1 Write the word.

2 Sort the words.

a Words that come from the Latin word *domus*

b Words that come from the Latin word *aqua*

c Words that come from the Latin word *bene*

d Words that come from the Latin word *habitare*

e Words that come from the Latin word *litera*

3 Underline the spelling mistake. Write the word correctly.

a The doume above the stadium was very high.
b The receptionist gave them a benine smile.
c The main benifit of exercise is a healthy heart.
d The gorillas' habitaytion at the zoo mimicked the jungle.
e Someone who can read and write is litirate.
f The litral translation made more sense than the altered version.
g The removal of mold made their house more habitabel.
h The ferel cat looked hungry and dirty.

L.5.2.E Spell grade-appropriate words correctly, consulting references as needed.

Week 12 Day 4 Spelling

Latin origins

1 **Revise your spelling list from page 64.** Fill in the missing syllables.

a a/quar/i/_____
b in/_____/it/ant
c _____/i/tat
d a/_____/en
e lit/_____/a/cy
f a/_____/plane
g lit/er/_____/cy
h _____/ral
i do/_____/tic
j hab/it/a/_____

Challenge words

2 **Write the word.**

aquamarine _____
uninhabitable _____
alias _____
alibi _____
beneficial _____
beneficially _____
benefactor _____
ferocious _____
domestically _____
alliteration _____

3 **Hidden words.** Find the challenge word.

a tasdaliasaseuy _____
b ciousferociousaug _____
c sadrdomesticallyi _____
d asudhyalibiasdu _____
e aquaquamariney _____
f fisibeneficiallylly _____

4 **Word clues.** Which challenge word matches?

a fierce _____
b favorable _____
c blue-green _____
d known by another name _____

5 **Complete the sentence.**

a The hospital had a wing named after its main _____.
b 'Penny picked pretty petals' is an example of _____.
c The water was a beautiful _____ color.
d He couldn't have committed the crime as he had an _____.
e Eating many fruits is _____ to your health.
f The desert wasteland was completely _____ to humans.
g The shark looked _____ because it had so many teeth.
h Her _____ was Marsha Mallow.

L.5.2.E Spell grade-appropriate words correctly, consulting references as needed.

Present and past perfect tense

Week 12 Day 5 Grammar

Tense is the form of a verb that shows **when an action happens**. The **present perfect tense** shows that an **action has been completed**. It has the auxiliary verbs **have** or **has** before the main verb; e.g., She **has finished** her ukulele practice. They **have made** their beds.

The **past perfect tense** shows that **something happened before something else** took place. It has the auxiliary verb **had** before the main verb; e.g., By the time we got there, someone **had eaten** all the food.

1 Use a blue check (✔) for sentences in the present perfect tense.
   Use a red check (✔) for sentences in the past perfect tense.

   a   She had taken the wrong turn before anyone noticed.
   b   When we saw them, they had already been for a swim.
   c   We have not seen our cousins for more than two years.
   d   He has practiced all week and is ready for his music exam.

2 Underline the verb that is wrong. Write the correction in the space.

   a   Before we ate dinner, I have already done all my chores.   _____
   b   She have drawn an illustration to go with her story.   _____
   c   She is happy because she have just heard the good news.   _____
   d   I has lived in the country for a very long time.   _____

3 Use the correct form of the main verb to complete each sentence.

   a   It has just (begin) _____ to rain.
   b   She had already (forgive) _____ us by that time.
   c   The sun had already (rise) _____ by the time we woke up.
   d   He has (hide) _____ his diary where no one will find it.
   e   The lake near our house has (freeze) _____ over completely.

4 Write the following sentences in the present perfect tense.

   a   They bent the wire.   _____
   b   Our puppy chewed Dad's slipper.   _____

Week 13 Day 1 Comprehension

The Village Blacksmith

Figurative language

Alliteration repeats consonant sounds. **Onomatopoeia** imitates sounds. A **simile** compares two things using the words *like* or *as*. **Metaphors** make a more direct comparison. They do not contain the words *like* or *as*.

Read the passage.

Circle the alliteration in line 2.

Underline the simile in line 6.

Highlight the alliteration in line 3.

Color the simile in line 8.

Under a spreading chestnut-tree
The village smithy stands;
The smith, a mighty man is he,
With large and sinewy hands;
And the muscles of his brawny arms
Are strong as iron bands.

His hair is crisp, and black, and long,
His face is like the tan;
His brow is wet with honest sweat,
He earns whate'er he can,
And looks the whole world in the face,
For he owes not any man.

Circle the correct answers.

1. Which of the following is an example of **alliteration**?
   a chestnut-tree   b brawny arms   c mighty man   d sinewy hands

2. What is the **clue** to question 1's answer?
   a The words imitate a sound.
   b A consonant sound is repeated.
   c One thing is compared to something else.
   d It contains the word *like*.

3. What figure of speech is "strong as iron bands"?
   a onomatopoeia   b metaphor   c alliteration   d simile

4. What is the **clue** to question 3's answer?
   a The words imitate a sound.
   b A consonant sound is repeated.
   c It compares two things using the word *as*.
   d It gives an object human qualities.

5. Which of the following is a **simile**?
   a His face is like the tan   b His brow is wet with honest sweat

L.5.5 Demonstrate understanding of figurative language, word relationships, and nuances in word meanings.

Week 13 Day 2 Comprehension

The Village Blacksmith

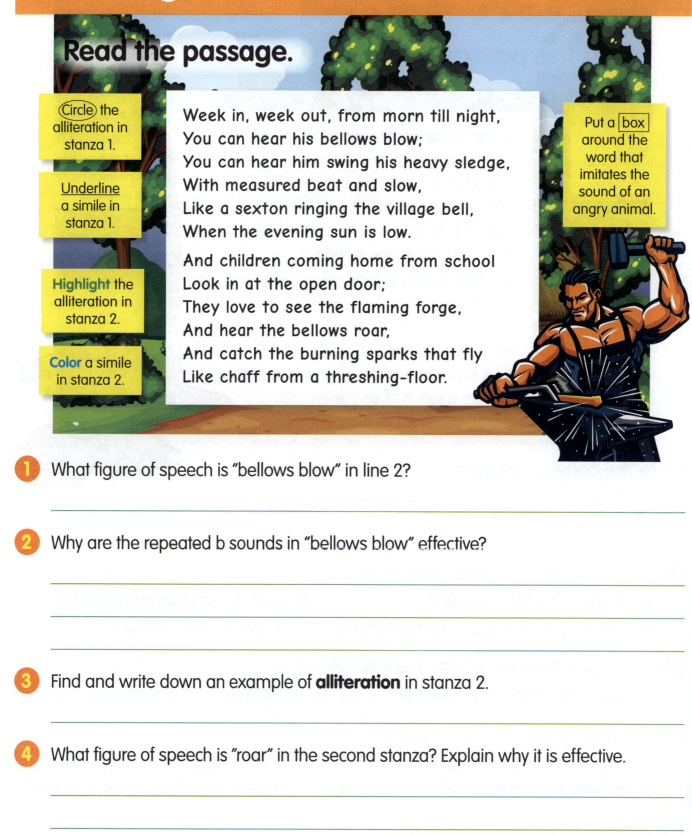

Read the passage.

Circle the alliteration in stanza 1.

Underline a simile in stanza 1.

Highlight the alliteration in stanza 2.

Color a simile in stanza 2.

Week in, week out, from morn till night,
You can hear his bellows blow;
You can hear him swing his heavy sledge,
With measured beat and slow,
Like a sexton ringing the village bell,
When the evening sun is low.

And children coming home from school
Look in at the open door;
They love to see the flaming forge,
And hear the bellows roar,
And catch the burning sparks that fly
Like chaff from a threshing-floor.

Put a box around the word that imitates the sound of an angry animal.

1. What figure of speech is "bellows blow" in line 2?

2. Why are the repeated b sounds in "bellows blow" effective?

3. Find and write down an example of **alliteration** in stanza 2.

4. What figure of speech is "roar" in the second stanza? Explain why it is effective.

L.5.5 Demonstrate understanding of figurative language, word relationships, and nuances in word meanings.

Week 13 Day 3 Spelling

Suffix: ive

Many words can be **turned into adjectives or nouns** by adding the suffix **ive**; e.g., digest → diges**t**ive.

When the base word ends in **e**, **drop the e** before adding **ive**; e.g., creat**e** → creat**ive**.

For words that end in **d** or **de**, **change the d** or **de** to **t** or **s** before adding **ive**; e.g., atten**d** → atten**t**ive, explo**de** → explo**s**ive.

Some words **change in other ways** before **ive** is added; e.g., form → form**at**ive, capt**ure** → cap**t**ive, exce**ed** → exce**ss**ive.

List

1 Write the word.

- active
- captive
- detective
- extensive
- creative
- intensive
- expensive
- explosive
- selective
- objective
- impulsive
- secretive
- attentive
- formative
- attractive
- narrative
- productive
- massive
- offensive
- connective

2 Write the list words in alphabetical order.

3 Rewrite the syllables in the correct order.

a nec/con/tive
b tive/ob/jec
c a/tive/cre
d cre/tive/se

4 Word clues. Which list word matches?

a busy, full of energy
b something that looks good
c something incredibly large
d costing a lot of money
e a person who follows clues to find the answer
f a story
g careful in choosing

L.5.2.E Spell grade-appropriate words correctly, consulting references as needed.

Week 13 | Day 4 | Spelling

Suffix: ive

1 Revise your spelling list from page 69. Which list word means?
  a Able to make something new or with imagination _____
  b Causing anger or hurt feelings _____
  c Acting without thinking or planning _____
  d A story _____
  e Held as a prisoner _____
  f Something that connects things _____
  g A goal that a person works towards _____
  h A person who solves crimes _____

Challenge words

2 Write the word.
  sensitive _____
  digestive _____
  expressive _____
  descriptive _____
  repetitive _____
  comparative _____
  possessive _____
  imaginative _____
  competitive _____
  excessive _____

3 Word clues. Which challenge word matches?
  a fanciful _____
  b detailed _____
  c not sharing _____
  d too much _____
  e easily hurt _____
  f ambitious _____

4 Hidden words. Find the challenge word.
  a petrepetitiveive _____
  b exivexcessivecess _____
  c tivedigestivedigi _____

5 Complete the sentence.
  a The boy wrote a _____ story about his vacation.
  b The girl was very _____ and always wanted to win.
  c There was an _____ amount of food at the party.
  d The little boy had a very _____ face.
  e The song had a very catchy and _____ beat.
  f I was very _____ of my favorite video game.

Week 13 Day 5 Grammar

Commas and tag questions

Commas are used to separate words and phrases from the rest of the sentence. They are used after the words yes and no; e.g. Yes, I know you're tired. They are used before a question tagged onto the end of the sentence; e.g., You will help me, won't you?

1 **Fill in the commas in the following sentences.**
   a Yes I've fed the dog and taken it for its walk.
   b They should be here by now shouldn't they?
   c No I haven't finished my other chores yet.
   d You know how to use the washing machine don't you?
   e You knocked on the door before entering didn't you?
   f Yes of course I did.

2 **Answer the following questions with Yes or No. Use full sentences.**

Are you in the fifth grade?

Yes, I am in the fifth grade.

   a Is the sun shining today?
   _____
   _____

   b Have you seen an interesting movie lately?
   _____
   _____

   c Do you like to read adventure stories?
   _____
   _____

3 **Fill in the missing commas in the following passage.**

"You will have a slice of cake won't you?" asked Mrs. Brown.
"Yes thank you," replied Ginny.
"And you're still going to your piano lesson aren't you?" said Mrs. Brown.
"No my teacher can't make it today," said Ginny.

L.5.2.C Use a comma to set off the words yes and no, and to set off a tag question from the rest of the sentence.

Week 14 · Day 1 · Comprehension

The Four Musicians

Drawing conclusions
To draw conclusions from a text, use clues to make your own judgments. The clues help you find the answers that are hiding in the text.

Read the passage.

<u>Underline</u> why Dog joined Donkey.

(Circle) the word that suggests that Cat was unhappy.

<mark>Highlight</mark> the words that show that Cat was eager to join Donkey and Dog.

Along the way Donkey met a dog.
"I am too old to hunt," sighed Dog.
"Join me," said Donkey. "I am off to town to be a singer."
Soon they came across a weary cat.
"My old teeth are worn, and I can no longer catch mice," sobbed Cat.
"Come with us," said Donkey. "We are off to town to be singers." Cat leaped at the offer.
Soon after, they met an old rooster.
"My mistress says tomorrow I am to be dinner!" Rooster wailed.

Color why Rooster was upset.

Put a box around the word that shows that Rooster was upset.

(Circle) the punctuation that emphasizes how upset Rooster was.

Circle the correct answers.

1 Which is the best **conclusion**? When Donkey and Dog came across Cat, Cat was …
  a excited.   **b** surprised.   **c** angry.   **d** upset.

2 Which word is the **clue** to question 1's answer?
  a weary   **b** sobbed   **c** worn   **d** old

3 Which is the best **conclusion**? When Donkey asked Cat to join them, Cat accepted …
  a enthusiastically.   **b** wearily.   **c** nervously.   **d** shyly.

4 Which group of words is the **clue** to question 3's answer?
  a no longer catch mice   **b** old teeth are worn
  c leaped at the offer   **d** a weary cat

5 Which is the best **conclusion?** Rooster's mistress plans to …
  a sell him.   **b** eat him.
  c give him dinner.   **d** make him cook dinner.

RL.5.1 Quote accurately from a text when explaining what the text says explicitly and when drawing inferences from the text.

The Four Musicians

Read the passage.

Highlight the words that are the clue to what Cat did to the robber.

Color the words that tell what Dog did to the robber.

Underline the words that tell what Donkey did to the robber.

Put **boxes** around who or what the robber thought had attacked him.

But the robbers were not happy. One of them crept back into the house. Cat leaped at the robber with her sharp claws. The robber tripped over Dog, who bit the robber on the leg. The robber fell onto the sleeping Donkey, who lashed out with his hooves. Rooster woke and crowed loudly, "Cock-a-doodle-do!"

The robber raced back to his gang, his face torn and bleeding, his leg sore, and his head swollen. "There is a horrible witch by the fire. She clawed me with her nails and stabbed me in the leg. A hairy monster clubbed me in the head, and from the roof a judge cried 'Catch the rascal, do!' I never want to go near the place again!"

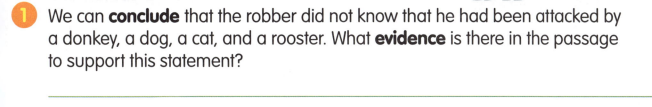

1 We can **conclude** that the robber did not know that he had been attacked by a donkey, a dog, a cat, and a rooster. What **evidence** is there in the passage to support this statement?

___
___
___
___
___
___
___
___
___

Week 14 | Day 3 | Spelling

Ending: ish

Many nouns and verbs **end in the letters ish**; e.g., varn**ish**. Sometimes **ish** is a suffix that is added to words to form adjectives. In these words, **ish** mean **somewhat like or having the characteristics of**; e.g., child**ish**. Some words that have the suffix **ish** show where someone or something comes from; e.g., Ir**ish**. These words always start with capital letters.

List
- English
- nourish
- sheepish
- reddish
- astonish
- furnish
- sluggish
- cherish
- childish
- skittish
- varnish
- stylish
- establish
- perish
- vanquish
- youngish
- demolish
- replenish
- flourish
- fiendish

1 Write the word.

2 Complete these list words.
- a sh_____
- b che_____
- c es_____
- d st_____
- e fi_____
- f En_____
- g fl_____
- h as_____

3 Unscramble these list words.
- a hpseri _____
- b ysthlis _____
- c espehhsi _____
- d lpenrihes _____
- e ifndseih _____
- f yhunogsi _____
- g aosinhts _____
- h hlsfuior _____

4 Complete each sentence with a list word.
- a They speak _____ as well as German in Germany.
- b He behaved in a _____ manner and was scolded for it.
- c The sky had a _____ tinge from the fire.
- d They had to _____ the building as it was ruined.
- e Once the chair was finished, they had to apply _____.
- f We eat fruit to _____ our bodies.
- g The coach wanted to _____ some ground rules for the game.
- h "It's okay, girl," said the farmer to the _____ mare.

Week 14 Day 4 Spelling

Ending: ish

1 **Revise your spelling list from page 74.** Write the list word that belongs in each group.

a young, younger, _____
b child, childlike, _____
c red, redder, _____
d style, styles, _____
e furniture, furnishings, _____

Challenge words

2 **Write the word.**

accomplish _____
anguish _____
distinguish _____
squeamish _____
extinguish _____
diminish _____
relinquish _____
feverish _____
embellish _____
amateurish _____

3 **Hidden words.** Find the challenge word.

a esqueamishsque _____
b fevefeverishsuiha _____
c turamateurisham _____
d dimmdiminishi _____
e llishembellishem _____
f accioaccomplisha _____

4 **Word clues.** Which challenge word matches?

a achieve _____
b burning up _____
c grief _____
d queasy _____

5 **Another way to say it.** Which challenge word could replace the underlined word/s?

a The firefighter had to put out the flame using special foam. _____
b The cooks were inexperienced, but were learning all the time. _____
c It was hard to differentiate between the identical twins. _____
d I will trim my hat with sequins and glitter. _____
e My sister wants to quit her role as swimming captain. _____
f Being sensible with scissors helps to decrease the chance of an accident. _____

L.5.2.E Spell grade-appropriate words correctly, consulting references as needed.

Using exclamation points

Exclamation points (!) are always used at the end of an exclamation sentence or phrase; e.g., **How** amazing was that**!** **What** a brilliant book**!** They are sometimes used **after interjections** and **sentences** that express strong feelings; e.g., **Ouch**! That was sore! **Warning!** Exclamation points should not be overused!

1 In each pair, change one of the periods to an exclamation point.
  a   I take my dog for a walk every morning and afternoon.
  b   What an exciting adventure they had.

  c   How fantastic that they both got into the team.
  d   Both May and Ella got into the soccer team.

  e   I can't wait to see my new bike.
  f   I'm getting a new bike for my birthday.

2 Turn each of the following sentences into an exclamation by starting it with What or How.

That documentary was excellent.

What an excellent documentary that was!

  a   It's exciting that you're going to see the Gateway Arch.
  _____
  _____

  b   They live in an enormous house.
  _____
  _____

3 In the following passage, change THREE periods to exclamation points.

Last weekend Harry, James, and I went camping at Eagle Valley. We had a great time. The weather was perfect, and we did lots of exciting things. On one of our hikes we saw an eagle swoop down and catch a rabbit. What an amazing sight. Another highlight was sitting around the campfire at night, telling ghost stories. Some of them were really scary. When we packed up to go home, we were already planning our next camping trip.

Week 15 Day 1 Comprehension

Volcano

Cause and effect
To find cause and effect, ask why something happens and what the result is.

Read the passage.

Highlight what happens to volcanic ash after it blasts into the air.

Underline how sulphur dioxide affects the environment.

Volcanic ash is deadly. It is hard and abrasive, like finely crushed glass. After blasting into the air, it forms an eruption plume, which settles over huge areas, suffocating people and animals.

Gases spewed out from volcanic eruptions, such as carbon dioxide and sulphur dioxide, are even more deadly. As carbon dioxide is heavier than air, it collects in low-lying areas and creates poisonous environments. Sulphur dioxide causes acid rain and air pollution.

Circle how volcanic ash affects people and animals.

Color the gases that spew out from volcanic eruptions.

Circle the correct answers.

1. During a volcanic eruption, what **causes** people and animals to suffocate?
   a crushed glass   b volcanic ash   c molten lava   d carbon dioxide

2. How does volcanic ash blasting into the air **affect** people and animals? It **causes** them to ...
   a cough.   b sneeze.   c perspire.   d suffocate.

3. What can **cause** acid rain during a volcanic eruption?
   a magma   b sulphur dioxide   c volcanic ash   d smoke

4. During a volcanic eruption, what **effect** does sulphur dioxide have on the environment? It **causes** ...
   a smoke and fires.   b power blackouts.
   c acid rain and air pollution.   d electric storms.

5. In the second last sentence, which word shows **cause** and **effect**?
   a As   b is   c collects   d out

RI.5.8 Explain how an author uses reasons and evidence to support particular points in a text, identifying which reasons and evidence support which point(s).

Week 15 | Day 2 | Comprehension

Volcano

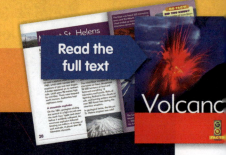

Read the passage.

Circle why volcanic soils are good for growing crops.

Highlight the sentence that shows how lava flows can affect farmers' lives.

Put a box around what caused the destruction of Pompeii.

Volcanic soils are very fertile, making them ideal for growing crops. Indonesian farmers grow rice near active volcanoes. However, thick lava flows are disastrous. It takes months for lava to cool, and then years for soil to form.

In Italy, previous eruptions provide daily benefits. The Roman city of Pompeii, buried when Mount Vesuvius erupted in 79 AD, now attracts thousands of visitors. Spending by these tourists helps the local economy.

However, Mount Vesuvius is still active. Millions could be affected by a new eruption. Volcanic activity has brought benefits to southern Italy, but eruptions are a constant threat.

Underline how people in southern Italy benefit from Pompeii.

Color why Mount Vesuvius continues to be a threat.

1 What **effect** have volcanoes had on the lives of modern Indonesian farmers?

2 What **caused** the destruction of Pompeii?

3 Carefully explain how the destruction of Pompeii continues to **affect** people's lives.

Week 15 Day 3 Spelling

Prefixes: un, dis, mis

> A **prefix** is added to the beginning of a word to make a new word with a slightly different meaning. Adding the prefix **un**, **dis**, or **mis** can turn a word into its opposite; e.g., known → **un**known, appear → **dis**appear, lead → **mis**lead.

List

1 Write the word.

unknown _____
unravel _____
mislead _____
dislocate _____
uncertain _____
disappear _____
unpleasant _____
dissolve _____
misplaced _____
misjudge _____
unfortunate _____
unusual _____
discourage _____
misconduct _____
miscalculate _____
unexpected _____
distasteful _____
unemployed _____
misguided _____
disapprove _____

2 Sort the words.

a *un*
_____ _____
_____ _____
_____ _____
_____ _____

b *dis*
_____ _____
_____ _____
_____ _____

c *mis*
_____ _____
_____ _____
_____ _____

3 Word clues. Which list word matches?

a melt _____
b surprise _____
c odd _____
d underestimate _____
e unappetizing _____
f disentangle _____

4 Fill the missing letters

a m___scon___u___t
b ___nf___rt___na___e
c ___ ___ ___pl___ ___s___nt
d d___st___s___ef___l
e ___ ___ ___expect___ ___ ___
f ___ne___p___o___ ___d
g d___ ___ap___ro___ ___ ___
h m___s___ ___ ___ad
i u___cer___ ___ ___in
j u___ra___e___

L.5.2.E Spell grade-appropriate words correctly, consulting references as needed.

Week 15 Day 4 Spelling

Prefixes: un, dis, mis

1 **Revise your spelling list from page 79.** Underline the mistake. Write the word correctly.

a She can disapear so quietly that no one notices. _____
b The mizguided boy followed his friends' example. _____
c It was unfortunete that we had to change our plans. _____
d There was an unplesant smell coming from the kitchen. _____
e I was worried I would dislocait my knee again. _____
f The vitamin tablet will disolv when I place it in water. _____
g I caught a thread on my jumper and it started to unraval. _____
h While my dad was unemploied, he started his own business. _____
i We were in unown territory. _____

Challenge words

2 **Write the word.**

unnatural _____
disinterested _____
discriminate _____
disobedient _____
unnecessary _____
unfamiliar _____
disentangle _____
unconscious _____
unacceptable _____
discontinue _____

3 **Hidden words.** Find the challenge word.

a unfamunfamiliars _____
b diisdiscontinuedic _____
c siousunconciousu _____
d dissdisinteresteds _____
e natuunnaturalun _____
f entadisentangled _____

4 **Word clues.** Which challenge word matches?

a separate _____
b naughty _____
c cease _____
d peculiar _____

5 **Complete the sentence.**

a The girl was punished because her behavior was _____ .
b They were unable to _____ between the two chocolate brands.
c Her dogs were very _____ and dug many holes.
d We had to _____ all the knots we made in the rope.

Week 15 Day 5 Grammar

Commas for direct address

When you **address someone or something directly**, use **a comma** to separate their name from the rest of the sentence; e.g., **Georgie,** where did you put my keys? I can't come to your house today**, Sammy**. No**, you greedy dog,** you can't have my cookie.

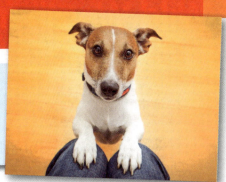

1 Check [✔] the sentences that have the correct punctuation.
- a ☐ Hurry up, Rosie or we'll be late.
- b ☐ Ben, I've put your socks in the drawer.
- c ☐ I don't know, Roxy, I've never heard of it.
- d ☐ Come here Allie, and Jamie, I want to speak to you.
- e ☐ Yes, Your Majesty, the prince has arrived.
- f ☐ When are you coming to visit us Grandpa?
- g ☐ It's cold outside, children, so make sure you dress warmly.

2 Fill in the commas in the following sentences.
- a Oh Julia what a mess you've made!
- b Do you think this will work Dad?
- c Yes son I'm sure it will work.
- d Carrie how many books have you read this year?
- e Come on Marcus you're wasting my time.
- f Ruby would like to speak to you Suzie.
- g Tessa that mitt belongs to Mateo.

3 Rewrite the following sentences with the correct punctuation.
- a Keep trying Noah and, you'll soon get it right.

_____

_____

- b Ava when are you going to visit, Auntie Mae?

_____

_____

L.5.2.C. Use a comma to indicate direct address.

Week 16 Day 1 Comprehension

Wild Weather

Drawing conclusions
To draw conclusions from a text, use clues to make your own judgments. The clues help you find the answers that are hiding in the text.

Read the passage.

Circle the time of day when the tornado struck.

Underline how long it took the tornadoes to merge and reach the Double Creek Estate.

Shortly before 3:45 p.m. on May 27, 1997, a violent tornado struck the small Texas town of Jarrell.

Jarrell's tornado alert siren sounded after a group of tornadoes was spotted 1.2 miles north of the town. Less than 20 minutes later the twisters had merged into a single tornado 0.7 miles wide, which bore down on the Double Creek Estate. Though massive, the tornado was slow moving, and spent the next half-hour destroying areas of Jarrell.

Highlight when the tornado alert siren sounded.

Color what was destroyed.

Circle the correct answers.

1. After reading the passage, which of the following **conclusions** can we draw? When the tornado struck, most people were …
   a awake.   b asleep.   c having dinner.   d having breakfast.

2. What is the **clue** to question 1's answer?
   a May 27   b 1997   c 3:45 p.m.   d 20 minutes

3. Which is the best **conclusion**? Before the tornado struck, people had …
   a lots of warning.   b no warning.   c very little warning.

4. What is the **clue** to question 3's answer?
   a 1.2 miles north   b 0.7 miles wide   c half-hour   d Less than 20 minutes

5. The passage **suggests** that Jarrell was not entirely destroyed. Which group of words is the **clue**?
   a slow moving   b areas of Jarrell
   c the Double Creek Estate   d merged into a single tornado

Week 16 Day 2 Comprehension

Wild Weather

Read the passage.

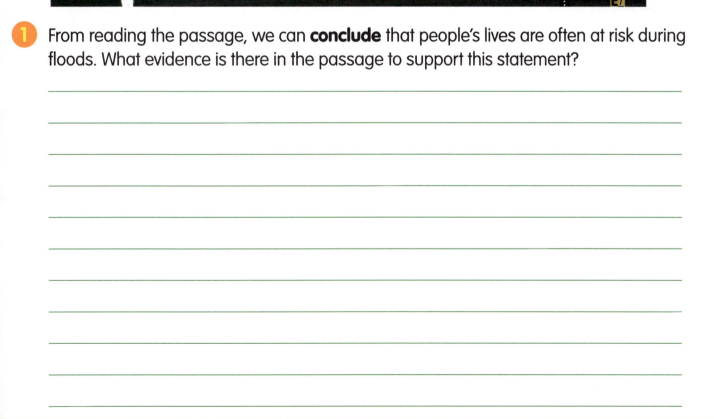

Underline the damage rushing walls of water can cause.

Circle what debris carried along by floodwaters can do to humans.

Highlight how people can be electrocuted during floods.

Color the damage polluted water can do to humans.

Floods are often destructive, but they can also have benefits. Some areas of the world rely on floods to keep their land fertile.

Floods cause enormous damage. Rushing walls of water wash people, animals, buildings, and vehicles away. The debris carried along by the floodwaters also causes havoc, battering humans and property. Floods burst sewage pipes and gas mains, causing pollution. They bring down electrical wires, which cause deaths by electrocution.

Floods also destroy agricultural crops. Floodwaters can lead to the spread of deadly, infectious diseases as drinking water becomes polluted.

FLASH FLOODING AHEAD

1. From reading the passage, we can **conclude** that people's lives are often at risk during floods. What evidence is there in the passage to support this statement?

_____
_____
_____
_____
_____
_____
_____
_____
_____

RI.5.1 Quote accurately from a text when explaining what the text says explicitly and when drawing inferences from the text.

Week 16 | Day 3 | Spelling

Plurals

Plurals are formed by adding **s** to singular nouns. For nouns that end in **s**, **sh**, **ch**, **x**, and **z**, add **es**; e.g., 3 atlas**es**, 2 sketch**es**, 5 box**es**, 3 quizz**es**. For some nouns that end in **o**, add **es**; e.g., 4 potato**es**. Other nouns that end in **o** can take either **s** or **es**; e.g., mango**s** or mango**es**.

List

1 Write the word.

- stitches
- lenses
- sleeves
- styles
- stretches
- weaknesses
- colleges
- clashes
- witnesses
- diseases
- approaches
- reserves
- routes
- vegetables
- magazines
- influences
- passages
- audiences
- obstacles
- tissues

2 Rewrite the words as plurals.

a vegetable
b stitch
c weakness
d influence
e disease
f sleeve
g witness
h audience
i lens
j college
k tissue
l clash
m style
n approach
o stretch
p route
q passage
r obstacle
s reserve
t magazine

3 Chunks. Rearrange the letters to make a list word.

a s yle st
b s lege col
c s sage pas
d serve re s
e ea dis ses
f itch es st
g es ness weak
h es proach ap
i sh a es cl
j es ness wit
k es ro ut
l es veg ta bl e
m ee ves sl
n ac ob les st

Week 16 Day 4 Spelling

Plurals

1 Revise your spelling list from page 84. Complete each sentence with a list word.

a We had to do three different _____ on each leg before we could run.
b It is important to eat five servings of _____ every day.
c I pulled my _____ down when it started to get cold.
d My mom cleaned the _____ of her glasses with a cloth.
e The orchestra was performing to _____ around the world.
f Your bones are formed from several different _____.
g It is said that rats carry many _____.
h There were many _____ to overcome on the course.
i We were collecting _____ to cut pictures from.

Challenge words

2 Write the word.

businesses _____
addresses _____
committees _____
references _____
performances _____
temperatures _____
certificates _____
disturbances _____
catalogs _____
privileges _____

3 Word clues. Which challenge word matches?

a locations _____
b diplomas _____
c brochures _____
d interruptions _____
e advantages _____
f work places _____

4 Hidden words. Find the challenge word.

a encereferencesre _____
b aturtemperaturest _____
c mmtcommitteese _____
d ceperformancese _____

5 Complete the sentence.

a We are putting on three _____ of the play.
b The nurse taught us to measure our _____ using a thermometer.
c We searched the store _____ to find the best deal on microwaves.
d My parents were on the board of many charity _____.
e We had to get five bronze _____ before we could receive a silver one.

L.5.2.E Spell grade-appropriate words correctly, consulting references as needed.

Week 16 Day 5 Grammar

Avoiding shifts in tense

Tense is the form of a verb that shows when an action happens. When a sentence contains **two or more verbs**, it is important to **keep the verbs in the correct tense**; e.g., She **is drawing** and he **is watching** television. I **told** him we **would help** him with the task.

1 Write the verb in parentheses in the correct tense.

a After the movie (is) _____ over, we all went home.
b The bird (flies) _____ away when I approached it.
c I (see) _____ you tonight when I come to your house.
d They (leave) _____ the cage open and the mouse escaped.
e After they had voted, they (wait) _____ to hear the results.

2 Complete each sentence with a verb from the box.

> had been   am starving   wanted   was starving
> have been   want   will starve

a It was nearly time for dinner and I _____.
b I thought we _____ through this before.
c You _____ if you don't have enough to eat.
d I hope it's nearly time for dinner because I _____.
e I _____ through your work and I like what you've done.
f I asked him if he _____ to help me, but he didn't want to get his hands dirty.
g The boys _____ to help us, but I don't think they're strong enough.

3 Circle the verbs in parentheses that correctly complete each sentence.

a He (go, went) for a swim even though the waves (are, were) rough.
b The athlete (leap, leaps) over the final hurdle and (wins, won) the race.
c I (have, will) to go to the doctor as I (have sprained, had sprained) my ankle.
d The coach (want, wants) you back in the team when your ankle (is, was) better.

Week 17 Day 1 Comprehension

Technological Wonders

Finding the main idea and supporting details
To discover what a text is about, look for the main idea or key point. Facts and details in the text can help you find the main idea.

Read the passage.

Underline what a GPS can do.

Highlight where a GPS gets its information from.

Circle how many satellites the GPS receives signals from.

The GPS (Global Positioning System) can pinpoint a location on Earth to within 0.3 of an inch.

GPS receivers gather information from 24 GPS satellites that orbit the Earth. First, a GPS receiver gets signals from at least four of the 24 satellites. It uses the time it takes for the signals to arrive to calculate the distance between it and the satellites. It can then work out its exact location, including its latitude, longitude, and height.

People use the GPS system to calculate their location accurately and precisely.

Color how a GPS is able to calculate the distance between it and the satellites.

Underline what the GPS is able to do once it has calculated the distance between it and the satellites.

Circle the correct answers.

1. In the passage above, what information do we get from paragraph 1?
   a. when to use a GPS
   b. what a GPS can do
   c. where to find a GPS
   d. how long it takes a GPS to work

2. What is the **main idea** of the passage? It tells us …
   a. why a GPS is important.
   b. when the GPS was invented.
   c. how a GPS works.
   d. where the satellites are positioned.

3. Which three **details** in paragraph 2 best support the main idea?
   a. First, a GPS receiver gets signals from at least four of the satellites.
   b. The GPS can pinpoint a location on Earth to within 0.3 of an inch.
   c. After receiving the signals, the GPS calculates the distance between it and the satellites.
   d. GPS stands for Global Positioning System.
   e. People use the GPS system to accurately calculate their location.
   f. The GPS then works out its exact location, including its latitude, longitude, and height.

Technological Wonders

Read the passage.

Underline what an organ transplant is.

Highlight how organ donors can help other people.

Circle what type of transplants were performed in the 1800s.

An organ transplant is an operation where a damaged or diseased organ is replaced with another person's healthy organ. Organ transplants have saved thousands of lives. One organ donor can save and improve the quality of life of up to 10 other people.

In the 1800s, doctors were able to perform skin transplants. The first organ transplant was a cornea transplant in 1905. In 1967, a South African heart surgeon, Christian Barnard, performed a successful heart transplant. He was able to take a healthy heart from a person who had just died, and implant it into a man who had a damaged heart.

The human body does not always accept a transplanted organ. Anti-rejection drugs help to stop the patient's body from rejecting the transplanted organ.

Put a box around the date of the first cornea transplant.

Underline a sentence that gives information about the world's first successful heart transplant.

Color what helps to stop a patient's body from rejecting a transplanted organ.

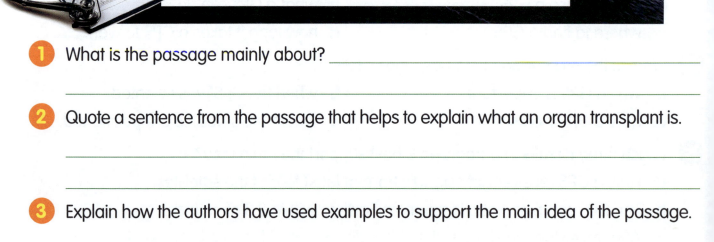

1. What is the passage mainly about? _____

2. Quote a sentence from the passage that helps to explain what an organ transplant is.

3. Explain how the authors have used examples to support the main idea of the passage.

Week 17 Day 3 Spelling

Suffix: ist

A **suffix** is added to the end of a word to make a new word with a slightly different meaning. When the suffix **ist** is added to a word, it indicates **someone who makes or does something**; e.g., novel**ist**. Sometimes we have to **drop the last one or more letters** before **adding ist**; e.g., cycle → cyc**list**, flor**al** → flor**ist**, opportun**ity** → opportun**ist**.

List

artist
tourist
florist
novelist
dentist
cyclist
cartoonist
finalist
soloist
motorist
pianist
journalist
violinist
machinist
vocalist
guitarist
botanist
zoologist
specialist
ecologist

1 Write the word.

2 Name.

a

b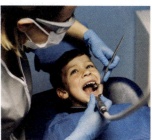

c

d

3 Complete these list words.

a gu_____   b zo_____
c ec_____   d ca_____
e to_____   f so_____
g pi_____   h mo_____

4 **Chunks.** Rearrange the letters to make a list word.

a ist-fin-al _____   b or-mot-ist _____
c e-gist-o-col _____   d chin-ma-ist _____
e lin-vi-ist-o _____   f el-nov-ist _____
g an-bot-ist _____   h o-ist-sol _____
i list-cyc _____   j cal-ist-vo _____
k ist-jou-al-rn _____   l ist-zoo-log _____
m ar-ist-t _____   n oo-ni-ca-st-rt _____

L.5.2.E Spell grade-appropriate words correctly, consulting references as needed.

Week 17 Day 4 Spelling

Suffix: ist

1 Revise your spelling list from page 89. Underline the mistake. Write the word correctly.

a The pianoist played a lovely piece at the recital. _____
b The flaurist placed the beautiful flowers in a vase. _____
c The artiste painted the scenery at the beach. _____
d The tourest took many photos of the Eiffel Tower. _____
e After I injured my knee, I had to see a specialest. _____
f The cartoonest drew a picture of me as a superhero! _____
g My dentast gave me a free toothbrush for being brave. _____
h The jounalest was ready to interview the celebrity. _____
i Before I was born, my dad was a guitarust in a band. _____
j The zoologast fed the crocodiles in front of an audience. _____

Challenge words

2 Write the word.

receptionist _____
opportunist _____
conservationist _____
archaeologist _____
psychologist _____
archivist _____
environmentalist _____
perfectionist _____
nationalist _____
traditionalist _____

3 Hidden words. Find the challenge word.

a torstarchivisterrsti _____
b pschpsychologisti _____
c strattraditionalistt _____
d aristarchaeologisti _____
e pposoopportunisti _____
f perscperfectionisti _____

4 Word clues. Which challenge word matches?

a secretary _____
b therapist _____

5 Another way to say it. Which challenge word could replace the underlined word?

a The <u>secretary</u> answered the phone in a professional manner. _____
b The <u>scientist</u> discovered a tomb in Egypt. _____
c The <u>curator</u> at the museum cataloged the information. _____

Week 17 Day 5 Grammar

Relative and interrogative pronouns

The **pronouns** Who, Which, and Whose can:
- introduce a **subordinate clause**; e.g., That's the man who sold us the tickets. (Relative pronoun)
- ask a **question**; e.g., Who baked this cake? (Interrogative pronoun)

1 Complete each sentence with *who, which,* or *whose*.

a _____ left the door open?

b _____ dirty socks are these?

c _____ dress should I wear to the party?

d I can't decide _____ flavor is best.

e I don't know _____ turn it is to set the table.

f I tried to work out _____ the card was from.

2 Complete each sentence so that it asks a question.

a Who _____

_____

b Which _____

_____

c Whose _____

_____

3 Complete each sentence with a subordinate clause.

a I have spoken to the girl who _____

_____

b I am not sure which _____

_____

c There are the children whose _____

_____

L.5.1 Demonstrate command of the conventions of standard English grammar and usage when writing or speaking.

Week 18 Day 1 Comprehension

Renewable Resources

Summarizing
A summary is a shortened version of the original text. To summarize a text, look for the points and details that contain the most important information.

Read the passage.

Tidal power is energy produced from tides and currents.

Tides are the changes in sea level that happen twice a day. They are caused by the gravitational effect of the moon.

A tidal power station uses the movement of water through a barrage to generate electricity. The water turns turbines inside the barrage, which power generators and produce electricity. Electricity is also made when the tide goes back and water flows the other way through the barrage.

Highlight the sentence that explains what tidal power is.

Underline the sentence that gives the most information about what a tidal power station does.

Circle the correct answers.

1 Which sentence contains the most information about tides and tidal power?
   a Tidal power is energy produced from tides and currents.
   b Tides are the changes in sea level that happen twice a day.
   c They are caused by the gravitational effect of the moon.

2 Which sentence contains the most information about what a tidal power station does?
   a A tidal power station uses the movement of water through a barrage to generate electricity.
   b The water turns turbines inside the barrage, which power generators and produce electricity.
   c Electricity is also made when the tide goes back and water flows the other way through the barrage.

3 Use the sentences you have chosen in questions 1 and 2 to write a **summary** of the passage.

_____

_____

RI.5.2 Determine two or more main ideas of a text and explain how they are supported by key details; summarize the text.

Week 18 Day 2 Comprehension

Renewable Resources

Read the passage.

Highlight the sentence that tells what biofuels are made from.

Put a box around two examples of biofuels.

Underline the sentence that tells what ethanol is made from.

Biofuels are fuels made from biomass material. The most common biofuels are ethanol and biodiesel.

Ethanol is made from the sugars in grains, such as corn, wheat, and sugar cane. Sugars are mixed with water and yeast. The mixture is left to ferment until the biomass is converted into ethanol. Ethanol can be mixed with petrol or used on its own.

Biodiesel is made from vegetable oils, fats, or greases. It can be used in diesel engines, either on its own or mixed with diesel fuel made from petroleum. Some engines can even run on pure vegetable oil.

Biodiesel performs much like diesel made from petroleum. However, using biodiesel reduces harmful exhaust gases, such as carbon monoxide and sulphur.

Circle what biodiesel is made from.

Color why biodiesel is better for the environment than diesel.

1 Use the annotations to help you write a **summary** of the passage.

_____
_____
_____
_____
_____
_____
_____
_____
_____
_____

RI.5.2 Determine two or more main ideas of a text and explain how they are supported by key details; summarize the text.

Week 18 | Day 3 | Spelling

Palindrones and portmanteaus

> A **palindrome** is a word or phrase that reads the same backwards as forwards; e.g., level.
>
> A **portmanteau word** combines the letters and meanings of two or more words to make a new word; e.g., **sm**oke + **f**og = smog.

List

madam
level
smog
newscast
motel
sagas
refer
racecar
taxicab
brunch
redder
squiggle
chortle
rotor
kayak
radar
ginormous
fortnight
cheeseburger
paratrooper

1 Write the word.

_____
_____
_____
_____
_____
_____
_____
_____
_____
_____
_____
_____
_____
_____
_____
_____
_____
_____
_____
_____

2 Sort the words.

a *Palindromes*

_____ _____
_____ _____
_____ _____
_____ _____
_____ _____

b *Portmanteau words*

_____ _____
_____ _____
_____ _____
_____ _____
_____ _____

3 Chunks. Fill in the missing letters.

a ___hort_____   b r___f___r
c s_____as   d r___d___e___
e ___ada___   f ___ew___ca___t
g s_____igg___e h r___c___c___r
i k___y___k   j l___ve___

4 Word clues. Which list word matches?

a chronicles   _____
b program   _____
c fog   _____
d sonar   _____
e speedy vehicle   _____
f huge   _____
g lady   _____
h boat   _____

94   L.5.2.E Spell grade-appropriate words correctly, consulting references as needed.

Week 18 Day 4 Spelling

Palindrones and portmanteaus

1 **Revise your spelling list from page 94.** Complete each sentence with a list word.

a We stayed overnight in a _____ .
b We had a _____ and fries for lunch.
c Another ship showed up on our ship's _____ .
d I picked the red _____ to drive on the video game.
e We had people coming over at 11 a.m. for a _____ of bacon and eggs.
f The _____ steered his parachute as best he could to land in the field.
g Our art teacher drew a _____ and we had to turn it into a picture.
h My family hired a _____ and we spent the day rowing on the river.
i Eloise gave a _____ at Ava's joke.

Challenge words

2 **Write the word.**

rotator _____
guesstimate _____
deified _____
emoticon _____
cyberspace _____
reviver _____
rotavator _____
simulcast _____
nanosecond _____
knowledgebase _____

3 **Hidden words.** Find the challenge word.

a waoyrotavatorva _____
b asdjksimulcastca _____
c sknowledgebase _____
d rottarotatortorea _____
e nonanoseconda _____
f funreviververyah _____
g timaguesstimatet _____
h ieonemoticonem _____
i defideifiedfied _____
j cyspcyberspacey _____

4 **Another way to say it.** Which challenge word could replace the underlined word/s?

a Sandra used a <u>smiley face</u> at the end of her text message. _____
b The computer performed the task in a <u>blink of an eye</u>. _____
c Some ancient tribes <u>idolized</u> their kings. _____
d The sporting event was <u>transmitted</u> on television and radio. _____
e My email got lost in a <u>virtual world</u>. _____

L.5.2.E Spell grade-appropriate words correctly, consulting references as needed.

Week 18 | Day 5 | Grammar

Adverbs of degree

An **adverb** gives information about a verb by telling **how, where,** or **when** something is done; e.g., He walks **slowly**. She sits **there**. They will arrive **soon**. **Adverbs** also show to what **extent or degree** something is done; e.g., I **almost** fell. Many adverbs of degree come before an adjective or another adverb; e.g., He is an **extremely** good player. She **hardly ever** comes to see us.

1. Complete each of the following sentences with an adverb from the box. Use each adverb once.

a. There were _____ any people at the show.
b. Everyone was exhausted after a _____ busy day.
c. My brother is an _____ fast runner.
d. He _____ got it right that time.
e. I tried on the shoes, but they were _____ big for me.

> too
> exceptionally
> hardly
> very
> almost

2. Circle the adverb in parentheses that correctly completes each sentence.

a. She knows (hardly, almost, perfectly) well what I mean.
b. He is feeling ill because he ate (too, very, really) much dessert.
c. That was the (more, most, much) exciting game of the season.
d. She gave us an (extremely, very, quite) difficult problem to solve.
e. This movie is even (most, more, much) amazing than the last one.
f. The river was flowing (almost, very, hardly) quickly after the heavy rains.

3. Complete each sentence with a suitable adverb.

a. I think your puppy is _____ cute.
b. He was fined for driving _____ fast.
c. I was so excited I could _____ breathe.
d. The strong winds did _____ a bit of damage.
e. They _____ disagreed with everything we said.

4. Make your own sentences with the following adverbs.

a. extremely _____
b. nearly _____

L.5.1 Demonstrate command of the conventions of standard English grammar and usage when writing or speaking.

REVIEW 2: Spelling

Spelling

> Use this review to test your knowledge. It has three parts—**Spelling**, **Grammar**, and **Comprehension**. If you're unsure of an answer, go back and read the rules and generalizations in the blue boxes.

You have learned about:
- suffix: ity
- suffix: ive
- plurals
- compound words
- ending: ish
- suffix: ist
- Latin origins
- prefixes: un, dis, mis
- portmanteau words

1 In each sentence, the spelling error has been underlined. Write the correct spelling. 2 marks

a There was an <u>displeasant</u> smell coming from the trash can. _____

b Last summer, I managed to <u>unlocate</u> my shoulder when I fell off my bike. _____

c The day celebrated <u>equallity</u> for all people around the world. _____

d I was feeling <u>slugish</u> after our Thanksgiving feast. _____

2 Which word correctly completes this sentence? 1 mark

The author advertised for a _____ agent to sell her new book to a publisher.

a literary   b literacy   c literate   d literal

3 This sentence has one word that is incorrect. Write the correct spelling. 1 mark

I hope to one day be a guitiarist in a rock and roll band. _____

4 Name the compound and portmanteau words. 2 marks

a [cheese] + [hamburger] = _____

b [runners] + [car] = _____

5 Circle the correct word to complete the sentence. 3 marks

a Over the years, scientists have been able to eliminate many (disease/diseases).

b I packed cheese, pickles, meat, and a loaf of (bread, breads) for the picnic.

c I had to unravel my knitting as I had dropped a few (stitch, stiches).

6 Which word correctly completes this sentence? 1 mark

My brother is very _____ about the contents of his diary.

a secret   b secretly   c secretive   d secrets

Your score ☐ / 10

REVIEW 2: Grammar

Grammar

You have learned about:
- interjections
- exclamation points
- adverbs of degree
- commas in sentences
- shifts in tense
- perfect tense
- pronouns

1 Write a sentence to match each interjection. 2 marks

  a Ouch! _____

  b Hey! _____

2 Join the following pairs of sentences with *so*, *and*, or *but*. Use each word once. 3 marks

  a I baked the cake. We ate it straight afterwards. _____

  b I tried on the shirt. It was too tight. _____

  c The shirt didn't fit. We took it back. _____

3 In each sentence, circle the verb that is wrong. Write the correction in the space. 1 mark

  a He have hurt his foot and can't take part in the competition. _____

  b By the time they arrived, I have already finished my chores. _____

4 Fill in the commas in the following sentences. 3 marks

  a No I have never been to Vietnam.

  b Yes that is the correct answer.

  c Theo you have taken the dog for a walk haven't you?

5 Fill in the missing commas and exclamation points in the following sentences. 2 marks

  a Wow What a brilliant jump

  b Oh no What happened Marty?

  c How exciting was that

  d Shoo Go away you pesky fly

REVIEW 2: Grammar

Grammar

6 In the following sentences, underline the verb that is in the wrong tense. Write it correctly in the space. 3 marks

a I will open my present when I will get home. _____
b He sat down and starts eating his dinner. _____
c I have finished my snacks before the train arrived. _____
d She goes to the shops while I was at dance practice. _____
e He was washing the dishes when he hears someone at the door.
   _____
f I will believe it when I saw it. _____

7 Complete each sentence so that it asks a question. 2 marks

a Who _____
b Which _____

8 In each sentence, circle the relative pronoun and underline the relative clause. 2 marks

a I was talking to the boy whose bike this is.
c Here is the pencil which I borrowed from you yesterday.
d The bird, whose wing was broken, was unable to fly.
b Our new neighbors, who moved in yesterday, are very friendly.

9 Circle the adverb in parentheses that correctly completes each sentence. 2 marks

a They have (extremely, almost, too) completed the task.
b This is the (much, more, most) amazing chocolate I have ever eaten.
c I was (very, almost, much) tired after running the cross-country race.
d That was an (very, quite, extremely) difficult decision to make.

Your score ☐ 20

REVIEW 2: Comprehension

The Importance of Family

Read the passage and then use the comprehension skills you have learned to answer the questions.

You can choose your friends, but you can't choose your relatives. This may be true, but does it mean that friends are more important just because you choose who they are? I don't think so, but not everyone will agree.

To many people, friends (in particular best friends) are the most important relationships in their lives. They spend more time chatting with friends over the phone, by email, or text messages than they do with their families. There are different reasons for this.

One reason is that people share so many special memories with friends as they grow up together. Friends are often similar in age, so they find themselves doing the same things at the same times and this gives enjoyment. Often families have only one child or children many years apart, so they don't share these special moments.

Another reason in favor of friends is that people spend their free time, their fun time, with friends. Often parents are working on weekends, so who do you spend time relaxing with? Good friends, of course!

Yet families are also very important. Within families people have a special bond of culture, beliefs, and, of course, love. These are not always shared by friends. The best thing about families is that they are always there for you. They look after you when you are sick, they help you learn all about life and they love you no matter what—even when you might sometimes be a little bit naughty.

So, even though it is great to have friends, it is much better to have family. You might not be able to choose who they are, but you certainly can rely on them to be there and help you out whenever you need it.

1 What does the text suggest is the main reason people become friends? 1 mark **INFERENTIAL**
  a They live next door to each other.
  b Their parents know each other.
  c They play on the same football team.
  d They enjoy each other's company.

100

REVIEW 2: Comprehension

The Importance of Family

2 In the writer's opinion, what is one of the main benefits of having friends? 1 mark
You can ... **LITERAL**
   a always rely on friends.
   b relax with friends.
   c be completely honest with friends.
   d borrow things from friends.

3 What is the purpose of the rhetorical questions the writer uses? 1 mark
The writer is ... **CRITICAL**
   a looking for answers.
   b showing how important the issues are.
   c making the reader think about the issues.
   d testing the reader's knowledge.

4 Who does the writer think is the most important in a person's life? 1 mark **LITERAL**
   a best friends
   b school friends
   c family
   d good friends

5 When are you most likely to need your family? 1 mark **LITERAL**
   a when you are sick
   b when you have a secret to share
   c when you just want to chat
   d when you go to the movies

6 Who does the writer believe people spend the most time chatting with on the phone? 1 mark
INFERENTIAL
   a their parents
   b their friends
   c their brothers or sisters
   d their cousins

7 Which activity can you do with friends but NOT usually your family? 1 mark **INFERENTIAL**
   a play sport
   b go to the movies
   c go to the beach
   d attend baseball practice

8 What is most likely to happen as you grow older? Choose two answers. 1 mark **INFERENTIAL**
   a You will have the same friends.
   b You will have the same family.
   c Your friends will change.
   d Your family will change.

9 What is the main purpose of this text? 1 mark **CRITICAL**
_____
_____

10 Why are families always there for you? 1 mark **LITERAL**
_____
_____
_____

Your score ☐ / 10

Your Review 2 Scores
Spelling ☐ /10 + Grammar ☐ /20 + Comprehension ☐ /10 = Total ☐ /40

Week 19 | Day 1 | Comprehension

Backstage Betrayal

Cause and effect
To find cause and effect, ask why something happens and what the result is.

Read the passage.

Put a box around what has made Kelly's bullying worse.

Color how often Kelly is saying or writing nasty things to Laura.

Laura stops at the mirrors. She gazes at her reflection above the hand basin. She wishes Mr. Mitchell hadn't given her the solo. Kelly's bullying has always been bad, but the play has made it much worse. The name-calling, lies, and nasty notes are now daily events.

Singing usually makes Laura feel better. Softly, she sings her song from the play. She begins to twirl on the tiled floor, pretending she is on the stage. Suddenly the lights go out. Laura can't see a thing.

Circle the word that is similar in meaning to *looks*.

Highlight what usually cheers Laura up.

Circle the correct answers.

1 **Why** does Laura wish Mr. Mitchell hadn't given her the solo to sing?
  a She doesn't think she's good enough.
  b She doesn't like being on the stage.
  c She prefers dancing to singing.
  d She doesn't like being bullied.

2 What **effect** has Kelly's bullying had on Laura? Kelly's bullying has …
  a made Laura angry.
  b confused Laura.
  c upset Laura.
  d made Laura determined to succeed.

3 What is the most likely **reason** Kelly's bullying has become worse? Kelly is …
  a afraid of Laura.
  b jealous of Laura.
  c disappointed in Laura.
  d worried about Laura.

4 What is the **clue** to question 3's answer?
  a Laura is prettier than Kelly.
  b Laura is a better singer than Kelly.
  c Laura is singing a solo in the play.
  d Kelly has never liked Laura.

Backstage Betrayal

Week 19 Day 2 Comprehension

Read the whole story

Read the passage.

Highlight words that show why Laura is still in the theater.

Circle who Laura thinks will help her.

Underline the sentence that shows Laura is certain her parents will find her.

Color why Laura believes she might have to spend the night in the theater after all.

> Surely, before leaving, they will check to make sure that no one is locked in the theater? Of course they will check!
>
> Shona wouldn't leave without her! Shona will look for Laura and ask if anyone has seen her. Shona's parents are supposed to be driving Laura home.
>
> Suddenly, Laura thinks of her own parents. When she doesn't come home, her parents will worry. They will wonder where she is. They'll ring Shona. They'll come to the theater. They won't rest until they find her.
>
> A balloon of happiness swells in Laura's chest. She won't have to spend all night in this spooky place after all. The balloon bursts. Will her parents think to look for her in the toilet?

1. From reading the passage, we can tell that Laura is frightened. What is **causing** her to feel afraid? Support your answer with a quote from the text.

___

2. What gives Laura hope that someone will find her soon?

___

3. What **causes** Laura to lose hope again?

___

RL.5.1 Quote accurately from a text when explaining what the text says explicitly and when drawing inferences from the text.

Week 19 Day 3 Spelling

Suffix: ous

Adding the suffix **ous** to a noun or verb turns it into an adjective; e.g., hazard → hazard**ous**.
If the base word ends in **e**, drop the e before adding **ous**; e.g., adventur**e** → adventur**ous**.
If the base word ends in **y** and there is a consonant before the **y**, change the y to i before adding **ous**; e.g., victo**ry** → victor**ious**.
Some adjectives that end in **ous** are not formed from verbs or nouns; e.g., generous.

List

- numerous
- glorious
- meticulous
- tedious
- ominous
- devious
- monstrous
- victorious
- envious
- outrageous
- religious
- marvelous
- hazardous
- hilarious
- vicious
- ambitious
- indigenous
- gracious
- courteous
- ferocious

1 Write the word.

2 Write the list words in alphabetical order.

3 Unscramble these list words.
   a suolevram
   b osumino
   c cisfreouo
   d mnstrouos
   e dtuosei
   f cviusio

4 Underline the spelling mistake. Write the word correctly.
   a I was envyous of my friend's trip to Japan.
   b Our neighbors have a ferrocious dog.
   c I have watched the hilerious movie many times.
   d The man acted in a deevius way.
   e There had been a hazerdus chemical spill.
   f Someone with a glorias voice was singing my favorite song.
   g Washing the dishes is such a teedious chore.

L.5.2.E Spell grade-appropriate words correctly, consulting references as needed.

Week 19 Day 4 Spelling

Suffix: ous

1 Revise your spelling list from page 104. Which word means?

a successful _____
b wonderful _____
c funny _____
d native _____
e polite _____
f boring _____
g many _____
h dishonest _____
i dangerous _____
j careful _____
k jealous _____
l fierce _____

Challenge words

2 Write the word.

suspicious _____
conscious _____
surreptitious _____
harmonious _____
conscientious _____
mischievous _____
righteous _____
superstitious _____
advantageous _____
miscellaneous _____

3 Word clues. Which challenge word matches?

a secretive _____
b assorted _____
c mistrustful _____
d peaceful _____
e virtuous _____

4 Hidden words. Find the challenge word.

a icousconsciousct _____
b ievemischievousi _____
c superstitiousous _____
d scieconscientioust _____

5 Complete the sentence.

a He is a _____ and very hard worker.
b My father never walks under ladders as he is _____.
c I thought the story sounded _____ as the timings didn't match up.
d Eating vegetables is _____ to your health.
e The girl was still _____ after the ball hit her head.
f The closet is filled with _____ board games.
g His actions helped make the day _____ and calm.
h The little girl often gets into trouble because of her _____ ways.

L.5.2.E Spell grade-appropriate words correctly, consulting references as needed.

Week 19 Day 5 Grammar

Commas to separate parts of sentences

Commas (,) show us where to pause in a sentence. They help us understand the sentence by breaking it down into **smaller parts**; e.g., Mary-Lou, the girl in the lemon T-shirt, is coming with us to the city, even though she doesn't like riding on buses.

1 In each sentence, fill in two commas.
  a Billy has two Labradors I have a poodle and a cat and Savannah has a parrot.
  b My sister who trained hard for the event won a gold medal.
  c The carnival which starts next week is going to be bigger than last year's.
  d We saw beautifully decorated floats people in colorful costumes and inflatable characters bobbing about.
  e Tom who is my best friend is letting me use his bike while he's on vacation.

2 In each sentence, fill in three commas.
  a Nathan has found his jacket which he thought he'd lost but now he can't find his shoes which were in his closet a moment ago!
  b Olivia the girl sitting next to my sister is an excellent pianist but she doesn't like to play in front of an audience.
  c Although some of them now have cell phones their way of life has changed very little in hundreds perhaps thousands of years.
  d Rudyard Kipling who won the Nobel Prize for Literature in 1907 wrote *Rikki-Tikki-Tavi* one of my favorite stories.
  e There are eight different parts of speech including conjunctions prepositions and interjections.

3 Write the following sentence with the commas in the correct places.
When I scored, the winning goal my grandparents who had come all the way, from Houston, to watch me applauded loudly.

_____

_____

L.5.2 Demonstrate command of the conventions of standard English capitalization, punctuation, and spelling when writing.

Week 20 Day 1 Comprehension

Egyptian Queen

Making connections
Linking a text to other texts you have read is a great way to build understanding. Look for key words and phrases in the texts to make the connections.

Read the passage.

Text 1

Flynn could hardly believe their bad luck. They were only in Cairo for one day and they had to spend it in a museum. Uncle Earl, world famous archaeologist, got to float down the Nile. How unfair! Flynn wanted to climb a pyramid, visit the Valley of the Kings, maybe even ride a camel.

Flynn groaned as he scanned the map of the museum. "OK, let's get this over with. How about we start in the Statue Room?"

- In both texts, **color** all references to the Cairo Museum.
- In both texts, **highlight** all references to the pyramids.
- In both texts, underline all references to camels.
- In both texts, put a boxed around all references to the Valley of the Kings.

Text 2

One of the most interesting countries I've ever visited is Egypt. Its capital, Cairo, is home to the famous Pyramids of Giza, one of the wonders of the ancient world, and the Cairo Museum, which houses the treasures of Tutankhamun, as well as thousands of other objects from Egypt's past. And I will never forget those camel rides! So much fun! Not to mention our visit to Luxor and the Valley of the Kings. What an amazing experience!

1 Write down whether the following information applies to **both** of the texts, or just **one** of the texts.

- **a** a reference to things to see and do in Egypt _____
- **b** a reference to camel rides _____
- **c** what it feels like to ride a camel _____
- **d** visiting the Valley of the Kings _____
- **e** a reference to the Cairo Museum _____
- **f** a reference to Tutankhamun _____
- **g** a reference to the pyramids _____
- **h** a reference to Cairo as Egypt's capital city _____

RL.5.1 Quote accurately from a text when explaining what the text says explicitly and when drawing inferences from the text.

Week 20 Day 2 Comprehension

Egyptian Queen

Read the passage.

Text 1

Queen Hatshepsut was one of the few female pharaohs to rule Egypt. When her husband died, she ruled as regent for her young stepson, Thutmose III, and then proclaimed herself pharaoh. Queen Hatshepsut ruled for almost 20 years in a period known as the 18th Dynasty (around 1489 to 1469 B.C.).

Queen Hatshepsut was a master politician and dressed like a king, even wearing a false beard. She left behind more monuments and works of art than any Egyptian queen to come.

Text 2

When Queen Hatshepsut's husband, Thutmose I died, the heir to the throne, Thutmose III, was still a young boy. At first, Hatshepsut was named regent, which meant she ran the country for Thutmose III. Before long, however, she took the title of pharaoh.

Hatshepsut was a clever and powerful ruler. During her reign of 20 years she had many buildings and monuments constructed throughout Egypt, including many statues of herself.

- In both texts, **highlight** all references to Queen Hatshepsut's husband.
- In both texts, <u>underline</u> all references to Thutmose III.
- In one of the texts, color the information we are given about when Queen Hatshepsut was pharaoh.
- In both texts, (circle) the phrases that tell what kind of a ruler Hatshepsut was.

1 What information do both texts give us about how Queen Hatshepsut became pharaoh?

_____

2 What information do both texts give us about the kind of ruler Hatshepsut was?

_____

3 What extra information does the first text give us about Queen Hatshepsut?

_____

Week 20 Day 3 Spelling

Plurals: s, ies

> If a noun ends in **y** and there is a **consonant before it**, change the **y** to **i** and add **es** to make it plural; e.g. ci**ty** → ci**ties**. If a noun ends in **y** and there is a **vowel before it**, add **s** to make it plural; e.g., Sund**ay** → Sund**ays**.

List

- rallies
- decoys
- allies
- highways
- essays
- volleys
- energies
- countries
- abilities
- quantities
- companies
- difficulties
- policies
- discoveries
- deputies
- penalties
- salaries
- journeys
- assemblies
- identities

1 Write the word.

2 Make the words plural.
- a quantity
- b rally
- c energy
- d assembly
- e highway
- f essay
- g ally
- h difficulty
- i salary
- j decoy
- k company
- l deputy
- m identity
- n discovery
- o ability
- p policy
- q volley
- r penalty
- s journey
- t country

3 Complete these words with *ys* or *ies*.
- a rall_____
- b identit_____
- c all_____
- d polic_____
- e casualt_____
- f energ_____
- g journe_____
- h deput_____
- i volle_____
- j assembl_____
- k deco_____
- l penalt_____
- m countr_____
- n compan_____
- o highwa_____
- p discover_____

4 Match the clue with the list word.
- a payments
- b trips
- c amounts
- d lands
- e businesses
- f punishments
- g traps
- h freeways

L.5.2.E Spell grade-appropriate words correctly, consulting references as needed.

Week 20 Day 4 Spelling

Plurals: s, ies

1 **Revise your spelling list from page 109.** Which list word belongs to each group?

a energy, energetic, _____
b rally, rallying, _____
c inability, ability, _____
d journey, journeyed, _____
e penalize, penalty, _____
f ally, allied, _____
g assemble, assembled, _____
h policy, political, _____
i difficult, difficulty, _____
j identify, identity, _____
k discover, discovers, _____
l decoy, decoyed, _____

Challenge words

2 Write the word.

opportunities _____
responsibilities _____
communities _____
universities _____
laboratories _____
casualties _____
similarities _____
attorneys _____
possibilities _____
personalities _____

3 **Hidden words.** Find the challenge word.

a comcommunitiesu _____
b borilaboratorieste _____
c sibepossibilitiesilit _____
d tiesuniversitiesun _____
e torneyattorneysa _____
f caseucasualtiesli _____

4 **Word clues.** Which challenge word matches?

a likeness _____
b scientific workshops _____
c probabilities _____

5 **Another way to say it.** Which challenge word could replace the underlined word?

a My eldest brother was choosing between two different <u>colleges</u>. _____
b The <u>resemblances</u> between the siblings far outweighed their differences. _____
c Her <u>tasks</u> at home included cleaning her room and helping with dinner. _____
d The two girls had similar <u>characteristics</u> and so got on very well. _____
e They had many <u>chances</u> to score a goal. _____
f The various <u>neighborhoods</u> joined together to help each other after the fire. _____

Week 20 Day 5 Grammar

Adverbials of time

Adverbs and adverbial phrases give information about verbs. They can tell us when or how often something is done; e.g., Your package will arrive **soon**. It will be here **in a minute**.

1 Match the word to the phrase.

a soon — in the past
b immediately — now and again
c afterward — on that occasion
d before — right away
e then — at all times
f sometimes — in a little while
g always — later on

2 Sort the phrases.

right now   at a later date   last week   at this time   the other day
in a moment   in time to come   a while back   this instant

Past	Present	Future

3 Circle the phrase that correctly completes the sentence.

a I brush my teeth (every day/not at any time).
b They should be here (several days ago/in about an hour).
c The concert started (at exactly seven o'clock/at any moment).
d (In the future/In days gone by) we may be able to travel to Mars.
e He visited his friend (the day after tomorrow/the day before yesterday).

4 Complete each adverbial with a word from the box.

a I saw him just a _____ ago.
b I said I would get there as _____ as possible.
c Everything seemed to happen _____ the same time.
d I don't like broccoli, so I only eat it _____ in a while.
e They worked around the _____ to get the venue finished.

clock   soon   once   at   moment

L.5.1 Demonstrate command of the conventions of standard English grammar and usage when writing or speaking.

Week 21 Day 1 Comprehension

Diving for the Ghost Galleon

Making predictions
Your can predict what is going to happen in a text based on clues in the words and pictures and what you already know.

Read the passage.

Circle the skill that most people on board had.

Put a box around the word that shows that some members of the crew knew a lot about shipwrecks.

Mia and Flynn were surprised to find out how many different skills were on board. While almost all the crew were divers, everyone seemed to have another field of expertise as well. There were researchers, oceanographers, shipwreck specialists, artifact conservationists, salvage experts, and a medical team. It seemed that Mel was leaving nothing to chance. He wanted this team to be the best.

Highlight the word that refers to an object of cultural or historical interest.

Underline the phrase that refers to people who rescue or recover objects from shipwrecks.

Circle your answers for each question.

1. Based on information in the passage, what is most likely going to happen? The people on the boat are going to ...
    - a collect underwater plants.
    - b look for sunken treasure.
    - c study underwater rock formations.
    - d measure the depth of the ocean.

2. Which words and phrases are the clues to question 1's answer? Choose four options.
    - a different skills
    - b divers
    - c field of expertise
    - d researchers
    - e oceanographers
    - f shipwreck specialists
    - g artifact conservationists
    - h salvage experts
    - i medical team

112   RL.5.1 Quote accurately from a text when explaining what the text says explicitly and when drawing inferences from the text.

Week 21 Day 2 Comprehension

Diving for the Ghost Galleon

Read the whole story

Read the passage.

Color the phrase that shows what Flynn expected Bloodbath the Pirate to do to him.

Highlight the words that show why Bloodbath the Pirate was interested in *The Atocha*.

Underline the reason Mia says *The Atocha* will make them rich.

"SILENCE!" yelled Bloodbath the Pirate. He was now only a hair's breadth away from Flynn's face. Flynn stood in terror, waiting for the strike of the sword. Then Bloodbath the Pirate began to speak slowly. "You come from *The Atocha*, eh? The Spanish ship we are after? Hmm. How very interesting. Tell me of its cargo."

"Why, it's a pirate's dream," cried Mia, diverting Bloodbath the Pirate's attention. "It's packed to the rafters with gold, silver, and gemstones! The booty on that ship will make rich pirates of us all, a thousand times over."

"All of us, hey?" He eyed her with his one good eye.

"Why of course! Spare us, and I will lead you to hidden treasures that only we know about."

Circle the word that shows that Mia was trying to get Bloodbath the Pirate's attention away from Flynn.

Highlight the reason Mia says Bloodbath the Pirate should spare her and Flynn.

1. What do you think Bloodbath the Pirate is going to do next? Give reasons for your answer.

_____
_____
_____
_____
_____

2. What do you think is going to happen to Mia and Flynn? Give reasons for your answer.

_____
_____
_____
_____

RL.5.1 Quote accurately from a text when explaining what the text says explicitly and when drawing inferences from the text.

Week 21 | Day 3 | Spelling

Adding to fer

> In two-syllable words that **end in fer**, **double the r** if **fer is stressed when the suffix is added**; e.g., prefer → prefe**rr**ed, prefe**rr**ing.
>
> **Do not double the r** if **fer is not stressed when the suffix is added**; e.g., prefer → prefe**r**ential, prefe**r**ence.

List

differ
offer
refer
prefer
transfer
infer
confer
defer
suffer
offering
differed
different
difference
referee
preferred
transferred
inferring
conferring
deferred
suffered

1 Write the word.

2 Sort the words.

   a Words with suffix *ing*

   b Words with suffix *ed*

   c Words with suffix *ent*

   d Words with suffix *ee*

3 Fill in the missing letters.

   a o____fe____i____g
   b tra____s____e____re____
   c r____f____r
   d t_____ns____er
   e co____f____r
   f in____e_____ing
   g di____f____re____

4 Complete each sentence with a list word.

   a We _____ red apples to green apples.
   b Dad didn't follow a recipe, so the meal tasted _____ each time.
   c The age _____ between my sister and me is three years.
   d The _____ blew his whistle at the end of the football match.
   e The price included a free _____ from the airport to the hotel.
   f Ben accepted the _____ to go to his friend's house.

Week 21 Day 4 Spelling

Adding to fer

1 **Revise your spelling list from page 114.** Add suffixes to build words.

a infer	b differ	c prefer	d suffer
s ____	s ____	s ____	s ____
ed ____	ed ____	ed ____	ed ____
ing ____	ing ____	ing ____	ing ____

e offer	f transfer	g confer	h defer
s ____	s ____	s ____	s ____
ed ____	ed ____	ed ____	ed ____
ing ____	ing ____	ing ____	ing ____

Challenge words

2 Write the word.

- referred ____
- reference ____
- preference ____
- referral ____
- transference ____
- inference ____
- inferential ____
- conference ____
- deference ____
- preferential ____

3 **Word clues.** Which challenge word matches?

- a quotation ____
- b interpretation ____
- c movement ____
- d meeting ____
- e favorite ____
- f favored ____

4 **Hidden words.** Find the challenge word.

- a fereinferentialial ____
- b encedeferencedef ____
- c refereferredferr ____
- d reffreferralrral ____

5 Complete the sentence.

a I like action movies, but my _____ is for comedies.
b We received _____ seating on the plane as we were frequent flyers.
c Dad attended a work _____ in another state.
d Her _____ skills made it possible for her to work out the answer.

Week 21 Day 5 Grammar

Future perfect tense

Tense is the form of a verb that shows when something happens. Verbs in the **future perfect tense** show that **an action will be completed** before something else happens; e.g., They **will have arrived** by the time we get there.

1 Complete each sentence with a verb from the box.

| will have labeled | will have realized | will have milked | will have repaired |

a By now they _____ their mistake.
b The farmer _____ the cows by then.
c The man _____ the broken bicycle by now.
d He _____ the parcel before sending it to his friend.

2 Write the verb in parentheses in the future perfect tense.

a Hopefully she (find) _____ the key by then.
b They (test) _____ the app many times before putting it on the market.
c The weather (warm up) _____ by the time we go on holiday.
d By the end of the season, I (play) _____ ten games for the team.
e She (rest) _____ by then and should be ready to continue working.
f They (leave) _____ the house long before you get there.
g By five o'clock, the doctor (see) _____ all her patients.

3 Make a sentence with each of the following verbs.

a will have returned _____

b will have closed _____

c will have removed _____

d will have started _____

Week 22　Day 1　Comprehension

The Goblin and the Grocer

Figurative language

Alliteration repeats consonant sounds. **Onomatopoeia** imitates sounds. A **simile** compares two things using the words *like* or *as*. **Metaphors** make a more direct comparison. They do not contain the words *like* or *as*.

Read the passage.

In paragraph 1, underline the simile.

In paragraph 1, circle two consecutive words that start with the letter *b*.

In paragraph 1, put a box around two consecutive words that start with the letter *l*.

Highlight the word that imitates the sound the student's stomach makes.

There once was a student who was as poor as a church mouse. He lived in an attic above a grocer's shop. A goblin lived with the grocer downstairs, happy that every year he was given a big bowl of oatmeal with a large lump of butter.

One evening the student was very hungry. To stop his stomach rumbling, he went downstairs to the grocer's shop to buy some cheese. The student noticed that the cheese was wrapped in pages from a book of poetry.

Circle the correct answers.

1 Which phrase is an example of a **simile**?
 a a big bowl of oatmeal
 b as poor as a church mouse
 c a large lump of butter
 d his stomach rumbling

2 Which groups of words are examples of **alliteration**? Choose two options.
 a stomach rumbling   b big bowl   c book of poetry   d large lump

3 Which phrase contains an example of **onomatopoeia**?
 a stop his stomach rumbling
 b wrapped in pages from a poetry book
 c lived in an attic
 d was very hungry

4 What is the **clue** to question 3's answer?
 a The phrase contains the word "like".
 b The phrase contains words in which consonant sounds are repeated.
 c The phrase contains a word that imitates a sound.
 d The phrase contains a direct comparison between two objects.

L.5.5 Demonstrate understanding of figurative language, word relationships, and nuances in word meanings.

Week 22　Day 2　Comprehension

The Goblin and the Grocer

Read the passage.

Highlight the object that the tree is compared to.

Circle the objects that the fruits are compared to.

The goblin listened as the student read from the book of poetry. He was entranced. A tree was a beam of light. The leaves were emeralds, and a flower was the face of a lovely girl. Fruits were shining stars and the air was filled with beautiful music. The goblin had never known such wonders. Great feelings swept over him.

"Such beauty! Maybe I should move into the attic," thought the goblin. "But the student is poor, and he doesn't have any porridge for me."

Underline the object that the flower is compared to.

Color the objects that the leaves are compared to.

1 Carefully explain **how** the author uses **metaphors** to help us understand the great **feelings** that swept over the goblin as he listened to the poetry.

_____
_____
_____
_____
_____
_____
_____
_____
_____

Week 22 Day 3 Spelling

Endings: age, idge

> Most words that end in the **ij sound** have the letters **age** at the end; e.g., vint**age**.
>
> Some words that end in the **ij sound** have **idge** at the end; e.g., r**idge**.

List

- heritage
- vintage
- bridge
- damage
- bondage
- hostage
- storage
- manage
- package
- leakage
- drainage
- coverage
- ridge
- savage
- voyage
- postage
- wastage
- stoppage
- marriage
- dosage

1 Write the word.

2 Sort the words.

a *age*

b *idge*

3 Unscramble these list words.

a gobedan
b egamad
c drgei
d edogsa
e ethgreia
f avsgae
g dgbrei

4 Underline the spelling mistake. Write the correct word.

a The network is providing live covrage of the game.
b The rain kept me hostege inside all day long.
c The postege stamps cost more than I expected.
d There was a leekage in the bathroom, so we weren't allowed to go inside.
e The astronaut hoped to make a voyege to the moon.
f My parents recently celebrated twenty years of mariege.

L.5.2.E Spell grade-appropriate words correctly, consulting references as needed.

Week 22 Day 4 Spelling

Endings: age, idge

1 **Revise your spelling list from page 119.** Which list word means?
  a Someone held prisoner _____
  b An amount of medicine _____
  c From an older time _____
  d Not tamed; wild _____
  e To direct or control _____
  f Chain of mountains _____

Challenge words

2 **Write the word.**
  luggage _____
  garbage _____
  plumage _____
  orphanage _____
  cartilage _____
  advantage _____
  beverage _____
  pilgrimage _____
  rummage _____
  sewerage _____

3 **Hidden words.** Find the challenge word.
  a garbaggarbagea _____
  b asdtrsewerageauit _____
  c sdafluggageoiasy _____
  d orpahorphanagea _____
  e aseugrummagea _____
  f poaopilgrimageor _____

4 **Word clues.** Which challenge word matches?
  a feathers _____
  b trash _____
  c search _____
  d drainage _____
  e baggage _____

5 **Complete the sentence.**
  a We checked in our _____ at the airport.
  b We threw the _____ into the trash can.
  c The _____ pipe had cracked and the smell was awful.
  d Some children have to live in an _____.
  e Male peafowls have beautifully colored _____.
  f A cool _____ is refreshing on a hot day.
  g The other team had the _____ of being tall.
  h Your nose is made from _____, not bone.

120   L.5.2.E Spell grade-appropriate words correctly, consulting references as needed.

Week 22 Day 5 Grammar

Commas to avoid misunderstanding

Commas can change the meaning of a sentence; e.g., Owen the dog is digging in the garden. Owen, the dog is digging in the garden. In the first sentence, Owen is a dog. In the second sentence, someone is speaking to a person named Owen.

1 Add commas to the following sentences to make their meaning clear.

a   Let's eat Grandma.
b   She bought a coat and a pie which she ate immediately.
c   In the chest were silver and gold rings and bracelets.
d   Suddenly baking a cake seemed like a good idea.
e   The road said the man was very busy.
f   The old lady chased the thief waving an umbrella.
g   The players said the coach played like a team.
h   When cars move fast drivers usually close their windows.
i   To be honest children don't read those books.
j   Jack the swimming teacher is calling us.

2 Change the meaning of each sentence by placing the comma in a different place. Write the new sentence.

a   As the shadows grew, long creatures emerged from their burrows.
_____
_____

b   After cleaning the dish carefully, place it back on the shelf.
_____
_____

c   If the patient's condition changes quickly, call the doctor.
_____
_____

L.5.2 Demonstrate command of the conventions of standard English capitalization, punctuation, and spelling when writing.

Week 23 Day 1 Comprehension

Muscles in the Body

Study the diagram.

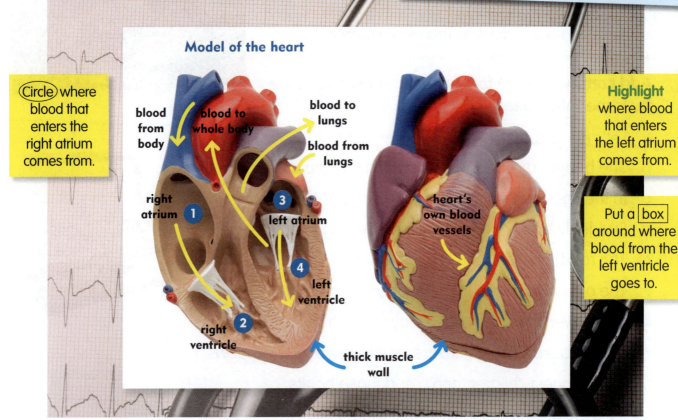

1. Use the diagrams to help you complete the following explanation of how the heart works.

   Blood from the body enters the **a** _____,

   which then contracts. A valve opens to let blood into the

   b _____, which contracts and pumps blood to the

   lungs. Blood full of oxygen returns from the **c** _____ and enters the

   d _____, which then contracts. A valve opens to let

   blood into the **e** _____, which contracts and pumps

   oxygen-filled blood to **f** _____. The heart

   is protected by **g** _____.

RI.5.1 Quote accurately from a text when explaining what the text says explicitly and when drawing inferences from the text.

Week 23 | Day 2 | Comprehension

Muscles in the Body

Study the diagram.

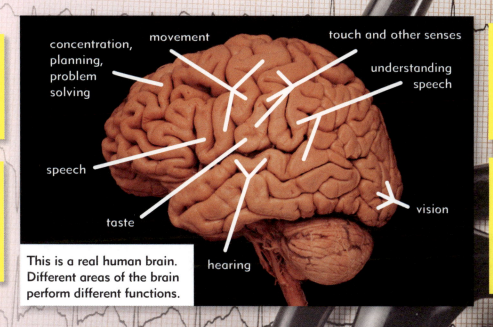

Highlight the part of the brain that controls our sense of sight.

Color the part of the brain that helps us focus when solving problems.

Color the part of the brain that controls our arm and leg muscles.

Highlight the part of the brain that helps us work out what people are saying.

This is a real human brain. Different areas of the brain perform different functions.

❶ Which parts of your brain would you use for the following activities?

a playing sport _____

b watching a movie _____

c reading a book _____

d eating an ice cream _____

e working on a math problems _____

f stroking a cat _____

RI.5.1 Quote accurately from a text when explaining what the text says explicitly and when drawing inferences from the text.

Week 23 Day 3 Spelling

ment, ship, hood, dom

Many verbs can be turned into nouns by adding the suffix **ment**; e.g., replace → replace**ment**.

Some words can be turned into abstract nouns by adding the suffixes **ship**, **hood**, or **dom**; e.g., citizen → citizen**ship**, mother → mother**hood**, chief → chief**dom**.

List
- stardom
- motherhood
- settlement
- chiefdom
- hardship
- wisdom
- kingdom
- assessment
- priesthood
- replacement
- attachment
- engagement
- achievement
- management
- assignment
- likelihood
- abandonment
- knighthood
- measurement
- citizenship

1 Write the word.

2 Sort the words.
- a ment
- b ship
- c hood
- d dom

3 Put the letter chunks in the right order.
- a ment/ace/re/pl
- b li/hood/like
- c ieve/ment/ach
- d dom/chief
- e t/hood/knigh
- f ment/en/gage
- g sure/ment/mea
- h hood/er/moth

4 Meaning. Which list word means?
- a The act of achieving
- b An area ruled by a chief
- c Time of suffering
- d The specific size of something
- e A judgment or evaluation
- f A person that takes the position of another

Week 23 Day 4 Spelling

ment, ship, hood, dom

1 **Revise your spelling list from page 124.** Match the clue with the list word.

a the status of belonging to a certain country
b chance or probability
c experience, knowledge, and good judgment
d a bond of fondness or loyalty to something
e to leave something without warning
f a task, usually with a deadline
g person or persons in charge of business
h celebrity status

Challenge words

2 **Write the word.**

environment
recruitment
embarrassment
apprenticeship
announcement
disappointment
encouragement
imprisonment
advertisement
companionship

3 **Word clues.** Which challenge word matches?

a captivity
b hiring
c broadcast
d shame
e commercial

4 **Hidden words.** Find the challenge word.

a tenvironmenterim
b acompanionshipin
c adisappointmentp
d papprenticeshipal

5 **Complete the sentence.**

a It caused her great _____ when she realized she had called him the wrong name.
b My mom went to a _____ agency to find a new job.
c I am always grateful for the support and _____ my parents give me.
d It was a big _____ to hear that my favorite band had canceled their tour.

L.5.2.E Spell grade-appropriate words correctly, consulting references as needed.

Week 23 Day 5 Grammar

Sequence adverbs

Adverbs give information about verbs. **Sequence adverbs** show the **order** in which **things** happen; e.g., **First** I combed my hair, and **then** I put on my cap. They include the following words and phrases.

after   after that   afterward   before   eventually   finally   first
last   last of all lastly   later   meanwhile   next   then

1 Complete the following procedure with sequence adverbs from the above.

a _____, butter two slices of wholemeal bread.

b _____, place some chopped lettuce and sliced avocado on one of the slices.

c _____, arrange the shredded chicken on top of the lettuce, cucumber, and tomato.

d _____, put the two slices together.

e _____, cut the sandwich into neat triangles.

2 Circle the word that correctly completes each sentence.

a Everyone was happy when it was (meanwhile, finally) time to go home.

b (First, Then) you have to fix your bicycle, and (first, then) you can ride it.

c If you leave a block of ice in the sun, it will (eventually, afterward) melt.

d Jack stood at the front of the line, Charlie was behind him, and I came (lastly, next).

e I started by pulling out the weeds and (afterward, before) I watered all the plants.

3 Write sentences that start with the following adverbs.

a First _____

b Eventually _____

c Later _____

d Afterward _____

e Finally _____

L.5.1 Demonstrate command of the conventions of standard English grammar and usage when writing or speaking.

Endangered Animals

Week 24 · Day 1 · Comprehension

Fact or opinion?
A fact is something that we can prove is true; e.g., A spider has eight legs. An opinion is a belief or feeling; e.g., Spiders are ugly.

Read the passage.

In paragraph 1, put a box around the sentence that expresses a fact.

In paragraph 1, highlight the sentence that expresses two opinions.

Zoos and wildlife sanctuaries are working to save endangered animals from extinction. Some people think animals shouldn't be kept in zoos and that sanctuaries take up valuable land.

Zoos are places where people can see wild animals in captivity. Modern zoos educate people about animals, conduct research, and encourage the conservation of endangered animals. Some animals, such as the California condor, have been saved from extinction by breeding programs in zoos.

Color what people can see in zoos.

Underline a fact about the California condor.

Circle the correct answers.

1 Which of the following statements about zoos is a **fact**?
  a Animals shouldn't be kept in zoos.
  b Animals in zoos are unhappy.
  c People can see wild animals in zoos.
  d Animals feel safe in zoos.

2 Which of the following statements about zoos is an **opinion**?
  a Zoos work to save endangered species.
  b Some people think zoos take up valuable land in cities.
  c Many zoos run special breeding programs.
  d Modern zoos educate people about animals.

3 Write down one **fact** about the California condor.
  _____
  _____

4 What is your **opinion** about zoos?
  _____
  _____

RI.5.1 Quote accurately from a text when explaining what the text says explicitly and when drawing inferences from the text.

Week 24 | Day 2 | Comprehension

Endangered Animals

Read the passage.

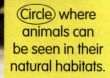
Read the full text

Underline why some people are against zoos.

Color why some people support zoos.

Circle where animals can be seen in their natural habitats.

Highlight the advantages of keeping animals in wildlife sanctuaries.

Some species don't breed in captivity. Some people object to zoos because they believe it is wrong to hold animals captive. They say that zoos keep animals in poor, cramped conditions. Zoo supporters say that animals are now kept in habitats as close as possible to their natural habitat.

You can see animals in their natural habitats in wildlife sanctuaries and national parks. Sanctuaries keep animals safe from poachers. African wildlife sanctuaries have increased the population of African elephants.

1. What are the different **opinions** that people have about zoos? Support your answer with quotes from the passage.

   _____
   _____
   _____
   _____
   _____

2. Many animals have benefited from being in wildlife sanctuaries. List two **facts** that support this statement.

   _____
   _____
   _____
   _____

Week 24 Day 3 Spelling

Vowel sounds

> The vowels **a**, **e**, **i**, **o**, **u** can make a **short** or **long** sound; e.g., c**a**t/c**a**ble, b**e**d/m**e**, l**i**d/f**i**nd, f**o**g/p**o**st, s**u**n/**u**nit.
> In words with **split digraphs**, the vowel makes a **long** sound; e.g. calcul**a**t**e**, stamp**e**d**e**, appet**i**t**e**, casser**o**l**e**, comm**u**t**e**.

List ① Write the word.

brigade
volume
athlete
conclude
stampede
accuse
costume
operate
cascade
control
hurricane
recognize
calculate
indicate
crocodile
commute
appetite
casserole
paradise
absolute

② Complete these words.

a cos_____
b app_____
c stam_____
d croc_____
e ath_____
f vol_____
g conc_____
h brig_____

③ Fill in the missing letters.

a i___d___ca_____
b a_____u___e
c ___b_____l___t___
d c___m___ut___
e o_____r___t___
f c_____s___r_____e
g ___ri_____de
h r___cog_____ze

④ Name.

Week 24 Day 4 Spelling

Vowel sounds

1 **Revise your spelling list from page 129.** Complete each sentence with a list word.

a The elephants began to _____, knocking down trees as they went.
b My parents told me to turn down the _____ of my music.
c Her hair was so long that it would _____ down her back.
d My favorite animal at the wildlife park was the _____ because I liked its big teeth.
e I loved my _____ for the concert so much I wanted to wear it all the time.
f In our house, we each have an hour in which we are in _____ of the TV.
g My grandma wasn't feeling well, so we took her a beef _____ for dinner.
h I tried to _____ the price of the items before the sales assistant.
i The _____ trained daily in the hope of making the Olympic team.

Challenge words

2 **Write the word.**

pronounce _____
balustrade _____
cellophane _____
palindrome _____
electrocute _____
scrutinize _____
demonstrate _____
diagnose _____
pantomime _____
insecticide _____

3 **Hidden words.** Find the challenge word.

a srdemonstrateas _____
b sdfinsecticideoai _____
c drbalustradeoiyb _____
d crysscrutinizeisse _____
e asdtpantomimeit _____
f opronounceaosu _____
g cypalindromepro _____
h deelectrocuteoua _____
i opcellophanehae _____
j adaidiagnoseose _____

4 **Another way to say it.** Which challenge word could replace the underlined word?

a I held onto the <u>handrail</u> on the stairs to help my balance. _____
b I watched my brother <u>perform</u> his karate skills at the tournament. _____
c The mechanic had to look under the hood to <u>determine</u> the problem. _____

Week 24 Day 5 Grammar

Prepositions

A **preposition** shows the **relationship** between a **noun or pronoun** and **other words** in a sentence. It often introduces a phrase that tells **where**, **when**, **why**, or **how** something happens; e.g., We went **to** Denver. He practices **in** the afternoon. They paint **for** fun. She arrived **on** horseback. A **phrase that starts with a preposition** can also give **information about a noun**; e.g., I live in the house **with** the red roof.

1 Complete the following sentences with prepositions from the box.

| in | about | over | into | beside | to | of | with | by | through | along | on | across | at |

a I went _____ the beach _____ my friends.
b A flock _____ birds flew _____ our house.
c My friend lives _____ the house _____ the corner.
d The book _____ Roald Dahl is _____ a boy called Charlie.
e She looked _____ the stars _____ a large telescope.
f I dove _____ the water and swam _____ the pool.
g I walked _____ the path that ran _____ the river.

2 Complete the puzzle with the missing prepositions.

Across:
2. We sheltered ___ the umbrella.
3. They are waiting ___ the house.
5. He fell ___ the stairs.
7. She drew a border ___ the picture.
8. The park is ___ my house.
9. They are walking ___ the path.

Down:
1. I told him to sit ___ me.
3. He walked ___ the room.
4. I woke up a lot ___ the night.
6. She is sitting ___ the bench.

L.5.1.A Explain the function of conjunctions, prepositions, and interjections in general and their function in particular sentences.

Week 25 Day 1 Comprehension

Earthquake

Identifying audience and purpose
To identify the author's purpose in writing a text, it helps to work out who the text was written for. The language the author uses will show what his or her purpose is—to inform, persuade, instruct, or entertain.

Read the passage.

Underline the cause of earthquakes.

Circle the word that is similar in meaning to *set free*.

Put a box around the word that tells that rock is hard, but can break easily.

Color the word that means *to move quickly to and fro*.

Most earthquakes are caused by the movement of tectonic plates. This movement can create enormous pressure. Earthquakes occur when this pressure is released.

As tectonic plates move, rock is pulled apart and pushed together. This creates stress in the rock. Rock is brittle and with enough force, will eventually break, slip, or shift. When this occurs, all the stored energy is released. This release of energy causes the surrounding rock to vibrate.

Circle the correct answers.

1. What is the main **purpose** of the text?
   - a to persuade
   - b to inform
   - c to entertain
   - d to warn

2. Who is the **target audience**? Choose the best answer.
   - a scientists
   - b geologists
   - c young children
   - d the general public

3. What type of **language** has the author used?
   - a humorous
   - b very simple
   - c formal and scientific
   - d informal

4. Which group of words is the best **clue** to question 3's answer?
   - a tectonic plates
   - b pulled apart
   - c pushed together
   - d the movement

Week 25 Day 2 Comprehension

Earthquake

Read the passage.

Circle the name of the instruments that measure vibrations in the ground.

Highlight the name of the instrument that turns the information recorded by seismometers into a visual record.

Although it is impossible to predict when an earthquake will happen, there are instruments such as seismometers that measure vibrations in the ground. As they record the tiniest of movements, seismometers can detect the minor vibrations that often occur just before a big quake. The digital information recorded by seismometers is turned into a visual record on a seismograph.

Seismographs display the vibrations caused by an earthquake as a series of lines.

The total energy released by an earthquake is measured on the Richter scale.

Underline the sentence that gives information about how seismographs display vibrations.

Color the name of the scale on which the total energy released by an earthquake is measured.

1 List all the scientific words in the text.

_____
_____

2 What is the main purpose of the text?

_____
_____
_____

3 Who do you think this text was written for? Give reasons for your answer.

_____
_____
_____
_____

RI.5.1 Quote accurately from a text when explaining what the text says explicitly and when drawing inferences from the text.

Week 25 Day 3 Spelling

Suffixes: ion, ian

Some verbs that end in **t** or **s** can be turned into nouns by adding the suffix **ion**; e.g., ac**tion**, discus**sion**. If a verb ends in **te** or **se**, drop the **e** before adding **ion**; e.g., celebra**te** → celebra**tion**, ten**se** → ten**sion**.

If a verb ends in **d** or **de**, drop the **d** or **de** before adding **ion**; e.g., exten**d** → exten**sion**, deci**de** → deci**sion**.

If the verb ends in **mit**, drop the **t** and add **ssion**; e.g., per**mit** → per**mission**.

Some nouns that end in **c** can be turned into other nouns by adding the suffix **ian**; e.g., magi**cian**.

List

action
protection
election
direction
connection
collection
relation
discussion
television
operation
conclusion
expansion
physician
admission
situation
population
attention
application
celebration
introduction

1 Write the word.

2 Sort the words.

a *tion*

b *sion*

c *cian*

3 Complete these words with *tion*, *sion*, or *cian*.

a direc_____ b popula_____ c celebra_____ d protec_____
e expan_____ f discus_____ g physi_____ h conclu_____

4 Underline the spelling mistake. Write the word correctly.

a The director called for acshun and we began the scene. _____
b My introduccian to karate was an enjoyable experience. _____
c We had a bad conection on the phone. _____
d Driving on a slippery road can lead to a dangerous situasion. _____

Week 25 Day 4 Spelling

Suffixes: ion, ian

1 **Revise your spelling list from page 134.** Which list word means?

a Something made larger
b A doctor of medicine
c Something planned in order to honor someone
d The process of choosing a leader by voting
e The end of something
f The people who live in an area
g Control or guidance
h A group of things of the same type

Challenge words

2 **Write the word.**

opposition
competition
concession
contribution
communication
institution
association
organization
tactician
mathematician

3 **Word clues.** Which challenge word matches?

a resistance to something
b an allowance or special rate
c an established custom
d someone who plans a strategy
e a conversation
f a partnership

4 **Complete the sentence.**

a My parents made a large _____ to the fundraiser.
b The _____ was capable of working out long and complex sums.
c There were eight teams in my basketball _____.
d The American Red Cross is an _____ that helps people in times of trouble.
e The army general was an excellent _____.
f They overcame all _____ to get into the finals.

L.5.2.E Spell grade-appropriate words correctly, consulting references as needed.

Week 25 Day 5 Grammar

Colons to introduce information

A **colon (:)** introduces a list, a definition, or an explanation; e.g., There are three countries I would like to visit**:** France, Italy, and Spain.

1 **In the following sentences, fill in the missing colons.**

a   There were only three items in her shopping basket tea, sugar, and milk.

b   Pacing up and down was a beautiful animal a sleek cat with a shiny black coat.

c   In the chest was a collection of precious stones diamonds, emeralds, sapphires, and rubies.

d   In the box was the present she'd always wanted a gold necklace with her name engraved on it.

e   Grandpa always says "Hard work never did anyone any harm."

f   These are my three favorite books The Phantom Tollbooth, Circus Mirandus, and Hidden Figures.

g   I couldn't believe it when I saw the address on the envelope 14 Gray Avenue, Hazel Park.

2 **Complete each sentence.**

a   I love all kinds of Italian food: _____

b   There is one main reason why I like to read books: _____

c   I can name a few breeds of cat: _____

d   We were given a list of items to add to our first aid kits: _____

e   There are many chores my little sister helps me with: _____

L.5.2 Demonstrate command of the conventions of standard English capitalization, punctuation, and spelling when writing.

Week 26 Day 1 Comprehension

Technological Wonders

Study the diagram and read the passage.

Reading diagrams
Diagrams are often used to explain scientific or technical ideas. They help us understand the text by representing information in a visual form.

In Step 1, circle the arrow that shows the direction in which the piston moves.

In Step 2, color the area that fills with fuel and gas.

In Step 4, put a box around the valve through which the burned gases leave the combustion chamber.

1. **Intake** – The piston moves down and opens a valve. This lets fuel and air into the combustion chamber.
2. **Compression** – The piston moves up, putting the fuel and air mixture under pressure.
3. **Combustion and Expansion** – The spark plug ignites the fuel and air mixture. It burns and forces the piston down again. This force drives the vehicle.
4. **Exhaust** – The piston hits the bottom. A valve opens and the burned gases leave the combustion chamber.

Circle the correct answers.

1. In which direction does the piston move? The piston moves …
   - a round and round.
   - b from side to side.
   - c up and down.
   - d backward and forward.

2. What happens to the valve when the piston moves down?
   - a It vibrates.
   - b It closes.
   - c It causes a spark.
   - d It opens.

3. What moves into the combustion chamber when the valve opens?
   - a fuel
   - b air
   - c gases
   - d fuel and air

4. Where is the spark plug situated?
   - a above the combustion chamber
   - b beneath the combustion chamber
   - c to the right of the combustion chamber
   - d to the left of the combustion chamber

RI.5.1 Quote accurately from a text when explaining what the text says explicitly and when drawing inferences from the text.

Week 26 | Day 2 | Comprehension

Technological Wonders

Study the images.

Astronauts repair part of the International Space Station.

Astronauts on the ISS work in zero gravity.

an illustration of the completed ISS

This is a robot that NASA will use to investigate whether there is life on the planet, Mars.

23

Underline the abbreviation for International Space Station.

Highlight the type of environment astronauts on the International Space Station work in.

Color the word that suggests that things sometimes go wrong on the International Space Station.

Circle a part of the Mars robot that shows how it will move across the planet.

Put a **box** around the part of the Mars robot that could contain a camera.

1 How does the illustration of the Mars robot add to our understanding of how it will move across and collect information from the planet?

_____
_____
_____
_____

2 What does the illustration tell us about the kind of terrain the Mars robot will have to cover?

_____
_____
_____
_____

RI.5.1 Quote accurately from a text when explaining what the text says explicitly and when drawing inferences from the text.

Week 26 Day 3 Spelling

Digraph: ch

Two or more letters that make a single sound are called a **digraph**. The **letters ch** can make the **sound ch**; e.g., **ch**uckle. Sometimes the letters **ch** make the single sound **k**. These words come mainly from Greek; e.g., **ch**iropractor. Sometimes the letters **ch** make the sound **sh**. The words come mainly from French; e.g., **ch**arade.

List

1 Write the word.

- aching
- attached
- detach
- chutney
- charcoal
- choral
- chrome
- cache
- anchovy
- chimpanzee
- brooch
- chemical
- cockroach
- bachelor
- check
- chariot
- echidna
- arachnid
- chiffon
- chameleon

2 Sort the words.

a ch as a 'k' sound

b ch as a 'ch' sound

c ch as a 'sh' sound

3 Unscramble these list words.

a eathdc
b ocbralhe
c aclrohac
d otcahir
e echca
f ehipcemnza
g khcraococ

4 Name.

a

b

c

d

L.5.2.E Spell grade-appropriate words correctly, consulting references as needed.

Week 26 Day 4 Spelling

Digraph: ch

1 **Revise your spelling list from page 139.** Which list word matches?

a spicy sauce or relish _____
b jewelry with a clasp or pin _____
c small, spiky mammal _____
d the bill in a restaurant _____
e sung by a choir _____
f sore _____
g small, salty fish _____
h a type of metal _____
i a spider _____
j a type of fabric _____

Challenge words

2 Write the word.

archaic _____
epoch _____
choreograph _____
charisma _____
chauffeur _____
cholesterol _____
chamomile _____
avalanche _____
chiropractor _____
crochet _____

3 **Word clues.** Which challenge word matches?

a era _____
b needlework _____
c attraction _____
d driver _____
e landslide _____
f ancient _____

4 **Hidden words.** Find the challenge word.

a irchiropractorpra _____
b pchoreographap _____
c rocholesterolloes _____

5 Complete the sentence.

a She drank _____ tea to help her upset stomach.
b The _____ drove us in a limousine.
c I helped my sister to _____ some dance moves for the show.
d Dad sees a _____ to help his sore back.
e The invention of the telephone started an important _____ in communication.

Commas and dashes

Extra information inserted into a sentence is separated from the rest of the sentence by **commas**, **dashes**, or **parentheses**; e.g., Jordy**,** my favorite cousin**,** is coming to visit next week. Some of the oranges—the ones I bought last week—are starting to go bad. The sentence makes sense without the extra information.

1. **In each sentence, fill in commas to show where extra information has been added.**
   a   Billy the boy next door is a very good athlete.
   b   Her collection of teddy bears the largest in the country is worth a lot of money.
   c   He stuffed everything and I mean everything into his backpack.
   d   Some of the spectators the ones who came late didn't get a seat.
   e   Sixteen players exactly half the squad didn't turn up for practice.

2. **Add the information in parentheses to each sentence. Use dashes to separate the extra information from the rest of the sentence.**
   a   There were hordes of people at the concert. (old and young)

   b   The buildings were impressive. (many made of granite)

   c   The novel is about a brother and sister who solve a great mystery. (her first)

   d   Alex walked up to the stage to receive his prize. (his head held high)

   e   All of the houses were painted blue. (from the smallest to the largest)

L.5.2 Demonstrate command of the conventions of standard English capitalization, punctuation, and spelling when writing.

Week 27 Day 1 Comprehension

Renewable Resources

Identifying audience and purpose
To identify the author's purpose in writing a text, it helps to work out who the text was written for. The language the author uses will show what his or her purpose is—to inform, persuade, instruct, or entertain.

Read the passage.

A solar power station uses either solar cells or concentrating solar power dishes.

Solar cells are also known as photovoltaic cells. They convert light directly into electricity.

Concentrating solar power dishes use hundreds of mirrors to focus the sun's energy into heat. It can concentrate the sun's rays thousands of times to produce temperatures more than 1,800°F. This heats a chemical, which in turn produces steam to power a generator, just like a fossil fuel-burning power station.

- **Circle** the adjective that means *relating to the sun*.
- **Highlight** the scientific name for solar cells.
- Put a box around the word that is similar in meaning to *change*.
- **Color** the words that describe a power station that burns coal.

Circle the correct answers.

1. What is the main purpose of the passage?
   a to warn   b to persuade   c to inform   d to entertain

2. What are the clues to question 1's answer? The passage contains many …
   a rhyming words.   b similes and metaphors.
   c opinions.   d facts.

3. Who is most likely the target audience for this text?
   a school students   b preschoolers   c retired people   d electricians

4. Which words best describe the language used in the passage?
   a humorous and informal   b factual and formal
   c descriptive and poetic   d simple and persuasive

Week 27 Day 2 Comprehension

Renewable Resources

Read the passage.

Highlight the heading.

Circle the word that is similar in meaning to use.

Underline the sub-heading.

Color a scientific word in step 1.

Put a box around the word that is similar in meaning to bump into.

Color three scientific words in Step 3.

How a solar cell works

Solar cells convert light from the sun into electricity. They have no moving parts, consume no fuel, and create no pollution.

From light to electricity

1. Light is made up of particles known as photons. Photons enter the cell.
2. Photons collide with electrons inside the cell.
3. Electrons pass from one semiconductor to the other, and then onto the metal-conductor strips. The flow of electrons produces electricity.

1 What is the purpose of the text?

___

2 What is the scientific name for particles of light?

___

3 What happens inside a solar cell?

___

4 List the scientific words in Step 3.

___

5 Who is most likely the target audience for this text?

___

RI.5.1 Quote accurately from a text when explaining what the text says explicitly and when drawing inferences from the text.

Week 27 Day 3 Spelling

Tricky words

Some words are trickier to spell than others. Sometimes we add letters that are not supposed to be there. Sometimes we leave out letters. Sometimes we write letters in the wrong order.

List

nervous
width
neither
similar
beginning
calendar
twelfth
variety
courage
people
definite
naturally
nuisance
government
yacht
harass
profession
original
recommend
persuade

1 Write the word.

2 Name.

a
b
c
d

3 Unscramble these list words.

a terenih
b tnemnrevog
c vnseuor
d yllarutan
e mrdnecemo
f etinifed
g gngnbneii

4 Put the syllables back together.

a ern/ment/gov
b ning/gin/be
c vous/ner
d i/o/nal/rig
e mend/om/rec
f ple/peo
g ther/nei
h nite/def/i
i rass/ha
j suade/per
k age/cour
l i/sim/lar

L.5.2.E Spell grade-appropriate words correctly, consulting references as needed.

Week 27 Day 4 Spelling

Tricky words

1 **Revise your spelling list from page 144.** Complete each sentence with a list word.
  a I can easily swim the _____ of the pool, but I struggle with the length.
  b I have _____ curly hair, but I can make it straight using a straightener.
  c My birthday was on October _____.
  d I loved the book from _____ to end.
  e The venue was filled with excited _____ waiting for the show to begin.
  f The shop has a _____ of different styles.
  g Doctors _____ eating two pieces of fruit each day.
  h The friends look very _____, even though they aren't related.

Challenge words

2 **Write the word.**
  guarantee   _____
  occurred   _____
  ceremony   _____
  restaurant   _____
  parallel   _____
  enough   _____
  immediately   _____
  temporary   _____
  unanimous   _____
  pronunciation   _____

3 **Hidden words.** Find the challenge word.
  a papapparallelllep   _____
  b sibunanimousun   _____
  c upronunciationpo   _____
  d asdutemporaryzs   _____
  e asrdenoughasdo   _____
  f monyceremonyas   _____

4 **Word clues.** Which challenge word matches?
  a sufficient   _____
  b makeshift   _____
  c united   _____
  d happened   _____

5 **Another way to say it.** Which challenge word could replace the underlined word?
  a We ordered 3 different pizzas at the <u>cafeteria</u>.   _____
  b The lines run <u>next</u> to one another.   _____
  c The athletes were honored at a special <u>function</u>.   _____
  d They could give us no <u>assurance</u> that the plan would work. _____

L.5.2.E Spell grade-appropriate words correctly, consulting references as needed.

Week 27 Day 5 Grammar

Correlative conjunctions

A **conjunction** is a word that **joins sentences**, **clauses**, or **words** within a clause; e.g., Jack **and** Jill went up the hill **because** they needed water.
Correlative conjunctions are **pairs of joining words** that work together; e.g., I did not know **whether** to pick it up **or** to leave it alone. Other correlative conjunctions are
either ... or   not ... but   both ... and   not only ... but also   neither ... nor

1 Complete each sentence with a pair of correlative conjunctions from the list. Use each pair of conjunctions once.

a You can wear _____ a cap _____ a sunhat.
b I have been overseas _____ just once _____ many times.
c We weren't sure _____ to get him a bicycle _____ a scooter.
d The child wanted _____ the caramel flavor _____ the mint flavor.
e We had to catch _____ a bus _____ a train to get to our destination.
f She managed _____ to unpack the pieces, _____ to put them back together.

2 Underline the conjunction that is incorrect in each sentence and write it correctly.

a Today I feel neither happy or sad.   _____
b He was wearing not one and two pairs of socks.   _____
c I wasn't sure whether to phone her but to email her.   _____
d I tried not only to juggle the balls and also to do some other tricks.   _____
e They have predicted that tomorrow will be both wet nor cold.   _____
f They said I could have either a milkshake nor an ice cream, but not both.   _____

3 Join the following sentences with the correlative conjunctions in parentheses.

a I don't like snakes. I don't like lizards. (neither... nor)

_____
_____

b She has longer hair. She has curlier hair. (not only... but also)

_____
_____

146 L.5.1.E Use correlative conjunctions.

REVIEW 3: Spelling

Spelling

Use this review to test your knowledge. It has three parts—**Spelling**, **Grammar**, and **Comprehension**. If you're unsure of an answer, go back and read the rules and generalizations in the blue boxes.

You have learned about:
- suffix: ous
- endings: age, idge
- suffixes: ion, ian
- plurals
- suffixes: ment, ship, hood
- diagraph: ch
- adding to fer
- vowels
- tricky words

1 **In each sentence, the spelling error has been <u>underlined</u>. Write the correct spelling.** 2 marks

  a Let's walk as far as the <u>brage</u>, and then we'll turn back for home. _____

  b The RMS Titanic sank on its maiden <u>voyidge</u> in the North Atlantic Ocean. _____

  c Rosa Parks showed <u>corage</u> when she refused to move on a Montgomery City bus in 1955. _____

  d It can be a real <u>nuisanse</u> to turn off the light when you're snuggled in bed with a good book. _____

2 **Which word correctly completes this sentence?** 1 mark

Many _____ have signed the UN Conventions on the Child.

  a country   b countries   c counties   d country's

3 **This sentence has one word that is incorrect. Write the correct spelling.** 1 mark

Nuclear waste is hazardeous and needs to be carefully disposed of. _____

4 **Write the suffix ment, ship, or hood to correctly complete these words.** 2 marks

  a attach _ _ _ _   b knight _ _ _ _
  c citizen _ _ _ _   d engage _ _ _ _

5 **Circle the correct word to complete each sentence.** 3 marks

  a We cooked a (casserole, casseroles) for our new neighbors.
  b The nation has big (celebration, celebrations) for Fourth of July weekend.
  c I'm a volunteer (referee, referees) for the junior soccer team.

6 **This sentence has one word that is incorrect. Write the correct spelling.** 1 mark

At the Colosseum we saw a replica shariot. _____

Your score ☐ / 10

147

REVIEW 3: Grammar

Grammar

You have learned about:
- commas in sentences
- sequence adverbs
- parentheses, commas, and dashes
- time adverbials
- prepositions
- correlative conjunctions
- future perfect tense
- colons

1 **In each sentence, fill in two commas.** 2 marks

  a The chimps were chasing each other around the enclosure the zebras were grazing beside the giraffes and the elephants were drinking from the pond.

  b The competitors whose ages ranged from eight to eighty were waiting for instructions.

2 **In each sentence, replace the underlined phrase with an adverb from the box.** 2 marks

> before   immediately   annually   soon

  a She wants to see you <u>right away</u>. _____
  b They should be arriving <u>in a little while</u>. _____
  c That would never have happened <u>in the past</u>. _____
  d They hold the fundraiser <u>once a year</u>. _____

3 **In each sentence, write the verb in parentheses in the future perfect tense.** 2 marks

  a By the time we get there, the show (start). _____
  b By five o'clock, everyone (go) home. _____

4 **Add commas to the following sentences to make their meaning clear.** 2 marks

  a The movie said the child was brilliant.
  b The swimming teacher is calling us Miranda.
  c While Grandma bakes the children draw pictures in the books.
  d We drove down the street looking left and right for the house.

5 **Complete each sentence with an adverb from the box. Use each adverb once.** 2 marks

> after   eventually   finally   then

  a Eat your dinner, and _____ you can watch TV.
  b If you read a page every day, you will _____ finish the book.
  c I always get dressed _____ I make my bed.
  d Everyone will be happy when it is _____ time to go home.

148

REVIEW 3: Grammar

Grammar

6 **Circle the prepositions in the following sentences.** 2 marks

    a My friend lives in that house.
    b My cat hides under my bed.
    c She hangs her coat behind the door.
    d The plane flies above the clouds.

7 **Complete each sentence with prepositions from the box. Use each preposition once.** 2 marks

past	for	with	on	of	to	from	in

    a She removed a sheet _____ paper _____ the pile.
    b The girl _____ the long brown hair is waiting _____ you.
    c I walk _____ their house when I go _____ soccer practice.
    d I put the coins _____ the box _____ the table.

8 **In each sentence, change one of the commas to a colon.** 1 mark

    a The following animals make excellent pets, dogs, cats, and rabbits.
    b The room was divided into four separate areas, a kitchen, a dining room, a living room, and a study.

9 **In the following sentences, insert a ^ to show where dashes are needed.** 3 marks

    a I watched helplessly as my boat it was really just a dinghy started drifting away.
    b I eat citrus fruits mainly oranges at least three times a week.
    c Early this morning before it got light, actually I was woken by a loud noise.

10 **Complete each sentence with the correct conjunction.** 2 marks

    a Both Maria _____ her sister were at the party.
    b I didn't know whether to laugh _____ cry.
    c Not one, _____ two whales emerged from the water.
    d You can have either the bike _____ the scooter, but not both.

Your score ☐ / 20

REVIEW 3: Comprehension

Cassan's Lesson

Read the passage and then use the comprehension skills you have learned to answer the questions.

Long ago there lived a beggar named Cassan. Once he had worked to earn his living, but he had fallen on hard times and now the only way he knew how to live was by begging for coins and food, or by stealing them from those who had more than he.

One day as he wandered through the marketplace he saw a traveler and his dog. Cassan knew the man was wealthy because of his fine clothes and the fat purse hanging from his belt. Cassan was very hungry. The purse looked even larger as he closed in on the stranger and reached out for it.

He was about to grab the object of his desire when a strange voice said, "Please do not steal my master's purse." The voice seemed to come from near his feet. Cassan looked down and, to his great surprise, saw that it was the stranger's dog who was speaking. Despite being startled, Cassan said, "If I don't steal, I won't have money for food."

"My master provides me with food for the services I provide him," replied the dog. "Why do you not seek work and thus not steal?" Cassan replied that since he had become a beggar, no one would give him work. He could not believe it; here he was, talking to a dog!

"I too was once a beggar like you, but was turned into a dog for my evil deeds," the dog told Cassan. "Do not follow my path. Speak to my master and he will help you."

Cassan nervously approached the stranger and told him what he had meant to do and how the dog had stopped him. The stranger replied, "You have done the right thing. Will you join me in my search for the wizard to turn my friend back into a human?" Cassan hesitated for only a moment before agreeing to accompany the stranger and his dog, but he had no idea of the adventures that were yet to come.

1 Why had Cassan become a beggar? 1 mark LITERAL
  a It was easier than working.
  b He had fallen on hard times.
  c He was good at it.
  d He enjoyed being a beggar.

REVIEW 3: Comprehension

Cassan's Lesson

2 What is the most likely reason Cassan was wandering through the marketplace? 1 mark
   He was ...   **CRITICAL**
   a buying food.
   b looking for his friends.
   c looking for work.
   d looking for something to steal.

3 In the story, which of the following services does the dog provide for
   his master? 1 mark   **INFERENTIAL**
   a He protects him.
   b He carries his purse.
   c He retrieves items for him.
   d He warns him of approaching danger.

4 What is the most likely reason the dog tried to help the beggar? 1 mark   **CRITICAL**
   a His master needed a servant.
   b He liked the beggar.
   c He knew what it was like to be a beggar.
   d He felt sorry for the beggar.

5 What does the dog mean when he says: "Do not follow my path."? 1 mark   **INFERENTIAL**
   a Do not walk behind me.
   b Do not do as I did.
   c Do not try to find me.
   d Do not ask me for directions.

6 In the story, which of the following emotions does Cassan NOT experience? 1 mark   **LITERAL**
   a surprise
   b nervousness
   c disbelief
   d amusement

7 Which words best describe the dog's master? 1 mark   **CRITICAL**
   a kind and understanding
   b stern and cruel
   c selfish and grumpy
   d clever and funny

8 Which sentence about the wizard is supported by evidence in the text? 1 mark
   The wizard ...   **INFERENTIAL**
   a is an evil genius.
   b has a high opinion of himself.
   c has superhuman powers.
   d uses lots of magic potions.

9 What are the text clues to support your answer to question 8? 1 mark   **CRITICAL**

_____

10 Why was the dog able to talk? 1 mark   **LITERAL**

_____

Your score / 10

Your Review 3 Scores

Spelling / 10 + Grammar / 20 + Comprehension / 10 = Total / 40

Week 28 Day 1 Comprehension

Operation Green Thumbs

Finding the main idea and supporting details
To discover what a text is about, look for the main idea or key point. Facts and details in the text can help you find the main idea.

Read the passage.

(Circle) the word that suggests that Mr. Piper wanted Alex to be his secret agent.

Put a [box] around the word that shows that Mr. Piper did not want anyone to hear what he was saying to Alex.

"Alex, this job is very important," he whispered. "It's undercover, so don't tell anyone. I'll leave your assignments near the compost bin out in the back."

Mr. Piper looked up and down the street. "First I need you to get me some soil samples from Old Man Oliver's garden and spare block. You can leave them by the trash can. Make sure no one sees you. Top-secret," he said as he tapped the side of his nose.

Color the word that is similar in meaning to *tasks*.

Underline a sentence that shows that Mr. Piper did not want anyone to know about Alex's assignment.

Circle the correct answers.

1 What is the passage mainly about?
- a the street Mr. Piper lives in
- b Alex's undercover assignment
- c Old Man Oliver's garden
- d the importance of the compost bin

2 Which three details from the passage support the main idea?
- a leave them by the trash can
- b up and down the street
- c this job is very important
- d Top-secret
- e near the compost bin
- f don't tell anyone

3 What would be the best title for this passage?
- a The compost bin
- b Undercover agent
- c Mr. Piper's street
- d Old Man Oliver's Garden

Week 28 Day 2 Comprehension

Operation Green Thumbs

Read the passage.

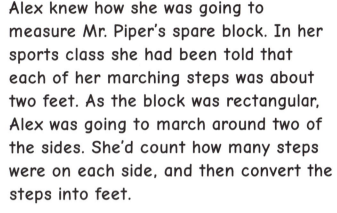

Underline how long each of Alex's marching steps was.

Alex knew how she was going to measure Mr. Piper's spare block. In her sports class she had been told that each of her marching steps was about two feet. As the block was rectangular, Alex was going to march around two of the sides. She'd count how many steps were on each side, and then convert the steps into feet.

If Mr. Piper caught her, Alex was going to say she was practicing her marching.

Color how Alex was going to measure Mr. Piper's spare block.

Put a box around the excuse Alex was going to give Mr. Piper if he caught her.

1. What is the passage mainly about?

2. Which three details in the passage support the main idea?

3. What would be a good title for this passage?

RL.5.1 Quote accurately from a text when explaining what the text says explicitly and when drawing inferences from the text.

Week 28 Day 3 Spelling

Digraphs: oo, ou

> Two letters that make a single sound are called a **digraph**.
> The letters **oo** make the single sound **oo**; e.g., ig**loo**.
> The letters **ou** can also make the single sound **oo**; e.g., c**ou**pon.

List

- igloo
- baboon
- lagoon
- snooze
- loosen
- wound
- mousse
- hooray
- through
- shampoo
- cocoon
- groove
- troupe
- noodle
- oozing
- coupon
- cuckoo
- routine
- ballooned
- boomerang

1 Write the word.

2 Sort the words.

a Words with *oo*

b Words with *ou*

3 Complete the words using *oo* or *ou*.

a igl_____
b coc_____n
c bab_____n
d gr_____ve
e lag_____n
f tr_____pe
g sn_____ze
h n_____dle
i l_____sen
j _____zing
k w_____nd
l c_____pon
m m_____sse
n ball_____ned

4 Put the letter chunks in the right order.

a ou-pe-tr
b oo-gr-ve
c ing-ooz
d tine-rou
e nd-woun
f oon-ball-ed
g oo-shamp
h oon-bab
i oon-lag
j ang-er-boom
k oo-dle-n
l ray-hoo
m sn-ze-oo
n oo-co-n-c

L.5.2.E Spell grade-appropriate words correctly, consulting references as needed.

Week 28 Day 4 Spelling

Digraphs: oo, ou

1 **Revise your spelling list from page 154.** Underline the mistake. Write the correct word.

a We walked thru the forest to get to the swimming pool. _____
b The cuckou clock will chime twelve times at midday. _____
c I always hit the snoze button when my alarm goes off for work. _____
d The babone liked to eat fruit. _____
e I was sad when I accidentally dropped a noudle on the ground. _____

Challenge words

2 **Write the word.**

tattoo _____
harpoon _____
mongoose _____
typhoon _____
hooligan _____
schooner _____
cockatoo _____
acoustics _____
souvenir _____
bassoon _____

3 **Hidden words.** Find the challenge word.

a typhntyphoonsia _____
b sdfyhooliganihu _____
c asdfftattooasdhs _____
d asdtmongooseas _____
e asdrschoonerasd _____
f asdrgrsouveniras _____

4 **Word clues.** Which challenge word matches?

a echoes _____
b cyclone _____
c bird _____
d boat _____

5 **Complete the sentence.**

a The _____ squawked loudly as it flew by.
b The _____ had injured the large whale.
c The hall had wonderful _____ that made listening to music special.
d She brought me back a _____ from her trip.
e We sailed in the harbor on a _____.
f The _____ is a large woodwind instrument.
g The warrior had a tribal _____ on his arm.
h The _____ killed the poisonous snake.

L.5.2.E Spell grade-appropriate words correctly, consulting references as needed.

Week 28 Day 5 Grammar
Relative clauses

A **clause** is a group of words that has its own verb. A **main clause** makes **sense by itself**; e.g., His socks are dirty and smelly.

A **subordinate clause** does **not make sense by itself**; it depends on the main clause for its meaning; e.g., **His socks, which are lying on the floor, are dirty and smelly**. The subordinate clause is which are lying on the floor.

Many subordinate clauses are introduced by the **relative pronouns who**, **whose**, **whom**, **which**, and **that**. They are sometimes called **relative clauses**.

1 Circle the relative pronoun that correctly completes the sentence.
   a Which is the stick (who, that) glows in the dark?
   b Jake and Julia, (who, which) live across the road, are coming to my party.
   c The actors, many of (who, whom) he recognized, were already on the stage.
   d The town, (which, whom) is close to our farm, has some interesting little shops.
   e Our new neighbors, (who, whose) daughter is the same age as my sister, moved in yesterday

2 Complete each of the following sentences with a relative pronoun.
   a The child _____ hurt herself is crying.
   b The girl _____ bag you are carrying is my sister.
   c The house _____ burned down has been rebuilt.
   d The book, _____ he read often, was about Greek mythology.

3 Match the clauses.

Main clause	Subordinate clause
a I will give the apple to the boy	which has won several awards.
b The pirates are looking for a chest	whom I invited.
c I went to the doctor	who left his post-game snack at home.
d Last night I watched a movie	that contains treasure.
e I have had a reply from the people	whose consulting rooms are close by.

Week 29 Day 1 Comprehension

Decoding the Mayan Marvels

Cause and effect
To find cause and effect, ask why something happens and what the result is.

Read the passage.

Circle a word that suggests that the heat was affecting Mia.

Underline the phrases that show that Mia and her companions were having trouble walking on the forest floor.

Highlight the sentences that show how the humidity made Mia feel.

Color the word that tells why they could not move quickly through the jungle.

Put a box around where Mia and her companions were headed.

Sweat poured from Mia's brow as she lifted the heavy machete to clear the jungle ahead. As they struggled on, the jungle became more treacherous. At times they could barely get a foothold in the soft mud of the rainforest floor. Mia stopped to catch her breath. "This humidity is too much. I'm melting. The jungle is so thick I don't think we'll ever get there!"

Flynn glanced at his watch. It was already 3 p.m. At this rate they'd be lucky to make it to the cliffs by sunset!

Mia stopped for some water and found a chocolate bar. She broke off pieces of chocolate for Flynn and Professor Drake.

Circle the correct answers.

1 How did the humidity affect Mia? The humidity caused Mia to …
- a start melting.
- b lose her breath.
- c feel hot and sticky.
- d slip in the mud.

2 Why were Mia and her companions making such slow progress? Choose three options. Mia and her companions were struggling to …
- a carry their machetes.
- b walk in the mud.
- c see the cliffs.
- d deal with the humidity.
- e keep the sun out of their eyes.
- f cut their way through the jungle.

3 What is the most likely reason Mia gave everyone a piece of chocolate?
- a to reward them with a treat
- b to eat it before it melted
- c to replenish their energies
- d to stop insects from eating it

RL.5.1 Quote accurately from a text when explaining what the text says explicitly and when drawing inferences from the text.

Week 29 Day 2 Comprehension

Decoding the Mayan Marvels

Read the whole story

Read the passage.

Underline why the people left Tayasal.

Highlight what the people of Tayasal took with them into the forest.

Color the information the Mayan scrolls are thought to contain.

The Mayan cities survived until 1697 when the last city, Tayasal, was overtaken by Spanish invaders. The king of Tayasal, King Can Ek, and his people vanished into the forest and were never found. They took with them the treasures of the city, including a huge library of Mayan scrolls. These scrolls apparently recorded ancient Mayan medicines, astrology, and the secrets of eternal life. It was believed that King Can Ek took his people and library to caves deep within the Mayan mountains.

In 1994 an American archaeologist stumbled upon a clue to the whereabouts of King Can Ek's library—an ancient glowing stone. Finding the library of the Maya would unravel the mystery surrounding South America's oldest civilization and answer some of *our* most puzzling questions.

Circle when the American archaeologist discovered the ancient glowing stone.

Underline why the archaeologist's discovery was important.

Highlight why archaeologists would like to find the library of the Maya.

1 What caused the people of Tayasal to go into the forest?
_____
_____

2 What is the most likely reason the people of Tayasal took their treasures into the forest with them?
_____
_____
_____

3 How would discovering the library of the Maya affect modern humans?
_____
_____
_____

158   RL.5.1 Quote accurately from a text when explaining what the text says explicitly and when drawing inferences from the text.

Week 29 Day 3 Spelling

Digraphs: wh, ph, gh

> A **digraph** is two consonants that make a single sound. The consonants **wh**, make the sound **w**; e.g., **wh**arf. The consonants **gh**, make the sound **g**; e.g., **gh**etto. The consonants **ph**, make the sound **f**; e.g., **ph**antom.

List

awhile
aghast
wharf
whiten
graphic
whistles
everywhere
whereby
whisker
whirlpool
whine
cartwheel
wheedle
pheasant
ghetto
somewhat
phantom
somewhere
headphones
geography

1 Write the word.

2 Sort the words.

a wh

b gh

c ph

3 Fill in the missing letters.

a s_____ewh___t
b w___e___d___e
c ge_____r___ph___
d ___e_____pho_____s
e g___et_____
f w_____te___
g c___rt___he___l
h ___han___om

4 Complete each sentence with a list word.

a I wore my _____ to listen to music on the bus.

b My grandfather had one white _____ on his chin.

c The ship docked next to the _____.

d We looked _____ to find the perfect present for my grandmother.

e She practiced a _____ routine on the grass every lunchtime.

f I asked them to wait _____ because I was busy.

Week 29 Day 4 Spelling

Digraphs: wh, ph, gh

1 Revise your spelling list from page 159. Which list word means?

a A large bird with a long tail and bright feathers _____
b To try to persuade or influence by flattery _____
c Something that seems real but is not _____
d Water turning rapidly about a center and pulling downward _____
e The science of the earth's surface and all life on it _____
f Described clearly and vividly _____
g Filled with alarm or horror _____
h A part of the city where a group of people live _____

Challenge words

2 Write the word.

lymph _____
decipher _____
metaphor _____
homophone _____
emphasize _____
cenotaph _____
periphery _____
asphalt _____
hieroglyphics _____
claustrophobia _____

3 Word clues. Which challenge word matches?

a point out _____
b ancient writing _____
c decode _____
d figure of speech _____
e monument _____
f bitumen _____

4 Hidden words. Find the challenge word.

a phlylymphymyl _____
b ohomophoneph _____
c hlemphasizeph _____

5 Complete the sentence.

a I went to the doctor because my _____ glands were swollen.
b He used many descriptive words to _____ the beauty of what he saw.
c The archaeologists discovered _____ on the wall of the tomb.
d Tim had to _____ the code to know where to meet his friend.
e My little brother was scared and stood on the _____ of the group.
f The _____ on the road gets very hot in the middle of summer.

Week 29 Day 5 Grammar

Capital letters in titles

A **title** before a person's name is written with a capital letter; e.g., Today I read a book about **P**resident **L**incoln. In a title that contains a **preposition**, only the **nouns** have **capital letters**; e.g., **Q**ueen **V**ictoria was also the **E**mpress **o**f **I**ndia.

1 In the following sentences, circle the words that need a capital letter.
   a   Yesterday doctor Wood sent me for an X-ray.
   b   We asked trooper Jackson for directions to the next town.
   c   When I went to the White House, I met vice president Smith.
   d   The person in the photo was president John F. Kennedy.
   e   My sister had to speak to professor Nunes about her assignment.
   f   The soldiers have to report to sergeant Romero.
   g   I am reading a book about chief Sitting Bull.

2 Write the following sentences with the correct capitalization.
   a   The pilot introduced himself to the passengers as captain edwards.
   _____
   _____

   b   The city of Houston in Texas was named after governor sam houston.
   _____
   _____

   c   My grandmother saw pope john paul II when he visited the United States.
   _____
   _____

   d   My uncle, colonel cooper, is stationed at Scott Air Force Base in Illinois.
   _____
   _____

   e   In 2016, queen elizabeth II celebrated her 90th birthday.
   _____
   _____

L.5.2 Demonstrate command of the conventions of standard English capitalization, punctuation, and spelling when writing.

Week 30 Day 1 Comprehension

Quest for the Cup

Making inferences
To make inferences while reading, use clues in the text. The clues help you find the answers that are hiding in the text.

Read the passage.

Heavy thumps and loud crashes filled the darkness. The strange noises jolted Flynn awake. Mia was already up looking for a flashlight. She grabbed a carved spear from the wall as she and Flynn crept down the hallway to Uncle Earl's study.

Mia raised her spear. "OK, Flynn, on the count of three, you fling open the door. Ready?"

Mia mouthed, "One... two... three!" and Flynn threw the door wide open.

Uncle Earl was standing at the top of a ladder leaning against a bookshelf. As he turned, startled, he dropped a small box. Mia and Flynn stared at the floor of the study. It was a gigantic mess of books, papers, folders, videos, cassettes, and overflowing boxes.

- **Underline** what woke Mia and Flynn.
- **Circle** what Mia used as a weapon.
- Put a **box** around the word that shows that Uncle Earl got a fright.
- **Highlight** where Uncle Earl was standing.
- **Color** what Uncle Earl was holding.
- **Underline** the list of objects on the floor of the study.

Circle the correct answers.

1. Which is the best **inference**? Mia and Flynn thought that Uncle Earl was a …
   a burglar.   b visitor.   c repairman.   d cleaner.

2. Which is the best **clue** to question 1's answer? Mia …
   a told Flynn to open the door.
   b looked for a flashlight.
   c armed herself with a spear.
   d crept down the hallway.

3. Which is the best **inference**? Uncle Earl had found the small box …
   a next to the bookshelf.
   b at the top of the bookshelf.
   c at the bottom of the bookshelf.
   d in a cupboard.

4. Which phrase is the **clue** to question 3's answer?
   a against a bookshelf
   b was standing
   c at the top of a ladder
   d a small box

Quest for the Cup

Read the passage.

Circle the word that suggests the photograph was old.

Highlight the sentence that shows that Uncle Earl had seen the photograph recently.

Color the words that tell us how old Uncle Earl was when the photograph was taken.

"Why do you need this photo right now?" asked Flynn. "It's 5 a.m.! Can't it wait?"

Mia held up a faded photograph of two men eating pizza. She had found it sticking out of the top of a book. "Is this it?" she asked.

"Yes, that's it!" Uncle Earl took the photograph and held it in the light. "Well done, Mia. I must have used it as a bookmark the other day when I was reading."

Mia and Flynn looked at the photograph to see what all the fuss was about. Uncle Earl looked very young and had a full head of curly hair. The other man was thin and wore a beaming smile. They were sitting at a café table with a glass raised in one hand and a slice of pizza in the other.

Underline the words that suggest that Uncle Earl has lost most of his hair.

Put a box around the description of Uncle Earl's companion.

Highlight what Uncle Earl and his companion were doing when the photograph was taken.

1 We can **infer** that the photograph Uncle Earl was looking for had been taken a long time ago. What are the **clues**?

_____

_____

_____

_____

_____

2 We can **infer** that Uncle Earl had seen the photograph recently. Support this statement with a quote from the passage.

_____

_____

_____

Week 30 Day 3 Spelling
Suffixes: ence, ance

Some verbs can be turned into nouns by adding the suffix **ance**; e.g., accept**ance**.
Adjectives that **end in ant** can be turned into nouns by changing **ant** to **ance**; e.g., dist**ant** → dist**ance**.
Some verbs can be turned into nouns by adding the suffix **ence**; e.g., interfer**ence**.
Adjectives that **end in ent** can be turned into nouns by changing **ent** to **ence**; e.g., sil**ent** → sil**ence**.

List
- distance
- absence
- existence
- persistence
- silence
- entrance
- elegance
- allowance
- evidence
- violence
- appearance
- arrogance
- difference
- brilliance
- importance
- obedience
- patience
- audience
- excellence
- resistance

1 Write the word.

2 Sort the words.
   a *ance*

   b *ence*

3 Complete these words with *ance* or *ence*.
   a obedi_____ b allow_____
   c persist_____ d evid_____
   e import_____ f excell_____
   g brilli_____ h sil_____

4 Match the clue with the list word.
   a a doorway
   b people who watch a show
   c refinement, taste, and grace
   d time away
   e to keep trying
   f the ability to spend time on a difficult task
   g opposing power of one force against another
   h not the same

164   L.5.2.E Spell grade-appropriate words correctly, consulting references as needed.

Week 30 Day 4 Spelling

Suffixes: ence, ance

1 **Revise your spelling list from page 164.** Which list word matches?

- a extreme brightness _____
- b looks _____
- c muteness _____
- d spectators _____
- e fighting _____
- f contrast _____
- g compliance _____
- h perfection _____
- i length _____
- j proof _____
- k defiance _____
- l determination _____

Challenge words

2 **Write the word.**

- acceptance _____
- interference _____
- inheritance _____
- innocence _____
- magnificence _____
- endurance _____
- fragrance _____
- ignorance _____
- annoyance _____
- intelligence _____

3 **Hidden words.** Find the challenge word.

- a zenduranceawdg _____
- b joeignoranceasu _____
- c nimagnificencea _____
- d nainnocenceasoi _____
- e nannoyancesen _____
- f frintelligenceasd _____

4 **Word clues.** Which challenge word matches?

- a legacy _____
- b cleverness _____
- c approval _____

5 **Another way to say it.** Which challenge word could replace the underlined word?

- a They were angered by my <u>intervention</u> in the matter. _____
- b I felt <u>displeasure</u> when he interrupted me for the third time. _____
- c The athlete's <u>stamina</u> in the marathon was unbelievable. _____
- d The house was filled with the <u>perfume</u> of roses. _____
- e They were awestruck by the <u>splendor</u> of the sunset. _____
- f My <u>heirloom</u> from my grandmother was her beautiful sapphire ring. _____

Week 30 Day 5 Grammar

Compound and complex sentences

> A **sentence** consists of one or more clauses. A **simple sentence** has one main clause; e.g., The clouds are gathering.
>
> A **compound sentence** has two or more main clauses; e.g., The clouds **are gathering** and thunder **is rumbling** in the distance. Compound sentences are formed using the conjunctions and, but, or, and so.
>
> A **complex sentence** has a main clause and a subordinate clause; e.g., The clouds, which **are gathering in the distance**, are dark and menacing. The subordinate clause which are gathering in the distance depends on the main clause for its meaning. Complex sentences are formed using:
> - the relative pronouns who, whose, whom, which, and that.
> - conjunctions like after, although, because, before, if, unless, until, when, and while.

1 Write down whether the following are compound or complex sentences.

a I don't know whose jacket that is. _____
b I will eat the apple if you don't want it. _____
c I took an umbrella because I thought it might rain. _____
d The ring, which is very valuable, is kept under lock and key. _____
e My sister went to the movies and I went to my friend's house. _____
f Jack won't take part in the competition unless Juan joins him. _____
g You can go to the dentist tomorrow, or you can wait a week. _____

2 Join each of the following sentences with the conjunction in parentheses;

e.g., We went out for dinner. It was her birthday. (because)
   We went out for dinner <u>because</u> it was her birthday.

a I've had lunch. I'm still hungry. (but) _____

b I will visit them. They are at home. (if) _____

c I made an appointment. I went to see him. (before) _____

d I will feed the dog. You unpack the dishwasher. (while) _____

166 L.5.1 Demonstrate command of the conventions of standard English grammar and usage when writing or speaking.

Week 31 Day 1 Comprehension

Coffee Creek

Figurative language
Alliteration repeats consonant sounds.
Onomatopoeia imitates sounds. A **simile** compares two things by using the words *like* or *as*. **Metaphors** make a more direct comparison. They do not contain the words *like* or *as*.
Personification is a type of metaphor that gives animals and objects human qualities.

Read the passage.

Highlight the metaphor.

Color an example of personification.

I remember fallen trunks
and the rings of growth revealed in death

Fallen yellow sorbet-colored leaves
over dusty paths just quelled by a storm
The blue-green firs, dusted with gray
in staggered rows, silent choristers* in stalls.

*choir members

Circle the word that the leaves are compared to.

Underline the words that the fir trees are compared to.

Circle the correct answers.

1 What figure of speech is "Fallen yellow sorbet-colored leaves"?
 a alliteration
 b simile
 c metaphor
 d personification

2 How does the figure of speech in question 1 help us create a picture of the leaves? It helps us imagine what the leaves …
 a look like.
 b taste like.
 c sound like.
 d smell like.

3 The poet compares the fir trees to choristers. What figure of speech is this?
 a a simile
 b alliteration
 c onomatopoeia
 d personification

4 What is the clue to question 3's answer?
 a Consonant sounds are repeated.
 b The words imitate sounds.
 c The trees are compared to humans.
 d The poet uses the word *like*.

L.5.5.A Interpret figurative language, including similes and metaphors, in context.

Coffee Creek

Read the passage.

Highlight an example of alliteration.

The blue-green firs, dusted with gray
in staggered rows, silent choristers in stalls.

I remember a sprinting squirrel
stopping mid-tree to eye my ride
and the patient inspection of rocks by my horse
as he picked our way across the stream.

Circle the adjective that describes the way the horse inspected the rocks.

Put a box around two words that show how the squirrel moved.

1. Write out the example of alliteration in the poem.

2. a Which two words in question 1's answer suggest movement?

   b How do these two words help us visualize the action?

3. Which human quality has the poet given the horse?

4. How does the poet's description of the horse make you feel about the animal?

Week 31 Day 3 Spelling

Eponyms

An **eponym** is a word that gets its name from a real or fictitious person, place, or thing; e.g., Daniel Gabriel Fahrenheit was a Dutch-German-Polish scientist who invented the mercury-in-glass thermometer. From his name we get the Fahrenheit scale that we use to measure temperature.

List

atlas
watt
volt
America
mentor
Tuesday
volcano
January
Saturday
python
martial
cardigan
sandwich
boycott
cannibal
vandal
marmalade
saxophone
diesel
Wednesday

1 Write the word.

2 Fill in the missing syllables.

a Sat/_____/day
b _____/wich
c mar/_____/lade
d _____/las
e vol/_____/no
f Tues/_____

3 Name.

a

b

c

d

4 Unscramble these list words.

a lmmadaear _____
b rotnem _____
c ramAcei _____
d wtat _____
e abcnailn _____
f elsdei _____
g olvt _____
h yadsendeW _____
i ldnava _____
j nohtyp _____
k tbotoyc _____
l sdeauyT _____

L.5.2.E Spell grade-appropriate words correctly, consulting references as needed.

Week 31　Day 4　Spelling

Eponyms

1 **Revise your spelling list from page 169.** Underline the mistake. Write the correct word.

a The volcanoe erupted and hot lava flowed out.
b I brought my cardigen as I was worried it would cool down later.
c The pithon curled around the tree in an elegant manner.
d I had orange marmalaid with cream on my scones.
e I usually have a cheese sanwicth for lunch.
f Janury is the first month of the Roman calendar.
g I found Africa in the atlass.
h On Saterday my brother and I play football.

Challenge words

2 Write the word.

Cartesian _____
Braille _____
algorithm _____
guillotine _____
mesmerize _____
silhouette _____
Fahrenheit _____
Jacuzzi _____
pasteurize _____
Herculean _____

3 **Hidden words.** Find the challenge word.

a zzjaJacuzziawdg _____
b dtaguillotineasuih _____
c tapasteurizeasdo _____
d dfihCartesianasdu _____
e asdrgsilhouetteas _____
f admesmerizeaso _____

4 **Word clues.** Which challenge word matches?

a temperature _____
b printing _____
c shadow _____

5 Complete the sentence.

a He uses a special _____ to make the computer run faster.
b The dairy will _____ your milk before they sell it you.
c Americans measure the temperature using _____.
d _____ is a special form of writing that allows blind people to read.
e Cleaning up our whole house would be a _____ task.

Commas and parentheses

Extra information that is inserted into a sentence is separated from the rest of the sentence by **commas**, **dashes**, or **parentheses**; e.g., Wuffles, my new puppy, is very cute. The Amazon (in South America) is the longest river in the world. The sentence makes sense without the extra information.

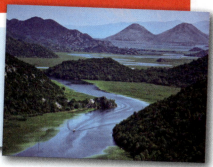

1 **Underline the unnecessary information in each sentence.**

a Patrick, the tallest of the triplets, was given the task of keeping the top shelf tidy.

b Myra, like her two older siblings, is an outstanding singer, dancer, and violinist.

c The latest model (it only came out last week) is the best one so far.

d I put on my hat (the one with the widest brim) before going for a walk.

e There is more information on the subject in this book (see page 32).

2 **Insert the extra information at the end into each sentence. Use parentheses to separate it from the rest of the sentence.**

a Danny Lopez will probably win the event again this year. last year's winner

b The last time we saw them was on our visit to Los Angeles. in California

c My little brother is crying because he can't find Bootsy. his teddy bear

d George and Cassie invited me to their birthday party. the twins next door

e We're spending the summer at Land's End. my grandparents' farm

Week 32 Day 1 Comprehension

The Emperor's New Clothes

Making connections
Linking a text to events in your own life is a great way to build understanding. Look for key words and phrases in the text to make the connections.

Read the passage.

There was once an Emperor who liked fine clothes more than anything. One day, two traders arrived in the kingdom. They said they could make beautiful cloth, invisible to anyone who was stupid or unfit for his job.

The traders set up looms and set about pretending to weave the invisible cloth. After a while, the Emperor sent his Chief Minister to check on their progress.

When the Chief Minister saw the looms, they looked empty. "I mustn't let anyone know I see nothing," he thought. So he said to the traders, "Wonderful patterns! Wonderful colors! I shall inform the Emperor."

- Highlight what the Emperor liked more than anything.
- Underline what the traders said to the Emperor.
- Circle the word that shows that the traders were not really weaving any cloth.
- Color who the Emperor sent to check on the traders.
- Put a box around what the Chief Minister saw when he looked at the looms.
- Highlight what the Chief Minister was going to tell the Emperor.

Circle the correct answers.

1. Which of the following have you done, or might you do?
   a wear fine clothes
   b wear clothes made from invisible cloth
   c play a trick on someone
   d lie about something because you don't want to appear foolish
   e weave cloth on a loom
   f rule over a kingdom

Week 32 Day 2 Comprehension

The Emperor's New Clothes

Read the passage.

Highlight the words that suggest that the people did not want to upset the Emperor.

Underline the child's words.

Circle the father's reaction to the child's words.

Color the words that show that the Emperor was a proud man.

The Great Procession began and the Emperor strode through the streets. No-one would dare admit that they couldn't see his fine set of robes, until a child called out, "He's got nothing on! The Emperor has nothing on!"

"Shhhh!" said the child's father.

The child's words moved through the crowd. The Emperor realized he had been tricked, but he held his head even higher and strode on, not wanting to spoil the procession, while his officials carried a long train that wasn't there at all!

1 Write about ONE of the following:
a) a time when you said or did something that embarrassed a family member or friend

b) a time when you said or did something that made you feel embarrassed afterward

_____
_____
_____
_____
_____
_____
_____
_____
_____

RL.5.1 Quote accurately from a text when explaining what the text says explicitly and when drawing inferences from the text.

Week 32 Day 3 Spelling

Suffix: ly

> Adding **ly** to an adjective turns it into an adverb; e.g., large → large**ly**. If the adjective has *two or more syllables* and ends in **y**, change the **y** to **i** if there is a consonant before it; e.g., ea/sy → ea**si**ly. If the adjective ends in **ic**, add **ally**; e.g., specif**ic** → specif**ically**.

List

- clearly
- simply
- largely
- quietly
- loosely
- daily
- totally
- formerly
- ideally
- hastily
- completely
- possibly
- basically
- enormously
- hurriedly
- privately
- beautifully
- thoroughly
- primarily
- legally

1 Write the word.

2 Write the list words in alphabetical order.

3 Fill in the missing syllables.

a thor/_____/ly
b e/_____/mous/ly
c i/de/al/_____
d hur/_____/ly
e leg/al/_____
f pri/mar/i/_____
g ba/si/_____/ly
h to/_____/ly
i loose/_____
j quick/_____
k pos/_____/bly
l pri/_____/ly

4 Complete each sentence with a list word.

a Her hair hung _____ on her shoulders.
b I wanted to talk to my friend _____ because I had a secret to tell her.
c The pathway was _____ covered in water.
d I eat three pieces of fruit _____.
e Our football team was _____ known as the Roosters, but now we are the Ravens.
f The venue was decorated _____ and looked beautiful.
g We walked _____ to our appointment so as not to be late.

Week 32 Day 4 Spelling

Suffix: ly

1 Revise your spelling list from page 174. Write the list word that belongs in each group.

a ideal, ideals, _____
b legal, illegal, _____
c haste, hasten, _____
d hourly, monthly, _____
e beauty, beautiful, _____
f simple, simplify, _____

Challenge words

2 Write the word.

particularly _____
especially _____
deliberately _____
surprisingly _____
approximately _____
remarkably _____
presumably _____
temporarily _____
automatically _____
occasionally _____

3 Word clues. Which challenge word matches?

a by itself _____
b now and then _____
c on purpose _____
d for a short time _____
e shockingly _____
f about _____

4 Hidden words. Find the challenge word.

a pecialespeciallyas _____
b beratdeliberatelya _____
c llyoccasionallyasd _____
d dapproximatelyas _____

5 Complete the sentence.

a I love ice cream, _____ chocolate ice cream.
b The door to the shop opened _____.
c I _____ enjoy summer when I can go to the beach.
d I was _____ two years older than him.
e The exhibit was _____ closed due to maintenance.
f Dad _____ lets us go to his office.
g He was _____ fit for his age.

L.5.2.E Spell grade-appropriate words correctly, consulting references as needed.

Week 32 Day 5 Grammar

Adverbs and prepositions

Some words that help to tell where or when something happens can be **adverbs** or **prepositions**; e.g., aboard, before, down, and inside.

If the word is an **adverb**, it **does not have a noun or pronoun after it**; e.g., They left their bags **behind**.

If the word is a **preposition**, it always has a noun or pronoun after it; e.g., They left their bags **behind** the wall.

1 **Is the underlined word an adverb, or a preposition?**
   a It was hard work cycling <u>up</u> the hill.   _____
   b When he saw her, he quickly jumped <u>up</u>.   _____
   c Have you been there <u>before</u>?   _____
   d I last saw him the day <u>before</u> yesterday.   _____
   e We had to swim <u>across</u> the river.   _____
   f Our house is <u>opposite</u> the park.   _____

2 **Complete each sentence with an adverb from the box.**

> above   after   inside   underneath   around   aboard

   a When I called her name, she turned _____.
   b The jacket feels tight because I'm wearing a thick sweater _____.
   c We are friends with the people who live on the floor _____.
   d It started to rain, so we went _____.
   e The driver announced that it was time to climb _____.
   f My grandparents are coming to visit us next week, or the week _____.

3 **Complete each sentence with a preposition from the box.**

   a I watched her as she walked _____ the corner.
   b She managed to keep her head _____ water.
   c The captain welcomed us _____ the ship.
   d The tears were running _____ her cheeks.
   e I found the toy _____ the bed.
   f The path continues _____ those trees.

> under
> down
> above
> around
> beyond
> aboard
> inside

Week 33 Day 1 Comprehension

Natural Wonders

Fact or opinion?
A fact is something we can prove is true; e.g., A spider has eight legs. An opinion expresses a belief or feeling; e.g., Spiders are ugly.

Read the passage.

In paragraph 1, **circle** the word that expresses an opinion.

Highlight the words that describe the appearance of the Polar Auroras.

Underline the cause of the Polar Auroras.

The Polar Auroras are a spectacular natural phenomena near the North and South Poles. They are colored lights that form ribbons and spirals in the sky.

The Polar Auroras are caused by solar winds flowing past the Earth. Solar wind is made up of particles from the Sun's atmosphere. These particles are very high in energy. When solar wind enters the Earth's atmosphere, it mixes with gases which then release light.

The Polar Auroras can only be seen at the most northern and southern parts of the Earth.

Color what solar wind consists of.

Underline what happens when solar wind enters the Earth's atmosphere.

Put a **box** around where the Polar Auroras can be seen.

Circle the correct answers.

1 Which word expresses an **opinion**?
- a North
- b South
- c spectacular
- d phenomena

2 Which sentence expresses a **fact**?
- a The Polar Auroras form an amazing pattern of ribbons and spirals in the sky.
- b The Polar Auroras are colored lights that form ribbons and spirals in the sky.
- c The Polar Auroras are a brilliant natural light display in the sky.
- d The Polar Auroras are a magnificent display of colored lights in the sky.

3 Find a **fact** about solar wind and write it down.

_____
_____
_____

RI.5.1 Quote accurately from a text when explaining what the text says explicitly and when drawing inferences from the text.

Week 33 Day 2 Comprehension

Natural Wonders

Read the full text

Read the passage.

Circle the words that mean *for* and *against*.

Highlight the reason some people want countries to stop buying timber from the Amazon.

Underline the reason some people are against the growing of crops in the Amazon.

Deforestation: pros and cons

Some people argue that deforestation in the Amazon destroys animal habitats. They want other countries to stop buying timber from the Amazon. Then, there would be no incentive for people to cut down the forest.

Deforestation is also bad for the environment. During heavy rains, pesticides from crops flow off the land and into rivers. This damages river wildlife.

Other people argue that deforestation helps the economy in South America. Farmers clear land to grow crops, such as coconuts, oranges, coffee, and soybeans. Agriculture and the timber industry provide jobs for people. The country also makes money from selling timber.

Color the reasons some people are in favor of the clearing of trees to make way for crops.

Put a box around why some people think the timber industry is good for South America.

1 In your own words, explain what different groups of people **believe** about deforestation in the Amazon.

_____

_____

2 Explain how the different groups use **facts** to support their beliefs.

_____

_____

_____

_____

_____

_____

Week 33 Day 3 Spelling

que

> The letters **que** make the sound **k** in some words that come from French; e.g., pla**que**.

List

1. **Write the word.**

plaque
mosque
bouquet
unique
opaque
antique
lacquer
conquer
pique
macaque
oblique
boutique
conqueror
grotesque
mystique
technique
brusque
physique
racquet
baroque

2. **Chunks.** Rearrange the letters in the right order.

a. mo-que-s
b. q-un-ue-i
c. br-que-us
d. q-con-uer
e. que-o-bar
f. si-ue-phy-q
g. es-gro-que-t
h. que-a-op
i. que-pla
j. que-pi
k. que-lac-r

3. **In a group.** Write the list word that belongs in each group.

a. church, temple,
b. monkey, ape,
c. flower, bunch,
d. diagonal, slanting,
e. original, special,
f. ugly, hideous,

4. **Meaning.** Which list word means?

a. A small shop, usually selling clothes
b. The particular method of doing something
c. An aura of mystery that surrounds certain people or activities
d. A liquid used on wood to protect and make it shiny
e. Being the only one of its type
f. A flat plate or tablet with writing on
g. Not able to be seen through

L.5.2.E Spell grade-appropriate words correctly, consulting references as needed.

Week 33 Day 4 Spelling

que

1 **Revise your spelling list from page 179.** Underline the mistake. Write the correct word.

a Many paintings from the Barocque era are from Italian and Dutch artists.
b I chose a pink racket to play tennis with on Saturday afternoon.
c I made a boucket of flowers from the plants in our garden.
d My room was always dark because of the opaike window.
e I have learned the techniqe of icing cupcakes.
f My dad likes to lacker the wooden deck outside once a year.
g My team received a placqe for winning the tournament.

Challenge words

2 Write the word.

critique
marquee
etiquette
masquerade
clique
croquette
statuesque
tourniquet
discotheque
marquetry

3 **Word clues.** Which challenge word matches?

a good manners
b canopy
c masked party
d fried food
e inlaid work

4 **Hidden words.** Find the challenge word.

a tqdldiscothequeas
b licilcliquequeli
c nqutourniquetquat
d crotcroquetteettec
e sttstatuesqueesqu

5 Complete the sentence.

a I ordered a _____ for lunch.
b We set up a _____ in the yard in case it rained.
c I was having a _____ party where everyone had to wear a mask.
d Having good manners is an important part of _____.
e The author was pleased with the glowing _____ of his new novel.
f The nurse used a _____ to stop my leg bleeding.

L.5.2.E Spell grade-appropriate words correctly, consulting references as needed.

Week 33 Day 5 Grammar

Sentences: subject, verb, object

A **simple sentence** can be divided into a **subject** (the person or thing that does the action), a **verb** (the action), and an **object** (the person or thing affected by the action); e.g.,
The child (subject) is catching (verb) the ball (object).

1 Is the underlined section the subject, verb, or object of the sentence?

a   The monkeys <u>are climbing</u> the trees.   _____
b   <u>The astronomer</u> has discovered a new star.   _____
c   <u>The kind boy</u> is helping the old lady.   _____
d   The choir is singing <u>a beautiful song</u>.   _____
e   The smart girl <u>has answered</u> the question.   _____
f   <u>My friend</u> has given me a big box of chocolates.   _____
g   The child has broken <u>her favorite toy</u>.   _____

2 Unscramble the clues to complete the puzzle.

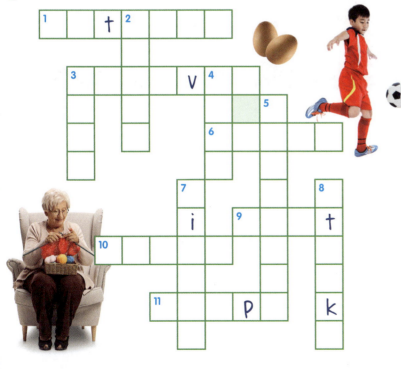

Across:
1. Soldiers fight <u>tablets</u>.
3. Grandma knits <u>sravecs</u>.
6. Soccer players score <u>agols</u>.
9. Lions eat <u>tame</u>.
10. Musicians write <u>nogss</u>.
11. Travelers go on <u>prits</u>.

Down:
2. Coaches train <u>mates</u>.
3. The sun melts <u>nows</u>.
4. Hens lay <u>gesg</u>.
5. Nurses look after <u>tapstine</u>.
7. Zookeepers feed <u>gitser</u>.
8. Restaurants serve <u>skates</u>.

3 Fill in subjects and objects to complete these sentences.

a   _____ is wearing _____.
b   _____ are making _____.

L.5.1 Demonstrate command of the conventions of standard English grammar and usage when writing or speaking.

Week 34 Day 1 Comprehension

Body Systems

Making connections
Linking a text to other texts you have read is a great way to build understanding. Look for key words and phrases in the texts to make the connections.

Read the passage.

Text 1

The respiratory system brings oxygen into the body and removes carbon dioxide from it.

The body's cells need oxygen to survive, and carbon dioxide is one of their waste products.

The air you breathe in moves down the trachea into the soft, spongy lungs. It flows through narrower and narrower tubes in the lungs. At the ends of the tubes are alveoli, which look like very small balloons.

*In both texts, **highlight** the sentences that contain the words* oxygen *and* carbon dioxide.

In both texts, underline the sentences that contain the word trachea.

*In both texts, **color** the sentences that contain the word* alveoli.

Text 2

Air travels through your nose to your lungs via the trachea (windpipe). It divides into two branches, one for each lung. The branches divide into narrower and narrower branches until they reach air sacs called alveoli. Alveoli look like tiny bunches of grapes.

When you breathe in, the lungs take up oxygen from the air. When you breathe out, carbon dioxide is released from your body.

Circle the correct answers.

1 Write down whether the following information appears in **both** texts, or in only **one** of the texts.

   a We breathe in oxygen and we breathe out carbon dioxide. _____
   b Air travels down the trachea into the lungs. _____
   c The trachea is also known as the windpipe. _____
   d We have two lungs. _____
   e The lungs are soft and spongy. _____
   f The alveoli look like tiny bunches of grapes. _____
   g The tubes in the lungs become narrower and narrower. _____
   h The air flows through tubes in the lungs to the alveoli. _____

Week 34 Day 2 Comprehension

Body Systems

Read the passage.

Text 1

The digestive system breaks food down into nutrients that the body absorbs. It expels whatever is left over.

Digestion starts in the mouth. Chewing breaks food into small pieces. Saliva contains an enzyme, which also helps to break food down. After swallowing, food moves down the esophagus to the stomach.

The stomach uses acids, enzymes and its own movements to turn the pieces of food into a thick liquid. It then squeezes small amounts of the liquid into the small intestine.

Text 2

The main function of your digestive system is to break down food, extract nutrients and water from that food, and to excrete waste.

Digestion breaks food into tiny parts called molecules. Your body uses these molecules as fuel to keep you healthy and active.

Chewing breaks up the food. When you chew, you produce a digestive juice called saliva. Saliva helps to break down the food into tiny parts.

When you swallow, your esophagus moves the food to your stomach.

In both texts, **highlight** the words that tell what the function of the digestive system is.

In both texts, underline the sentences that tell what happens to food when we chew it.

In both texts, color the sentences that tell what happens to the food when we swallow it.

---

1. What do **both** texts tell us about the function of the digestive system?

2. What do we learn from **both** texts about what happens when we chew our food?

3. According to **both** texts, what happens to our food when we swallow it?

RI.5.1 Quote accurately from a text when explaining what the text says explicitly and when drawing inferences from the text.

Week 34 Day 3 Spelling

Word building

Many new words can be built from a base word. The new words are formed by altering the spelling of the base word, or by adding **prefixes** or **suffixes**; e.g., using the base word, *simple*, we can form the words: simply, simplify, simplest, simplification.

List

1 Write the word.

- flat
- flatter
- flattest
- flatten
- flattened
- reside
- residing
- resided
- resident
- residential
- simple
- simply
- simplify
- simplest
- simplification
- horror
- horrible
- horrify
- horrifying
- horrified

2 Write the list words in alphabetical order.

3 Fill in the missing letters.

- a s___mpli_____cati_____
- b fl_____te___t
- c s___m___le___t
- d re___i___i___g
- e ___im_____y
- f re_____d_____
- g h___rr___f___
- h re_____de

4 Complete each sentence with a list word.

- a The dress that my sister wore was _____ and elegant.
- b I watched in _____ as the car drove over my football.
- c I had to _____ the instructions so my little brother could understand them.
- d As I was a _____ of the building, I had to attend the meeting.
- e She _____ the sandcastle with her foot.
- f The price of gas always seems to _____ my mother.
- g The speed limit in the _____ zone is lower to keep people safe.

Week 34 Day 4 Spelling

Word building

1 Revise your spelling list from page 184. Word building. Add suffixes to build words.

a flat
   er _____
   est _____
   en _____
   ened _____

b simple
   y   _____
   ify _____
   st _____
   ification _____

c reside
   ing _____
   ed _____
   ent _____
   ntial _____

d horror
   ible _____
   ify _____
   ifying _____
   ified _____

Challenge words

2 Write the word.

benefit _____
benefited _____
benefiting _____
beneficial _____
beneficiary _____
receive _____
receiving _____
received _____
reception _____
receipt _____

3 Hidden words. Find the challenge word.

a aduybenefitingtin _____
b wiohareceptionre _____
c asdrbenefitedaosi _____
d asdasreceiveasdi _____
e asbeneficiaryasld _____
f asdreceivingasod _____

4 Unravel these challenge words.

a prtecie _____
b deviecer _____
c lbaeinceif _____
d noitpecer _____

5 Complete the sentence.

a I _____ my pocket money once I had cleaned my room.
b Exercising regularly will _____ your heart.
c The shop assistant handed me a _____ for the items I had purchased.
d I was excited to be _____ my parcel in the mail.

L.5.2.E Spell grade-appropriate words correctly, consulting references as needed.

Active and passive voice

Verbs have two voices: active and passive. They are **active** when the subject of the sentence is responsible for the action; e.g., **Raccoons are eating the acorns.**

They are passive when the person or thing having the action done to them is the subject of the sentence; e.g., **The acorns are being eaten by racoons**. The passive voice has a form of the verb to be (e.g., be, being, been) plus the past form of the main verb (e.g., eaten).

1 Check (✔) the sentences in the passive voice.
- a ☐ The radio host welcomed the guest.
- b ☐ The guest was welcomed by the radio host.
- c ☐ The problem was solved by the scientist.
- d ☐ The scientist solved the problem.
- e ☐ The rude man interrupted his speech.
- f ☐ His speech was interrupted by the rude man.
- g ☐ They converted the kilograms into pounds.
- h ☐ The kilograms were converted into pounds.

2 Complete the second sentence in each pair so that it is in the passive voice.
- a He has added an egg to the mixture.
  An egg has _____.
- b They are expanding their empire.
  Their empire is _____.
- c We could hear a hissing sound.
  A hissing sound could _____.
- d They are producing lots of new cars.
  Lots of new cars are _____.
- e Someone has stolen the valuable painting.
  The valuable painting has _____.

L.5.1 Demonstrate command of the conventions of standard English grammar and usage when writing or speaking.

Week 35 Day 1 Comprehension

Letter of Complaint

Identifying audience and purpose
To identify the author's purpose in writing a text, it helps to work out who the text was written for. The language the author uses will show what his or her purpose is—to inform, persuade, instruct, or entertain.

Read the passage.

Circle Belinda Tochner's job title.

Put a box around the company the complaint is being made against.

Underline the sentence that expresses the purpose of the letter.

Color the date of the first phone call.

Highlight the reason the writer made a second phone call.

18 Main Street, Los Angeles, CA 90012
Belinda Tochner
Consumer Relations Manager
SuperSafe Insurance Ltd

Dear Ms. Tochner
COMPLAINT
Policy No: 98765432

I am writing to complain about my car insurance claim being rejected.

On November 22nd, 2009, I arranged car insurance with your company by telephone. On November 25th, I telephoned again to ask that my insurance also cover my 20-year-old daughter, as she would also be driving the car.

Circle the correct answers.

1 Who is the target audience for the letter?
  a the owner of SuperSafe Insurance
  b the Consumer Relations Manager of Supersafe Insurance
  c the Chief Executive Officer of SuperSafe Insurance
  d an accountant at SuperSafe Insurance

2 What is the purpose of the letter? The writer is complaining that ...
  a her daughter is driving her car.
  b Ms. Tochner did not answer her phone call.
  c SuperSafe Insurance wrongfully rejected her insurance claim.
  d SuperSafe Insurance wrongfully rejected her daughter's insurance claim.

3 What is the tone of the letter?
  a firm and polite
  b angry and abusive
  c lighthearted and friendly
  d nervous and embarrassed

RI.5.1 Quote accurately from a text when explaining what the text says explicitly and when drawing inferences from the text.

Week 35 Day 2 Comprehension

Letter of Complaint

Read the passage.

Circle how the writer feels about having her claim rejected.

Highlight how the writer attempts to prove that her claim was mistakenly rejected.

I am most upset that when I telephoned on January 14th this year to make a claim for an accident that my daughter had had in my car, I was informed that my claim was rejected. The reason provided was the policy did not cover my daughter. Furthermore, the claims consultant said there was no record that my policy had been extended, to my daughter or to anyone else.

However, as I noted earlier, I did call SuperSafe Insurance to extend the insurance. To prove this, I have included with this letter a copy of my telephone bill, which shows that the call was made to your company. I have underlined the call on the bill. The claims consultant I spoke to was Ben Wilkinson.

I believe you made a mistake in not changing my insurance policy, and I would like you to fix this and pay the claim I have made. I look forward to hearing from you and to having this matter resolved as quickly as possible.

Underline a clause that shows that the writer is certain that SuperSafe Insurance is in the wrong.

Color what the writer expects SuperSafe Insurance to do about her claim.

1. Which word in the passage expresses how the writer feels about her claim being rejected?

2. Carefully explain how the writer attempts to persuade the person she is writing to that SuperSafe Insurance was mistaken in rejecting her claim.

3. If you were Ms. Tochner, would you be offended by the language the writer has used in her letter? Give reasons for your answer.

Week 35 Day 3 Spelling

Loan words

> **Loan words** are words that have **come into a language from another language**; e.g., from Italian we have the words: opera, gelato, soprano. The word has the same meaning in both languages.

List

1 Write the word.

café _____
pasta _____
ballet _____
studio _____
gelato _____
genre _____
opera _____
pizza _____
mousse _____
croissant _____
cliché _____
sauté _____
macaroni _____
soprano _____
sabotage _____
brunette _____
rapport _____
dossier _____
scenario _____
baguette _____

2 Fill in the missing syllables.

a crois/_____
b _____/la/to
c bru/_____
d _____/er/a
e bal/_____
f _____/port
g so/_____/no
h gen/_____

3 Name.

a

b

c

d

4 Unscramble these list words.

a acraomin _____
b droesis _____
c étuas _____
d logeta _____
e doutis _____
f zapiz _____
g ponosar _____
h prtapro _____
i stapa _____
j otbagase _____
k uebteagt _____
l oiranecs _____

L.5.2.E Spell grade-appropriate words correctly, consulting references as needed.

Week 35 Day 4 Spelling

Loan words

1 Revise your spelling list from page 189. Match the clue with the list word.

a a person with brown hair _____
b a specific type of movie _____
c a play that is entirely sung _____
d dough base with tomato and cheese _____
e an expression that is overused _____
f a form of dance _____
g to fry lightly in oil _____
h a place to eat _____
i a long, thin loaf of bread _____
j the workshop of an artist _____
k Italian ice cream _____

Challenge words

2 Write the word.

spaghetti _____
lasagne _____
saboteur _____
entrée _____
staccato _____
chauffeur _____
entrepreneur _____
restaurateur _____
extravaganza _____
reconaissance _____

3 Word sort. These words are based on other languages. Put them in the correct list.

a **Italian**

_____   _____
_____   _____

b **French**

_____   _____
_____   _____
_____   _____

4 Another way to say it. Which challenge word could replace the underlined word?

a My sister and I put on a musical <u>spectacular</u>. _____
b First I had a <u>starter</u>, then I had a main course. _____
c The <u>driver</u> drove us from our house to the wedding. _____

190 L.5.2.E Spell grade-appropriate words correctly, consulting references as needed.

Week 35 Day 5 Grammar

Sentence fragments

A **sentence** is a group of words that makes complete sense. It contains a **subject** and a **verb**. A **sentence fragment** does not make sense on its own; it relies on other sentences for its meaning; e.g., Where is the book? **On the top shelf.**

1 Write down whether the following are sentences, or sentence fragments.
   a   He parked the car in the garage.
   b   The children were racing up and down the corridor.
   c   In a little while when the sun goes down.
   d   The boy wearing the pink shirt.
   e   At the back of the cupboard.
   f   Put your dirty socks in the laundry basket.
   g   Do you think it will rain later today?

2 Rewrite the following sentence fragments as full sentences.
In the flower bed.
The ball landed in the flower bed.
   a   To the beach.

   b   Because I missed the bus.

3 In the following passage, underline the sentence fragments.

Clouds drifted slowly across the night sky, occasionally blotting out the moon.
"Scared?" asked Nicholas.
"Not really," said Naomi. "You?"
"A bit nervous," admitted Nicholas. "I wish they'd hurry so we can get this over with."
As if in reply, the noise of an engine sounded in the distance. Naomi felt Nicholas tense beside her. Not long now.

L.5.1. Demonstrate command of the conventions of standard English grammar and usage when writing or speaking.

Week 36 | Day 1 | Comprehension

On the Edge of Extinction

Word study
You can often use clues in the text to work out the meaning of words you do not understand.

Read the passage.

(Circle) where thylacines once lived.

Put a box around where thylacines were last seen in large numbers.

We know that the thylacine once lived in New Guinea and mainland Australia because fossils have been found in these places. But these populations died out—killed by the introduced dingoes, or wild dogs, of the Aboriginal peoples. The island of Tasmania then became the thylacine's last refuge.

When European farmers arrived in Tasmania, they believed the thylacines were responsible for killing sheep. In 1888, a bounty was put on the thylacine's head. Killing them was now a profitable business encouraged by the government.

Color the word that shows that dingoes were not always native to Australia.

Underline a word that shows that people received payment for killing thylacines.

Circle the correct answers.

1. Which word in the passage suggests that dingoes have not always been native Australian animals?
   - a Aboriginal
   - b fossils
   - c introduced
   - d populations

2. What does the word *refuge* mean?
   - a something that is worthless
   - b a place of protection or safety
   - c to disagree with something
   - d someone from another place

3. What is the **clue** to question 2's answer? The word *refuge* refers to the island of Tasmania, which was …
   - a where European farmers hunted thylacines.
   - b where thylacines started killing sheep.
   - c where people made money out of thylacines.
   - d the last place thylacines lived in large numbers.

4. What is a bounty?
   - a a reward
   - b a cover
   - c a rope
   - d a leash

L.5.4.A Use context as a clue to the meaning of a word or phrase.

Week 36 Day 2 Comprehension

On the Edge of Extinction

Read the full text

Read the passage.

Circle the word that suggests that the Siberian tigers were difficult to find.

Put a box around the word that describes people who care for the environment.

More tigers lurked in the Siberian woods than anyone thought. Finding 600 instead of an expected 300 has increased the chance that the magnificent Siberian tiger will survive.

Conservationists were thrilled to find out that the Siberian tiger population was twice as big as believed. Siberian tigers live in the dense forests of Siberia. This cold and wild area is called the taiga (TIE-ga) and is vast enough to help the tigers hide from us. Poachers kill some, and forestry and mining have an impact on their habitat. But for now, the tiger seems safe.

Underline the word that suggests that the trees in the Siberian forest grow close together.

Color the word that suggests that the Siberian tigers have plenty of space to move around in.

1 Use the **clues** in the boxes to help you explain the meanings of the following words:

a lurked _____

b dense _____

c vast _____

2 Which word in the passage names people who care about the natural environment?
_____

3 Which word in the passage names people who kill wild animals illegally?
_____

L.5.4.A Use context as a clue to the meaning of a word or phrase.

Week 36 Day 3 Spelling

anti, circum, extra, semi

> The prefix **anti** means against; e.g., **anti**biotic.
> The prefix **circum** means around or circling; e.g., **circum**ference.
> The prefix **extra** means beyond or outside; e.g., **extra**ordinary.
> The prefix **semi** means half or partly; e.g., **semi**precious.

List

semifinal
semicircle
extramural
circumvent
antismoking
antidote
semiformal
antifreeze
antihero
semidarkness
semicolon
semiskilled
antisocial
anticlimax
semiprecious
antislavery
antiseptic
semidetached
antibiotic
circumscribe

1 Write the word.

2 Sort the words.

a *anti*

b *circum*

c *extra*

d *semi*

3 Fill in the missing syllables.

a sem/i/_____/ness
b ex/_____/mur/_____
c _____/i/cir/_____
d sem/____/_____/lon
e _____/i/de/tached
f sem/i/_____/nal
g an/_____/he/ro
h an/_____/smok/_____

4 Meaning. Which list word means?

a A substance that stops poison from working
b One half of a circle
c To find a way around an obstacle
d A substance that lowers the freezing point of a liquid such as water
e Against slavery
f A disappointingly weak conclusion to an event

Week 36 Day 4 Spelling

anti, circum, extra, semi

1 Revise your spelling list from page 194. Underline the mistake. Write the word correctly.

a The antedote to a snake's bite must be administered quickly. _____
b We are playing our football semefinal on the weekend. _____
c The pharmacist told me to take the antebiotc with food. _____
d After I fell over, I cleaned my knee with an anteseptik wipe. _____
e The United Kingdom and the United States passed an international antislavary law in 1807. _____
f My cousin's wedding was semiformale, so I could wear my new dress. _____
g I didn't want to be anticsocel, so I went and spoke to our guests. _____

Challenge words

2 Write the word.

antibacterial _____
circumference _____
semipermanent _____
extraordinary _____
semiconscious _____
antihistamine _____
circumnavigate _____
extraterrestrial _____
extracurricular _____

3 Word clues. Which challenge word matches?

a to sail around the world _____
b outside regular hours _____
c a line around a circle _____
d something to treat allergies _____
e exceptional _____
f sterile _____
g Martian _____

4 Complete the sentence.

a The boy takes part in many _____ activities at camp.
b I used a _____ marker to write my name on the label.
c I cleaned the kitchen bench with _____ wipes.
d The football player was still _____ as we took him to hospital.

L.5.2.E Spell grade-appropriate words correctly, consulting references as needed.

Week 36 Day 5 Grammar

Punctuating sentences

Punctuation helps readers understand text by breaking it down into smaller parts. The main rules to remember when punctuating sentences are:
- Start each sentence with a **capital letter** and end it with a **period**, **question mark**, or **exclamation point**.
- Start **proper nouns** with a **capital letter**.
- Use **commas** to show **pauses** in a sentence.
- Use **quotation marks** to show the exact words someone says.

1 Fill in the commas and end punctuation in the following sentences.
  a   Mandy why are you wearing your best shoes
  b   When we drove through the forest we saw maple pine and fir trees
  c   You have completed all your chores haven't you
  d   I ordered him a hamburger but he refused to eat it
  e   Yes I've been to New York and so has Ruby

2 Fill in the missing punctuation in the following sentences.
  a   How good was that exclaimed Alex, as he stepped off the ride
  b   When she saw the creature, Jemma asked What is it
  c   The clouds are gathering said the man and I think it might rain
  d   I'd like some roast potatoes said Aunt Lydia and a spoonful of mashed pumpkin
  e   Is this your wallet asked the girl or does it belong to someone else

3 Write the following sentences with the correct punctuation.
  a   my cousins, max and sophie harris, are coming to visit us on saturday.

  b   they have been to yosemite national park in californias sierra nevada mountains

  c   did you see the statue of liberty when you went to new york

196   L.5.2 Demonstrate command of the conventions of standard English capitalization, punctuation, and spelling when writing.

REVIEW 4: Spelling

Spelling

> Use this review to test your knowledge. It has three parts—**Spelling**, **Grammar**, and **Comprehension**. If you're unsure of an answer, go back and read the rules and generalizations in the blue boxes.

You have learned about:
- digraphs: oo, ou
- eponyms
- word building
- digraphs: wh, ph, gh
- suffix: ly
- loan words
- suffixes: ence, ance
- que
- prefixes: anti, circum, extra, semi

1 In each sentence, the spelling error has been underlined. Write the correct spelling. 2 marks

a Our team was in the <u>semefinal</u> for the third year in a row. _____

b "We have the <u>dossiar</u> ready for you, Captain," reported the detective. _____

c The doctor prescribed an <u>antebiotic</u> for my tonsillitis. _____

d Our coach tries hard to build <u>rappore</u> with each player. _____

2 Which word correctly completes this sentence? 1 mark

People once believed that the Earth was _____.

a flatter   b flattened   c flat   d flattering

3 This sentence has one word that is incorrect. Write the correct spelling. 1 mark

In Italy we ate lots of pizza, pasta, and gellato. _____

4 Complete each word with **oo** or **ou**. 2 marks

a cuck ___   b igl ___   c w ___ nd   d n ___ dle

5 Circle the correct word to complete the sentence. 2 marks

a I always try to find the (simplify, simply, simplest) solution.

b (Idea, Ideal, Ideally) I'd like to move to Washington D.C.

6 Which word correctly completes this sentence? 1 mark

On Thursday afternoons I take _____ arts lessons with Sally.

a maritime   b martian   c martial   d marital

7 This sentence has one word that is incorrect. Write the correct spelling. 1 mark

For my birthday, I got a new pair of bright orange headfones. _____

Your score ☐ / 10

REVIEW 4: Grammar

Grammar

You have learned about:
- relative clauses
- proper nouns
- compound and complex sentences
- parentheses
- adverbs and prepositions
- subjects, verbs, and objects
- active and passive voice
- sentence fragments
- punctuating sentences

1 In each sentence, circle the relative pronoun and underline the relative clause. 2 marks

   a She spoke to the man who had helped her once before.

   b The dog, which was large and fierce, frightened me.

2 In each sentence, circle the words that have been written incorrectly. Write the correction in the space. 2 marks

   a My mother is visiting mrs. jones, our next door neighbor. _____

   b Our pilot, captain reynolds, told us to fasten our seatbelts. _____

3 State whether the following are compound, or complex sentences. 2 marks

   a I put on a jacket because I was cold. _____

   b She was cold, but she wouldn't put on a jacket. _____

   c Alex was swimming, and Rosy was building sandcastles. _____

   d I have apologized to the boy whose baseball bat I used. _____

4 In the following sentences, add parentheses where they are needed. 2 marks

   a I put the book the one with the leather cover back on the shelf.

   b They have another car a very old one that they keep in the garage.

5 In each sentence, circle the adverb and underline the preposition. 2 marks

   a The children were playing outside when we drove past their house.

   b He walked to my house because he lives nearby.

6 In each sentence, underline the subject, and circle the verb. 2 marks

   a The little girl is singing her favorite song.

   b The police have arrested the thieves.

198

REVIEW 4: Grammar

Grammar

7 **In each sentence, underline the object.** 1 mark

a The hot sun was burning the grass.

b The men are fixing the roofs.

8 **In each pair, complete the second sentence.** 2 marks

a Benjamin Franklin invented the lightning rod.

_____ was invented by Benjamin Franklin.

b The fire fighters rescued the people on the top story.

The people on the top story were rescued _____

c A pilot has spotted the missing hikers.

The missing hikers _____ by a pilot.

d The conference was attended by doctors from all over the country.

Doctors from all over the country _____

9 **In the following conversation, underline the sentence fragment and write it as a full sentence.** 2 marks

"Where did you put your dirty washing, Jay?" asked Mom.

"On my bed," he replied.

_____

10 **Fill in the missing punctuation in the following sentences.** 3 marks

a "When is their train due to arrive asked Ryan.

b There was so much food on the table platters of meat salads fruit and little cakes.

Your score

☐

20

REVIEW 4: Comprehension
The Dark and Silent World

Read the passage and then use the comprehension skills you have learned to answer the questions.

Helen Keller is one of the most inspiring examples of someone who rose above their challenges to lead a commendable life.

Born in Alabama in 1880, Helen contracted an illness when she was 19 months old that resulted in her losing her sight and hearing. Unable to talk, she communicated her needs by making basic signs. Helen was like a prisoner inside her own body. She was frustrated and angry and would often fly into uncontrollable tempers.

Helen's parents were determined to find a teacher for their daughter, and when she was seven, Anne Sullivan was sent to help her. Anne immediately started teaching her young student by giving her the doll she had brought as a present and spelling out the letters 'd-o-l-l' into her hand. At first, Helen did not understand that objects had names and she became extremely frustrated, sometimes even throwing the object she was holding onto the floor. In fact, Helen's tantrums became so severe, Anne insisted she be isolated from her family for a time so that she could focus completely on her teacher's instructions. Anne and Helen moved into a nearby cottage.

The breakthrough came soon afterwards when Anne poured water over Helen's hand, at the same time spelling out the word into her palm. Once Helen grasped the concept, she wanted to know the names of all the things in her immediate world.

Helen later attended a school for the deaf, where she learned to talk. Despite her disability, she went to college, became a famous speaker and author, and dedicated her life to helping others.

1 What does the opening paragraph suggest about the way people view Helen Keller? 1 mark
People … CRITICAL

    a disapprove of Helen Keller.   **b** admire Helen Keller.
    c are critical of Helen Keller.   **d** are shocked by Helen Keller.

REVIEW 4: Comprehension

The Dark and Silent World

2 Where was Helen Keller born? 1 mark **LITERAL**
- a in Alaska
- b in Arizona
- c in Arkansas
- d in Alabama

3 Helen was like a prisoner inside her own body. This means ... 1 mark **INFERENTIAL**
- a she was isolated from the world.
- b she had to stay indoors.
- c it felt like she was being punished.
- d her parents were very protective.

4 Why did Helen often become frustrated and angry? She ... 1 mark **INFERENTIAL**
- a did not like her teacher.
- b could not make sense of the world.
- c often felt sick.
- d was forced to stay indoors.

5 As a result of her tantrums, Anne insisted that Helen be separated from her family for a time. What does this suggest about Helen's relationship with her family? 1 mark **CRITICAL**
- a They let her get her own way.
- b They were too strict with her.
- c They did not love her.
- d They gave her too many chores to do.

6 Which was the first word Helen associated with an object? 1 mark **LITERAL**
- a doll
- b water
- c cottage
- d bucket

7 Which of the following words would Helen most likely have learned first? 1 mark **INFERENTIAL**
- a sky
- b stars
- c light
- d ground

8 Which sentence does NOT apply to Helen Keller? 1 mark **CRITICAL**
- a She overcame many challenges.
- b She made a success of her life.
- c She was stubborn and lazy.
- d She was curious and intelligent.

9 What type of text is this? 1 mark **CRITICAL**
- a a narrative
- b an autobiography
- c a biography
- d an argument

10 Explain how Anne Sullivan taught Helen to understand words. 1 mark **LITERAL**

Your score /10

Your Review 4 Scores

Spelling	Grammar	Comprehension	Total
+	+	=	
10	20	10	40

ANSWERS • Weeks 1–3

Week 1, Day 1
Pg 2

> Jakob led Tibalt through the tunnels. There were guards all the way along. There wasn't much need for guards in this peaceful <u>underground</u> city, but they added to Zelig's power.
> Jakob and Tibalt arrived at the crystal gardens. The huge cave was filled with beautiful limestone formations. The strange, pale shapes glittered in the light from the firefly (lanterns). Long, thin (stalactites) hung from the roof, and chunky (stalagmites) rose up from the floor.

1 b
2 a are different shapes.
  b grow in different directions.
3 c grow on different parts of the cave.

Week 1, Day 2
Pg 3

> **Below world**
> Jakob walked slowly home. From the (tunnel) he could smell supper cooking on the fire. He opened the door to his dark, damp rock chamber. Della, Jakob's mother, was pouring mushroom stew into three bowls. "Supper will be ruined if we don't eat it now."
>
> **Above world**
> Felda lived in a large cottage in a small village. Her (father) Baldric, was the village chief. Jakob and Tibalt sat down with the villagers. They ate food with the most amazing tastes. Bread was mixed with herbs, and the fruits were sweet and juicy.

1 both live with a parent
2 it's above ground/it's a real house
3 food: more variety/tastier/fresher

Week 1, Day 3
Pg 4

1 Check for correct spelling of each word.
2 a deaf, head, idea, meant, bread, thread, great, wealth, really, break, dread, already, heavy
  b four, famous, cousin, nourish
  c said, bargain, curtain
3 Missing letters are <u>underlined</u>
  a w<u>ea</u>lth b br<u>ea</u>d c m<u>ea</u>nt d c<u>ou</u>sin
  e br<u>ea</u>k f n<u>ou</u>rish g f<u>a</u>mous h d<u>ea</u>f
  i alr<u>ea</u>dy j gr<u>ea</u>t
4 a bread b break c wealth d thread

Week 1, Day 4
Pg 5

1 a <u>curtein</u> curtain b <u>hevy</u> heavy
  c <u>def</u> deaf d <u>ideea</u> idea
  e <u>fore</u> four f <u>welth</u> wealth
  g <u>sed</u> said h <u>hed</u> head
  i <u>bargin</u> bargain
2 Check for correct spelling of each word.
3 a meadow b haiku c captain
  d trouble e deadly f boulder
  g dreamed h aisle i couple
  j knead
4 a deadly b aisle c boulder d dreamed

Week 1, Day 5
Pg 6

1 **red**: ears, hair **blue**: puzzlement, confusion
  green: Rosh, Canadian
2 a wisdom b success c anger d poverty
3 a American b Italy c Portugal d Russian
4 a hat b eggs c apple d lamb e tea f hole
  Abstract noun: health

Week 2, Day 1
Pg 7

> No way! Can't be! Please tell me this isn't happening. Help me someone! I look at my dad. His smile is so wide it covers his whole face. Mom is (crying). My sister, Georgia, seems pretty upset too. Her mouth hangs open. Her eyes are bulging.
> "Welcome to your new home," announces Dad. "What do you think, Oscar?"
> "I … I … I don't know what to say," I stammer.

1 c 2 b 3 d 4 a 5 b

Week 2, Day 2
Pg 8

> We've been in our new home in the jungle for about two months now. It seems like forever though.
> Georgia has discovered writing and writes great long letters to Tania. She's even started a novel—well she calls it a novel. Georgia doesn't care about Richard anymore. Not since she discovered Nell's earthy grandson. He's the same age as Georgia and she thinks he's gorgeous. Mom and Dad are pretty happy too. Dad's veggie garden is thriving and Mom's really into cooking.

1 he doesn't think it's any good—"well she calls it a novel"
2 she's discovered Nell's earthy grandson
3 Mom is now "pretty happy" about living in the jungle

Week 2, Day 3
Pg 9

1 Check for correct spelling of each word.
2 a rse: horse, worse, purse, verse, reverse, sparse, adverse, course, diverse, converse, immerse, averse, terse
  b rce: force, scarce, fierce, source, divorce, resource, pierce
3 Missing letters are <u>underlined</u>
  a <u>reverse</u> b <u>divorce</u> c <u>diverse</u> d <u>source</u>
  e <u>immerse</u> f <u>sparse</u> g <u>purse</u> h <u>fierce</u>
  i <u>resource</u> j <u>verse</u>
4 a horse b fierce c verse d sparse
  e converse f adverse g force h worse

Week 2, Day 4
Pg 10

1 a source b pierce c scarce d force
  e immerse f diverse
2 Check for correct spelling of each word.
3 a traverse b disperse c coarse
  d coerce e commerce f reinforce
4 a rehearse b enforce c reimburse
  d reinforce

5 a reimburse b rehearse c coarse
  d coerce e disperse f enforce
  g traverse h reinforce

Week 2, Day 5
Pg 11

1 a This b these c that d This e Those
2 a thing b thing c thing d person e person
3 a This, that b These, those
4 a <u>that</u> b <u>this</u> c <u>these</u>, <u>those</u>

Week 3, Day 1
Pg 12

> The novel is set against a backdrop of muddy roads and mournful cows in modern-day, rural Australia. The story of Hitler's daughter is told by Anna, one of four children who wait at the same bus shelter every morning. One of the children usually chooses a character and Anna makes up a story about the character. But one morning Anna decides that she will choose the character. The other children are surprised when she announces who the subject of her story will be. Ben thinks it's a "cool" choice. Mark protests that Hitler did not have a daughter; and little Tracey does not know who Hitler is.

1 a, c 2 b 3 d 4 c

Week 3, Day 2
Pg 13

> The story unfolds over a series of gray, wet mornings, and like the children at the bus stop, the reader can't wait to hear what happens next. French explores the effect that Anna's story has on Mark, a naturally curious boy. Anna's story gets him thinking, and he begins to take a greater interest in news bulletins about suffering in some faraway country. He fears that, like Hitler's daughter, he could be part of something evil without realizing it.
> But the character who is really at the center of this novel is Heidi, Hitler's daughter. Heidi is a young girl who loves her father, even though he publicly rejects her.

1 like the children, the reader will be eager to hear what happens next
2 he is worried that, like Hitler's daughter, he might be part of something evil without knowing it
3 Mark is a character in French's novel and Heidi is a character in Anna's story/Mark is a contemporary character and Heidi is historical/Mark is a boy and Heidi is a girl

Week 3, Day 3
Pg 14

1 Check for correct spelling of each word.
2 a ent: rodent, urgent, fluent, violent, evident, serpent, ancient, magnificent, apparent, opponent
  b ant: tenant, instant, pendant, tyrant, entrant, assistant, elegant, applicant, significant, radiant
3 Missing letters are <u>underlined</u>
  a eleg<u>a</u>nt b urg<u>e</u>nt c radi<u>a</u>nt
  d tyr<u>a</u>nt e magnific<u>e</u>nt f entr<u>a</u>nt
  g viol<u>e</u>nt h evid<u>e</u>nt i ten<u>a</u>nt
  j serp<u>e</u>nt k applic<u>a</u>nt l signific<u>a</u>nt
4 a <u>serpant</u> serpent b <u>aincient</u> ancient
  c <u>rodant</u> rodent d <u>assistent</u> assistant
  e <u>pendent</u> pendant f <u>vilent</u> violent
  g <u>opponant</u> opponent

ANSWERS • Weeks 3–6

Week 3, Day 4
Pg 15

1 **a** tyrant **b** violent **c** radiant **d** opponent **e** apparent **f** serpent **g** ancient **h** assistant **i** magnificent **j** fluent **k** significant **l** rodent
2 Check for correct spelling of each word.
3 **a** inhabitant **b** persistent/adamant **c** equivalent **d** extravagant **e** turbulent **f** participant
4 **a** warrant **b** instrument **c** nutrient **d** extravagant
5 **a** nutrient **b** participant **c** turbulent **d** warrant **e** extravagant **f** instrument **g** inhabitant **h** persistent

Week 3, Day 5
Pg 16

1 Insert a comma after **a** Phoenix **b** Drive, Richmond **c** Avenue, Monica **d** Saturday **e** 14 **f** Tuesday, 6
2 Circle comma after **a** 2387 **b** August **c** September **d** April, May **e** 6396
3 **a** Answers will vary. Suggested answer: January 12, 2010.
b Answers will vary. Suggested answer: 874 62nd Street, New York City, New York.
c Answers will vary. Suggested answer: January 12, 2022.

Week 4, Day 1
Pg 17

One day when the mother goat was (out) her kids heard a gruff voice outside.
"Open the door," said the gruff voice. "Your mother is home with food."
The little kids were hungry, but they remembered their mother's warning.
"You are not our mother," they bleated. "Your voice is too gruff!"
The wolf went away and chewed on a lump of chalk to make his voice softer. Then he returned to the goats' cottage.

1 3, 1, 4, 6, 5, 8, 2, 7

Week 4, Day 2
Pg 18

The wolf went away and rubbed chalk on his feet. He returned to the cottage a third time.
"My little treasures, it's your mother with yummy treats."
The kids saw the white feet, heard the soft voice, and flung the door open. The wolf chased the terrified kids, catching them one by one and putting them in a sack. When he caught the sixth kid, he threw the sack over his shoulder and made for his lair. The seventh, smallest kid remained hidden.
When the mother goat returned, she found the frightened kid and left at once to find the others.

1 The wolf rubbed chalk on his feet. He came back to the cottage a third time. The kids let the wolf in. The wolf chased the terrified kids. He caught six of them and placed them in a sack. The wolf then threw the sack over his shoulder and made for his lair. The seventh kid, who had remained hidden, told his mother what had happened.

Week 4, Day 3
Pg 19

1 Check for correct spelling of each word.
2 **a** and: husband, island, thousand, garland, command, demand
b end: legend, depend, intend, pretend, defend, amend, suspend, descend, attend, offend
c ond: second, beyond, almond, diamond
3 Missing letters are underlined **a** sec*ond* **b** gar*land* **c** husb*and* **d** alm*ond* **e** int*end* **f** susp*end* **g** pret*end* **h** comm*and* **i** dem*and* **j** off*end*
4 **a** diamond **b** almond **c** husband **d** descend **e** pretend **f** defend **g** island **h** garland

Week 4, Day 4
Pg 20

1 **a** thousand **b** pretend **c** attend **d** suspend **e** depend **f** command
2 Check for correct spelling of each word.
3 **a** errand **b** commend **c** vagabond **d** correspond **e** reverend **f** comprehend
4 **a** reprimand/reprehend **b** apprehend **c** correspond
5 **a** apprehend **b** comprehend **c** reprimand/reprehend **d** reprimand **e** Holland **f** commend **g** correspond **h** vagabond

Week 4, Day 5
Pg 21

1 **a** ironing **b** catch **c** dance **d** trust **e** see **f** slip **g** sleeping **h** swimming **i** work
2 **a** can trust **b** could see **c** is ironing **d** was trying to work **e** will dance **f** will be sleeping **g** might slip **h** have been swimming **i** is hoping to catch
3 **a** should **b** am **c** has **d** were **e** are **f** might

Week 5, Day 1
Pg 22

On Tuesday, May 11, 1813, Mr. Gregory Blaxland, Mr. William Wentworth, and Lieutenant Lawson, attended by four servants, with five dogs, and four horses laden with provisions, ammunition, and other necessaries, left Mr. Blaxland's farm at the South Creek, for the purpose of endeavouring to effect a passage over the Blue Mountains, between the Western River, and the River Grose.
They crossed the Nepean, or Hawkesbury River, at the ford, on to Emu Island, at four o'clock p.m., and having proceeded through forest land and good pasture, encamped at five o'clock at the foot of the first ridge.

1 Answers will vary. Suggested answer: drawing of three men and four servants with five dogs, and four horses, setting out on their exploration.

Week 5, Day 2
Pg 23

On the following morning (May 12), as soon as the heavy dew was off, which was about nine o'clock, the exploration party proceeded to ascend the ridge at the foot of which they had camped the preceding evening. Here they found a large lagoon of good water, full of very coarse rushes.
The high land of Grose Head appeared before them at about seven miles distance, bearing north by east. They proceeded this day about three miles and a quarter, in a direction varying from south-west to west-north-west, but, for a third of the way, due west. The land was covered with scrubby brush-wood, very thick in places, with some trees of ordinary timber, which much incommoded (inconvenienced) the horses.

1 Answers will vary. Suggested answer: drawing of information outlined in the passage

Week 5, Day 3
Pg 24

1 Check for correct spelling of each word.
2 Missing letters are underlined
a sim*plify* **b** gra*tify* **c** cla*rify* **d** jus*tify* **e** am*plify* **f** sig*nify* **g** li*quefy* **h** bea*utify* **i** i*dentify* **j** my*stify*
3 **a** satisfy **b** liquefy **c** modify **d** terrify **e** mystify **f** simplify **g** signify **h** gratify **i** justify **j** notify **k** magnify **l** certify
4 **a** *amlifie* amplify **b** *magnyfy* magnify **c** *notefy* notify **d** *horify* horrify **e** *bewtify* beautify **f** *identifie* identify **g** *classifie* classify **h** *justifie* justify

Week 5, Day 4
Pg 25

1 **a** identify **b** verify **c** notify **d** glorify **e** magnify **f** verify
2 Check for correct spelling of each word.
3 **a** dignify **b** electrify **c** specify **d** unify **e** personify
4 **a** crucify **b** diversify **c** pacify **d** rectify
5 **a** personify **b** electrify **c** pacify **d** rectify **e** diversify **f** specify **g** unify/crucify **h** dignify

Week 5, Day 5
Pg 26

1 **a** Mon. **b** Mont. **c** e.g. **d** Rd. **e** R.I. **f** M.D. **g** Md. **h** mi. **i** Miss. **j** fwy.
2 Insert a period after **a** Dr, Fla **b** Pa, Bell **c** oz, tsp, mixture **d** Dr, Mrs, Butler **e** Jan, April, year **f** D,C, U, S **g** Prof, J, S, Wright
3 **a** (calif) Calif. **b** (capt) Capt. **c** (jr) Jr.

Week 6, Day 1
Pg 27

On January 24, 1848, James Marshall found flakes of gold while building a timber mill at Coloma in California. News of the find soon spread, and there followed the (first) and biggest gold rush in America.
After Marshall's discovery, about 400,000 people traveled to California in search of gold. Before the gold rush, San Francisco was a small town. It quickly became a city. People built roads, churches, and schools. They also built new steamships and railroads.

1 c 2 b 3 a 4 d

203

ANSWERS • Weeks 6–8

Week 6, Day 2
Pg 28

> Gold is a useful decorative metal. It does not tarnish or corrode. It is extremely **malleable** so artists can easily shape it. Other metals, such as iron, are not very malleable.
> People measure the purity of gold in carats. Pure gold is 24 carats.
> Gold in jewelry is usually gold alloy, which is **harder** than pure gold. The three most popular gold alloys are white gold, yellow gold, and rose gold. White gold is gold mixed with **silver**, **nickel**, or **palladium**. Yellow gold is gold mixed with copper and silver. Rose gold is gold mixed with **yellow gold** and 25% **copper**.

5 it is malleable—can be shaped easily; does not tarnish or corrode
6 There are different types of gold—yellow, rose and white. Different metals are added to pure gold to achieve different effects.

Week 6, Day 3
Pg 29
1 Check for correct spelling of each word.
2 a guest, guessed   b suite, sweet
  c piece, peace   d horde, hoard
3 a you   b horde   c piece   d steal
  e passed   f suite   g wary   h bridal
  i patients j guessed
4 a horde hoard   b passed past
  c bridal bridle   d guessed guest
  e piece peace   f you ewe
  g suite sweet   h wary weary

Week 6, Day 4
Pg 30
1 Missing syllables are underlined a pa<u>tience</u>
  b <u>wea</u>ry c <u>bri</u>dle d <u>bri</u>dal e wa<u>ry</u>
2 a ewe   b steel   c piece
3 Check for correct spelling of each word.
4 a compliment   b weather   c morning
  d stationary   e principle f stationery
5 a morning   b whether   c principal
  d compliment
6 a whether, weather
  b compliment, complement
  c morning, mourning
  d stationery, stationary

Week 6, Day 5
Pg 31
1 a <mark>flashing</mark>   b <mark>mewling</mark>   c <mark>chilled</mark>
  d <mark>worried</mark>
2 a laughing   b amusing   c surprised
  d burning
3 a Verbs: has been <u>changing</u>, was <u>damaged</u>, to <u>confuse</u>, has been <u>completed</u>
  b Adjectives: a <u>changing</u> situation, <u>damaged</u> goods, a <u>confusing</u> story, a <u>completed</u> task
4 a The <u>flowering</u> tree made a beautiful sight.
  b The <u>damaged</u> spoons are in the packet.

Week 7, Day 1
Pg 32

> The **marathon** is the longest running race in athletics.
> The first Olympic marathon was held in **Athens** in **1896**. It was based on the legend of **Pheidippides**, a Greek soldier who ran approximately 25 miles carrying a message from the town of Marathon to Athens in 490 BC.
> At the 1908 Olympic Games, the distance was set at **26.2 miles**, which was the distance from **Windsor Castle** to the stadium in London.

1 c   2 b   3 d   4 a   5 b

Week 7, Day 2
Pg 33

> Some athletes take **performance-enhancing drugs** to gain an advantage over their competitors. This is illegal.
> Some drugs are legal for athletes, such as those for **treating injuries**. Others are banned because they improve performance and are dangerous to an athlete's health. Taking these drugs is called **doping**—it is a way of cheating.
> **The World Anti-Doping Agency** promotes the fight against doping in sport. National anti-doping agencies regularly test athletes to find out if they are taking banned drugs.

6 those that improve performance and are dangerous to an athlete's health
7 those that treat injuries
8 The World Anti-Doping Agency
9 they regularly test athletes

Week 7, Day 3
Pg 34
1 Check for correct spelling of each word.
2 a or: vapor, armor, flavor, clamor, valor, rigor, tumor
  b ure: culture, pasture, texture, future, lecture, figure, nurture, furniture, sculpture, leisure, moisture, creature, torture
3 Missing letters are underlined a fu<u>r</u>niture
  b l<u>e</u>isure   c ar<u>m</u>or   d t<u>u</u>mor
  e <u>p</u>asture f <u>v</u>apor/<u>v</u>alor   g m<u>o</u>isture
  h <u>t</u>orture
4 a armor   b furniture   c sculpture   d pasture

Week 7, Day 4
Pg 35
1 a texture   b moisture   c leisure   d future
  e flavor   f honor/valor g rigor   h sculpture
  i figure   j creature
2 Check for correct spelling of each word.
3 a signature   b temperature   c agriculture
  d departure   e miniature   f neighbor
4 a exposure   b fervor   c composure
  d rupture
5 a rupture   b composure   c exposure

Week 7, Day 5
Pg 36
1 a "What are you doing with that spade?" I asked.
  b "I'm going to dig for treasure," replied my little brother.
  c "Oh, yes," I said, "and where do you think it's buried?"
  d "In the vegetable patch," said Marco, "under the cabbages."
2 a "Where's Marco?" asked Mom.
  b "In the garden," I said, "digging for treasure."
  c "Not in my vegetable patch, I hope," said Mom.
3 a "What do you think you're doing?" yelled Mom.
  b "Digging for treasure," replied Marco, innocently.
  c "My beautiful cabbages!" wailed Mom. "You've destroyed them!"
  d "But they were in the way," said Marco. "I had to dig them up to find the treasure."

Week 8, Day 1
Pg 37

> Is there a chance you could have **misplaced** more than $550,000 from **lost** bank accounts or life insurance policies? That's how much is waiting to be claimed by three Americans who are living or who have lived in Jefferson County, Texas, and we want to **reunite** these people with their money.
> The total unclaimed money pool has risen to a record **$610 million** with 20,000 new additions to the database in the past year. So even if you have searched before, now is the time to search again and be **reunited** with your lost money.

1 b   2 d   3 a   4 c

Week 8, Day 2
Pg 38

> Ms. Delia Rickard, a **Chairwoman at the Federal Reserve Bank of Dallas**, said, "If you've changed addresses **frequently**, or had a number of bank accounts or life insurance policies, there might be money waiting to be claimed by you."
> "There might also be money to be claimed by you under the deceased estate of **somebody who has died and left you money**."
> "**Searching for** the lost money is quick and easy, and you could soon find money that you had long forgotten about," Ms. Rickard said.

5 Chairwoman at the Federal Reserve Bank of Dallas
6 often   7 they are dead
8 "somebody who has died"

ANSWERS • Weeks 8–10

Week 8, Day 3
Pg 39
1 Check for correct spelling of each word.
2 a music b public c historic d basic
  e magnetic f symbolic g topic h plastic
3 syllables are underlined   a poetic
  b horrific   c academic   d artistic
  e angelic   f tonic   g fantastic
  h romantic   i tragic   j heroic
4 academic, angelic, artistic, basic, dramatic, fantastic, heroic, historic, horrific, magic, magnetic, music, plastic, poetic, public, romantic, specific, symbolic, tonic, topic

Week 8, Day 4
Pg 40
1 a heroic   b academic   c music
  d tonic   e fantastic   f artistic
2 Check for correct spelling of each word.
3 a optimistic b photographic c enthusiastic
  d sympathetic e realistic f scientific
  g democratic h mechanic i automatic
  j strategic
4 a scientific   b strategic
  c automatic   d photographic
  e mechanic   f realistic/optimistic
  g sympathetic   h enthusiastic

Week 8, Day 5
Pg 41
1 a some b something c none d most
2 a dances b have c want d was
3 Across: 2 one, 4 none, 7 anybody, 8 any
  Down: 1 everybody 3 nobody 5 each 6 both

Week 9, Day 1
Pg 42
Modern skyscrapers are the tallest buildings in the world. Modern building materials make it possible to build such tall structures.
Developers built the first modern skyscrapers in New York City during the 1800s. The population in the city was growing rapidly, but because it sat on an island, there wasn't much space for new buildings. The only way to make room was to build taller buildings.

1 b 2 a 3 c 4 d 5 a

Week 9, Day 2
Pg 43
Burj Dubai is a modern skyscraper in the United Arab Emirates. It is the tallest human made structure in the world.
Burj Dubai is 2,683 feet tall. The tower contains apartments, hotels, shops, swimming pools, and offices. It has an observation deck on level 124. More than 7,000 people, mainly from India, Pakistan, Bangladesh, China, and the Philippines, worked to build Burj Dubai.
The architects invented a new structural system to build the tower. They had to consider differences between ground level and the building's final height—the temperature can vary up to 46°F, humidity can differ by 30%, and the air can be 10% thinner.

6 apartments

7 they came from many different countries—India, Pakistan, Bangladesh, China and the Philippines.
8 the architects had to invent a new structural system to build the tower because of differences in temperature and humidity between ground level and the building's final height

Week 9, Day 3
Pg 44
1 Check for correct spelling of each word.
2 a d b n   c b   d c   e b   f t   g w   h h
  i t   j t   k t   l n   m b   n c   o w   p d
  q b   r c   s t   t b
3 a solemn   b doubt   c thistle
  d crescent   e succumb   f moisten
  g soften   h debt   i whose
  j subtle   k sandwich   l whistle
  m answer   n muscle
4 a Wenesday Wednesday
  b musle muscle   c sanwich sandwich
  d glissen glisten   e wistle whistle
  f ryme rhyme   g colum column
  h fasinate fascinate

Week 9, Day 4
Pg 45
1 a succumb   b moisten   c doubt
  d fascinate   e solemn   f thistle
2 Check for correct spelling of each word.
3 a campaign   b pneumonia
  c government   d receipt
  e mortgage   f assignment
4 a assignment b government c abscess
  d foreign
5 a assignment   b foreign   c raspberry
  d psychology   e receipt   f abscess

Week 9, Day 5
Pg 46
1 a obviously b possibly c surely
  d clearly e undoubtedly f evidently
2 a certain   b uncertain   c certain
  d uncertain   e certain
3 b
4 a Answers will vary. Suggested answer: will definitely help protect your skin from harmful rays.
  b Answers will vary. Suggested answer: will probably give you more free time for reading after the meal.

REVIEW 1
Spelling
Pg 47
1 a fierce b ancient c attend d culture
2 c   3 famous
4 Missing letters are underlined
  a said   b cousin   c heavy   d thread
5 a specific   b horrific   c magnify
6 fascinate

Grammar
Pg 48–49
1 a maturity Ava   b childhood Chicago
  c idea Friday   d talent Michelangelo
2 a This   b these   c That   d those
3 Insert a comma after   a Denver
  b December   c Avenue, Atlanta
  d Tuesday, 27
4 a are/were   b will   c have   d been
5 a mrs Mrs.   b dr Dr.
6 a boring   b devastating   c challenging
  d amazing   e damaged   f boiled
7 a "What would you like for dinner?" asked Mom.
  b "Fold your clothes," said Margie, "and then put them in the drawer."
8 a everybody   b nobody
9 a Perhaps   b definitely/undoubtedly
  c probably   d definitely/undoubtedly

Comprehension
Pg 50–51
1 c
2 d 3 b 4 d 5 b 6 a 7 c 8 d
9 Answers will vary. Suggested answer: "the only reason I had carried on with the teasing was because of the laughs I got from other campers."
10 Responses will differ. Talk through answers together.

Week 10, Day 1
Pg 52
Shane shook himself free. Had Tony eaten mush for breakfast? It must have gone straight to his brain. "What do you mean, she's not hurting anyone? First she stole my hamburger and then she took my towel."
"Right," snapped Tony. "You ask her but leave me out of it." He stomped off. Sand sprayed everywhere as he kicked at clumps of grass.

1 d 2 a 3 c 4 b 5 c

Week 10, Day 2
Pg 53
The girl hugged Ruby, who was sobbing. "Are you OK?" the girl asked him.
Shane wasn't sure, but he nodded. "Is she... she OK?" he spluttered, pointing to Ruby.
"Yeah, she's just in shock. She thought you were dead."
Ruby wouldn't look at Shane. She had no breath for talking anyway. The three of them staggered back to shore and collapsed onto the sand.

1 it suggests that she was crying uncontrollably
2 it suggests that Shane was trying to catch his breath while asking the question
3 the children were unsteady on their feet
4 it emphasizes how exhausted the children were

205

ANSWERS • Weeks 10–12

Week 10, Day 3
Pg 54

1 Check for correct spelling of each word.
2 ability, brutality, clarity, continuity, curiosity, electricity, equality, hostility, identity, intensity, majority, maturity, minority, mobility, normality, personality, prosperity, publicity, reality, security
3 Missing letters are underlined **a** m<u>o</u>bility
 b <u>h</u>ostility **c** c<u>o</u>ntinuity **d** m<u>i</u>nority
 e <u>p</u>rosperity **f** p<u>u</u>blicity **g** <u>c</u>larity
4 **a** ability **b** intensity **c** electricity
 d security **e** majority **f** personality
 g curiosity

Week 10, Day 4
Pg 55

1 **a** mobility **b** ability **c** brutality **d** reality
 e clarity **f** publicity **g** curiosity
2 Check for correct spelling of each word.
 a productivity **b** flexibility **c** necessity
 d uniformity **e** simplicity **f** opportunity
 g sensitivity
4 **a** community **b** uniformity **c** opportunity
5 **a** responsibility **b** possibility **c** flexibility
 d simplicity **e** necessity **f** sensitivity
 g opportunity

Week 10, Day 5
Pg 56

1 **a** Ugh **b** Wow **c** Hooray **d** Oh, no
 e Yum **f** Phew
2 **a** Shhh! **b** Boo! **c** Hello! **d** Whoa!
 e Sure **f** Yay! **g** Huh? **h** Awesome!
3 Answers will vary. Suggested answers:
 a Brrr! It's really cold today!
 b Hmmm! Now where did I put those keys?
 c Uh-oh! I've spilled the milk all over the rug.

Week 11, Day 1
Pg 57

> The tingling sensation at the back of Sally's head was intense. "Don't worry, Faisal. I'll find out who Venny is."
> Faisal shuddered, "You're my only hope."
> Sally and Corinne walked to their first class. Corinne was one of the seven students on the list.
> "Are you a member of a chatroom?" Sally asked.
> Corinne was surprised. "Why? You think the Internet's a waste of time!"
> "Well, I do, but that doesn't answer my question." Corinne shrugged. "Sure I am."
> "You know chatrooms aren't safe," Sally warned.

1 b 2 c 3 a 4 d 5 b

Week 11, Day 2
Pg 58

> Sally said, "People will find out your secret one day. You'll go somewhere high and … you'll faint. Then everyone will know."
> "Maybe," Faisal didn't want to think about that.
> "Faisal, you'll have to tell people for your own safety. No matter what you do, Julian could still tell someone at any time," Sally said.
> Faisal scowled.
> "You can tell people in your own way, in your own time. But you have to do it," Sally concluded.
> Faisal kicked the ground. "I can't. It's just too embarrassing."

1 Faisal must tell people his secret
2 people will find out Faisal's secret eventually—he'll go somewhere high and faint, and Julian could still tell someone at any time
3 he doesn't want to tell people his secret—"it's just too embarrassing"

Week 11, Day 3
Pg 59

1 Check for correct spelling of each word.
2 **a** cart<u>wheel</u> **b** space<u>walk</u> **c** time<u>table</u>
 d news<u>stand</u> **e** good<u>bye</u> **f** high<u>way</u>
 g butter<u>fingers</u> **h** dead<u>line</u> **i** sky<u>scraper</u>
 j ware<u>house</u> **k** table<u>spoon</u> **l** water<u>melon</u>
 m eye<u>sight</u> **n** back<u>ground</u> **o** team<u>mate</u>
 p text<u>book</u> **q** head<u>ache</u> **r** book<u>case</u>
 s day<u>break</u> **t** week<u>night</u>
3 **a** time/ta/<u>ble</u> **b** head/ache
 c sky/<u>scra</u>/per **d** but/<u>ter</u>/fin/gers
 e wa/<u>ter</u>/mel/<u>on</u> **f** ta/<u>ble</u>/spoon
 g text/<u>book</u> **h** book/<u>case</u>
4 **a** spacewalk **b** headache **c** eyesight
 d bookcase **e** weeknight **f** goodbye
 g teammate **h** deadline

Week 11, Day 4
Pg 60

1 **a** watermelon **b** skyscraper **c** cartwheel
 d tablespoon
2 Check for correct spelling of each word.
3 **a** bodyguard **b** blindfold **c** candlelight
 d superhuman **e** thunderbolt **f** wastepaper
 g undercurrent **h** earthworm **i** courthouse
 j earthbound
4 **a** courthouse **b** superhuman **c** undercurrent
 d bodyguard **e** earthworm **f** blindfold
 g earthbound

Week 11, Day 5
Pg 61

1 Comma after: **a** sandwich **b** times
 c book **d** show **e** rain
2 **a** I enjoy science fiction movies, but I don't like horror movies.
 b Our water bottles were empty, so we filled them at the next camp.
 c We have packed the car, and we are ready to go.
 d You can have a chocolate milkshake, or you can try the new caramel flavor.
 e I have asked the children to be quiet, yet they continue to make a noise.

3 Answers will vary. Suggested answer: Our train has arrived, but it is not due to leave for another hour.

Week 12, Day 1
Pg 62

> "The islanders are very worried about what is causing the red rain. They think it will damage the Moai," whispered Uncle Earl.
> "Mo… what?" Flynn tried to say the word.
> "MOW-I." Mia sounded the word out slowly for Flynn.
> "The famous statues of Easter Island. Don't tell me you've never heard of them?"
> Flynn shrugged. Mia pulled a book out of her bag and showed Flynn the photograph on the back cover. It was of a long, stone face with a pointed nose, wearing a kind of crown, attached to a short, stone body.
> "So this is how you know about all of this?" asked Flynn. He wasn't surprised. No matter how little warning they had, Mia still managed to fit in some research.

1 b 2 c 3 a 4 b

Week 12, Day 2
Pg 63

> The woman nodded as though she understood it all. She looked at Flynn very seriously. "Makemake has chosen you to protect the treasured egg."
> "WHAT?" cried Flynn, jumping to his feet.
> The woman took her hand away from his arm. Flynn's mouth gaped when he saw the burn there. A deep red outline formed the shape of a bird.
> The woman pointed to a mask on the wall. Flynn thought he looked just like a god of thunder.
> "He is the one making the red rain," said the woman. "He is trying to warn us of danger. Makemake wants Flynn to make sure that the true Birdman finds the sooty tern's first egg of the season."
> "Danger?" croaked Flynn.

1 Flynn is shocked and cries out "WHAT?"
2 Flynn is horrified—his "mouth gaped"
3 Flynn repeats the word "danger" as a question and his throat is croaky.

Week 12, Day 3
Pg 64

1 Check for correct spelling of each word.
2 **a** dome domestic domain
 b aquatic aquarium aquaplane aquanaut
 c benefit benign
 d habitat inhabit habitable habitation inhabitant
 e literacy literate literal literary
3 **a** <u>doume</u> dome **b** <u>benine</u> benign
 c <u>benifit</u> benefit **d** <u>habitaytion</u> habitation
 e <u>litirate</u> literate **f** <u>litral</u> literal
 g <u>habitabel</u> habitable **h** <u>ferel</u> feral

Week 12, Day 4
Pg 65

1 Missing syllables are underlined
 a a/quar/i/<u>um</u> **b** in/<u>hab</u>/i/tant **c** <u>hab</u>/i/tat
 d a/<u>li</u>/en **e** lit/<u>er</u>/a/cy **f** a/<u>qua</u>/plane
 g lit/er/<u>a</u>/cy **h** <u>fe</u>/ral **i** do/<u>mes</u>/tic
 j hab/it/a/<u>ble</u>
2 Check for correct spelling of each word.
3 **a** alias **b** ferocious **c** domestically
 d alibi **e** aquamarine **f** beneficially
4 **a** ferocious **b** beneficial **c** aquamarine
 d alias
5 **a** benefactor **b** alliteration **c** aquamarine
 d alibi **e** beneficial **f** uninhabitable
 g ferocious **h** alias

ANSWERS • Weeks 12–15

Week 12, Day 5
Pg 66

1 a ✓   b ✓   c ✓   d ✓
2 a <u>have</u> had   b <u>have</u> has   c <u>have</u> has
   d <u>has</u> have
3 a begun   b forgiven   c risen
   d hidden   e frozen
4 a They have bent the wire.
   b Our puppy has chewed Dad's slipper.

Week 13, Day 1
Pg 67

> Under a spreading chestnut-tree
> The village (smithy stands;)
> The smith, a mighty man is he,
> With large and sinewy hands;
> And the muscles of his brawny arms
> <u>Are strong as iron bands.</u>
> His hair is crisp, and black, and long,
> <u>His face is like the tan;</u>
> His brow is wet with honest sweat,
> He earns whate'er he can,
> And looks the whole world in the face,
> For he owes not any man.

1 c   2 b   3 d   4 c   5 a

Week 13, Day 2
Pg 68

> Week in, week out, from morn till night,
> You can hear his (bellows blow)
> You can hear him swing his heavy sledge,
> <u>With measured beat and slow,</u>
> <u>Like a sexton ringing the village bell,</u>
> <u>When the evening sun is low.</u>
> And children coming home from school
> Look in at the open door;
> They love to see the flaming forge,
> And hear the bellows (roar)
> And catch the <u>burning sparks that fly</u>
> <u>Like chaff from a threshing-floor.</u>

1 alliteration
2 when you make the "b" sound, you blow air. The repeated "b" sounds emphasize the blowing sound the bellows make.
3 flaming forge
4 onomatopoeia—it is a loud sound that imitates the noise the bellows make

Week 13, Day 3
Pg 69

1 Check for correct spelling of each word.
2 active, attentive, attractive, captive, connective, creative, detective, expensive, explosive, extensive, formative, impulsive, intensive, massive, narrative, objective, offensive, productive, secretive, selective
3 a connective   b objective   c creative
   d secretive
4 a active   b attractive   c massive
   d expensive   e detective   f narrative
   g selective

Week 13, Day 4
Pg 70

1 a creative   b offensive   c impulsive
   d narrative   e captive   f connective
   g objective   h detective
2 Check for correct spelling of each word.
3 a imaginative   b descriptive   c possessive
   d excessive   e sensitive   f competitive
4 a repetitive   b excessive   c digestive
5 a descriptive   b competitive   c excessive
   d expressive   e repetitive   f possessive

Week 13, Day 5
Pg 71

1 *Commas after:* a Yes   b now   c No
   d machine   e entering   f Yes
2 a Yes,/No, the sun is/is not shining today.
   b Yes,/No, I have/haven't seen an interesting movie lately.
   c Yes,/No, I like/don't like to read adventure stories.
3 *Commas after:* a cake   b Yes   c lesson   d No

Week 14, Day 1
Pg 72

> Along the way Donkey met a dog.
> "I am too old to hunt," sighed Dog.
> "Join me," said Donkey. "I am off to town to be a singer."
> Soon they came across a weary cat.
> "My old teeth <u>are worn,</u> and I can no longer catch mice," (sobbed) Cat.
> "Come with us," said Donkey. "We are off to town to be singers." Cat leaped at the offer.
> Soon after, they met an old rooster.
> "My mistress says <u>tomorrow I am to be dinner</u>!" Rooster (wailed.)

1 d   2 b   3 a   4 c   5 b

Week 14, Day 2
Pg 73

> But the robbers were not happy. One of them crept back into the house. Cat leaped at the robber with her sharp claws. The robber tripped over Dog, who <u>bit the robber on the leg.</u> The robber fell onto the sleeping Donkey, who <u>lashed out with his hooves.</u> Rooster woke and crowed loudly, "Cock-a-doodle-do!"
> The robber raced back to his gang, his face torn and bleeding, his leg sore and his head swollen. "There is a horrible witch by the fire. She clawed me with her nails and stabbed me in the leg. A hairy monster clubbed me in the head, and from the roof a judge cried 'Catch the rascal, do!' I never want to go near the place again!"

1 The robber thought that the cat and the dog were a horrible witch who had clawed and stabbed him. He thought the donkey was a hairy monster that had clubbed him in the head. He thought the rooster was a judge crying out, "Catch that rascal, do!"

Week 14, Day 3
Pg 74

1 Check for correct spelling of each word.
2 Missing parts of words are <u>underlined</u>
   a sheep<u>ish</u>   b cher<u>ish</u>   c establ<u>ish</u>
   d styl<u>ish</u>   e f<u>iend</u>ish   f Engl<u>ish</u>
   g f<u>l</u>ourish   h as<u>ton</u>ish
3 a perish   b stylish   c sheepish
   d replenish   e fiendish   f youngish
   g astonish   h flourish
4 a English   b childish   c reddish
   d demolish   e varnish   f nourish
   g establish   h skittish

Week 14, Day 4
Pg 75

1 a youngish   b childish   c reddish   d stylish
   e furnish
2 Check for correct spelling of each word.
3 a squeamish   b feverish   c amateurish
   d diminish   e embellish   f accomplish
4 a accomplish   b feverish   c anguish
   d squeamish
5 a extinguish   b amateurish   c distinguish
   d embellish   e relinquish   f diminish

Week 14, Day 5
Pg 76

1 b What an exciting adventure they had!
   c How fantastic that they both got into the team!
   e I can't wait to see my new bike!
2 a How exciting that you're going to see the Gateway Arch!
   b What an enormous house they live in!
3 *Answers will vary. Talk through responses with students. Suggested answers:* We had a great time! What an amazing sight! Some of them were really scary!

Week 15, Day 1
Pg 77

> Volcanic ash is deadly. It is hard and abrasive, like finely crushed glass. After blasting into the air, it forms an eruption plume, which settles over huge areas, (suffocating people and animals.)
> Gases spewed out from volcanic eruptions, such as <u>carbon dioxide and sulphur dioxide,</u> are even more deadly. As carbon dioxide is heavier than air, it collects in low-lying areas and creates poisonous environments. Sulphur dioxide <u>causes acid rain and air pollution.</u>

1 b   2 d   3 b   4 c   5 a

Week 15, Day 2
Pg 78

> Volcanic soils are (very fertile,) making them ideal for growing crops. Indonesian farmers grow rice near active volcanoes. However, thick lava flows are disastrous. It takes months for lava to cool, and then years for soil to form.
> In Italy, previous eruptions provide daily benefits. The Roman city of Pompeii, buried when Mount Vesuvius erupted in 79 AD, now attracts thousands of visitors. Spending by these tourists helps the local economy. However, Mount Vesuvius <u>is still active.</u> Millions could be affected by a new eruption. Volcanic activity has brought benefits to southern Italy, but eruptions are a constant threat.

1 they have made the soil fertile and ideal for growing crops, especially rice
2 the eruption of Mount Vesuvius in 79AD
3 Pompeii has become a tourist attraction and when tourists spend money it helps the local economy; however, it is still an active volcano and therefore eruptions are a constant threat for residents

ANSWERS • Weeks 15–17

Week 15, Day 3
Pg 79
1 Check for correct spelling of each word.
2 a unknown   unravel   uncertain
   unpleasant   unfortunate   unusual
   unexpected   unemployed
  b dislocate   disappear   dissolve
   discourage   distasteful   disapprove
  c mislead   misplaced   misjudge
   misconduct   miscalculate   misguided
3 a dissolve   b unexpected   c unusual
  d miscalculate   e distasteful   f unravel
4 Missing letters are underlined   a misconduct
  b unfortunate   c unpleasant   d distasteful
  e unexpected   f unemployed   g disapprove
  h mislead   i uncertain   j unravel

Week 15, Day 4
Pg 80
1 a disapear disappear
  b mizguided misguided
  c unfortunete unfortunate
  d unplesant unpleasant
  e dislocait dislocate
  f disolv dissolve
  g unraval unravel
  h unemploied unemployed
  i unown unknown
2 Check for correct spelling of each word.
3 a unfamiliar   b discontinue   c unconscious
  d disinterested   e unnatural   f disentangle
4 a disentangle   b disobedient   c discontinue
  d unnatural
5 a unacceptable   b discriminate
  c disobedient   d disentangle

Week 15, Day 5
Pg 81
1 Check b, c, e, g
2 Commas after: a Oh, Julia   b work
  c Yes, son   d Carrie   e on, Marcus
  f you   g Tessa
3 a Keep trying, Noah, and you'll soon get it right.
  b Ava, when are you going to visit Auntie Mae?

Week 16, Day 1
Pg 82

> Shortly before 3:45 p.m on May 27, 1997, a violent tornado struck the small Texas town of Jarrell.
> Jarrell's tornado alert siren sounded after a group of tornadoes was spotted 1.2 miles north of the town. Less than 20 minutes later the twisters had merged into a single tornado 0.7 miles wide, which bore down on the Double Creek Estate. Though massive, the tornado was slow moving, and spent the next half-hour destroying areas of Jarrell.

1 a   2 c   3 c   4 d   5 b

Week 16, Day 2
Pg 83

> Floods are often destructive, but they can also have benefits. Some areas of the world rely on floods to keep their land fertile.
> Floods cause enormous damage. Rushing walls of water wash people, animals, buildings, and vehicles away. The debris carried along by the floodwaters also causes havoc, battering humans and property. Floods burst sewage pipes and gas mains, causing pollution. They bring down electrical wires, which cause deaths by electrocution.
> Floods also destroy agricultural crops. Floodwaters can lead to the spread of deadly, infectious diseases as drinking water becomes polluted.

1 The text explains how rushing walls of water can wash away people, animals, buildings, and vehicles, and how debris carried by floodwaters batters humans and property. It goes on to explain how floods can burst sewerage pipes and gas mains, causing pollution, and how floodwaters can bring down electrical wires, causing death by electrocution. It ends by explaining how floods can destroy crops and pollute drinking water, causing deadly diseases.

Week 16, Day 3
Pg 84
1 Check for correct spelling of each word.
2 a vegetables   b stitches   c weaknesses
  d influences   e diseases   f sleeves
  g witnesses   h audiences   i lenses
  j colleges   k tissues   l clashes
  m styles   n approaches   o stretches
  p routes   q passages   r obstacles
  s reserves   t magazines
3 a styles   b colleges   c passages
  d reserves   e diseases   f stitches
  g weaknesses   h approaches   i clashes
  j witnesses   k routes   l vegetables
  m sleeves   n obstacles

Week 16, Day 4
Pg 85
1 a stretches   b vegetables   c sleeves
  d lenses   e audiences   f tissues
  g diseases   h obstacles   i magazines
2 Check for correct spelling of each word.
3 a addresses   b certificates   c catalogs
  d disturbances   e privileges   f businesses
4 a references   b temperatures   c committees
  d performances
5 performances   b temperatures   c catalogs
  d committees   e certificates

Week 16, Day 5
Pg 86
1 a was   b flew   c will see   d left   e waited
2 a was starving   b had been   c will starve
  d am starving   e have been   f wanted
  g want
3 a went, were   b leaps, wins
  c have, have sprained   d wants, is

Week 17, Day 1
Pg 87

> The GPS (Global Positioning System) can pinpoint a location on Earth to within 0.3 of an inch. GPS receivers gather information from 24 GPS satellites that orbit the Earth. First, a GPS receiver gets signals from at least four of the 24 satellites. It uses the time it takes for the signals to arrive to calculate the distance between it and the satellites. It can then work out its exact location, including its latitude, longitude, and height.
> People use the GPS system to calculate their location accurately and precisely.

1 b   2 c   3 a, c, f

Week 17, Day 2
Pg 88

> An organ transplant is an operation where a damaged or diseased organ is replaced with another person's healthy organ. Organ transplants have saved thousands of lives. One organ donor can save and improve the quality of life of up to 10 other people.
> In the 1800s, doctors were able to perform skin transplants. The first organ transplant was a cornea transplant in 1905. In 1967, a South African heart surgeon, Christian Barnard, performed a successful heart transplant. He was able to take a healthy heart from a person who had just died, and implant it into a man who had a damaged heart.
> The human body does not always accept a transplanted organ. Anti-rejection drugs help to stop the patient's body from rejecting the transplanted organ.

1 organ transplants
2 "An organ transplant is an operation where a damaged or diseased organ is replaced with another person's healthy organs."
3 The authors describe where, when and how the first successful heart transplant was performed. They also mention that the first organ transplant was a cornea transplant in 1905.

Week 17, Day 3
Pg 89
1 Check for correct spelling of each word.
2 a artist   b dentist   c florist   violinist
3 Missing letters are underlined
  a guitarist   b zoologist   c ecologist
  d cartoonist   e tourist   f soloist
  g pianist   h motorist
4 a finalist   b motorist   c ecologist
  d machinist   e violinist   f novelist
  g botanist   h soloist   i cyclist
  j vocalist   k journalist   l zoologist
  m artist   n cartoonist

Week 17, Day 4
Pg 90
1 a pianoist pianist   b flaurist florist
  c artiste artist   d tourest tourist
  e specialest specialist
  f cartoonest cartoonist
  g dentast dentist   h journalest journalist
  i guitarust guitarist   j zoologast zoologist
2 Check for correct spelling of each word.

ANSWERS • Weeks 17–19

3 a archivist **b** psychologist
c traditionalist **d** archaeologist
e opportunist **f** perfectionist
4 a receptionist **b** psychologist
5 a receptionist **b** archaeologist
c archivist

Week 17, Day 5
Pg 91
1 a Who **b** Whose **c** Which **d** which
e whose **f** who
2 Answers will vary. Suggested answers:
a Who called me earlier?
b Which bag is yours?
c Whose fluffy jacket is this?
3 Answers will vary. Suggested answers:
a I have spoken to the girl who <u>called me earlier</u>.
b I am not sure which <u>dessert I should order</u>.
c There are the children whose <u>bags are still on the bus</u>.

Week 18, Day 1
Pg 92

> Tidal power is energy produced from tides and currents.
> Tides are the changes in sea level that happen twice a day. They are caused by the gravitational effect of the moon.
> A tidal power station uses the movement of water through a barrage to generate electricity. The water turns turbines inside the barrage, which power generators and produce electricity. Electricity is also made when the tide goes back and water flows the other way through the barrage.

1 a **2** a
3 Tidal power is energy produced from tides and currents. Tidal power stations use the movement of water through a barrage to generate electricity.

Week 18, Day 2
Pg 93

> Biofuels are fuels made from biomass material. The most common biofuels are ethanol and biodiesel.
> Ethanol is made from the sugars in grains, such as corn, wheat, and sugar cane. Sugars are mixed with water and yeast. The mixture is left to ferment until the biomass is converted into ethanol. Ethanol can be mixed with petrol or used on its own.
> Biodiesel is made from vegetable oils, fats, or greases. It can be used in diesel engines, either on its own or mixed with diesel fuel made from petroleum. Some engines can even run on pure vegetable oil.
> Biodiesel performs much like diesel made from petroleum. However, using biodiesel reduces harmful exhaust gases, such as carbon monoxide and sulphur.

1 Biofuels are fuels made from biomass material. The most common biofuels are ethanol and biodiesel. Ethanol is made from the sugars in grains and sugar cane, while biodiesel is made from vegetable oils, fats or greases. Biodiesel is better for the environment than diesel because it reduces harmful exhaust gases.

Week 18, Day 3
Pg 94
1 Check for correct spelling of each word.
2 a madam level sagas refer racecar redder rotor kayak radar
b smog newscast motel taxicab brunch squiggle chortle ginormous fortnight cheeseburger paratrooper
3 Missing letters are underlined
a chortle **b** refer **c** sagas
d redder **e** madam **f** newscast
g squiggle **h** racecar **i** kayak
j level
4 a sagas **b** newscast **c** smog
d radar **e** racecar **f** ginormous
g madam **h** kayak

Week 18, Day 4
Pg 95
1 a motel **b** cheeseburger **c** radar
d racecar **e** brunch **f** paratrooper
g squiggle **h** kayak **i** chortle
2 Check for correct spelling of each word.
3 a rotavator **b** simulcast
c knowledgebase **d** rotator
e nanosecond **f** reviver
g guesstimate **h** emoticon
i deified **j** cyberspace
4 a emoticon **b** nanosecond **c** deified
d simulcast **e** cyberspace

Week 18, Day 5
Pg 96
1 a hardly **b** very **c** exceptionally
d almost **e** too
2 a perfectly **b** too **c** most
d extremely **e** more **f** very
3 Answers will vary. Suggested answers:
a very, extremely, exceptionally
b too, very, extremely, exceptionally
c hardly **d** quite
e completely, totally
4 Answers will vary. Suggested answers:
a It is extremely hot today.
b I nearly bumped into a tree when I lost control of my bike.

REVIEW 2
Spelling
Pg 97
1 a unpleasant **b** dislocate **c** equality
d sluggish
2 a
3 guitarist
4 a cheeseburger **b** racecar
5 a diseases **b** bread **c** stitches
6 c

Grammar
Pg 98–99
1 Answers will vary. Suggested answers:
a Ouch! That was really sore!
b Hey! What do you think you're doing?
2 a I baked the cake and we ate it straight afterwards.
b I tried on the shirt, but it was too tight.
c The shirt didn't fit, so we took it back.

3 a have has **b** have had
4 a No, I have never been to Vietnam.
b Yes, that is the correct answer.
c Theo, you have taken the dog for a walk, haven't you?
5 a Wow! What a brilliant jump!
b Oh no! What happened, Marty?
c How exciting was that!
d Shoo! Go away, you pesky fly!
6 a will get – get **b** sat sits/starts started
c have had **d** goes went/was am
e hears heard **f** saw see
7 Answers will vary. Suggested answers:
a Who is going to help me eat this pie?
b Which bag belongs to you?
8 a whose bike this is
b which borrowed from you yesterday
c whose wing was broken
d who moved in yesterday
9 a almost **b** most **c** very **d** extremely

Comprehension
Pgs 100–101
1 d **2** b **3** c **4** c **5** a **6** b **7** d **8** b, c
9 The main purpose of this text is to persuade/to put forward a point of view.
10 Talk through responses. Suggested answer: You usually share a closer bond with family members like parents, brothers, and sisters than with friends, so they are much more likely to give you help when you need it.

Week 19, Day 1
Pg 102

> Laura stops at the mirrors. She gazes at her reflection above the hand basin. She wishes Mr. Mitchell hadn't given her the solo. Kelly's bullying has always been bad, but the play has made it much worse. The name-calling, lies, and nasty notes are now daily events.
> Singing usually makes Laura feel better. Softly, she sings her song from the play. She begins to twirl on the tiled floor, pretending she is on the stage. Suddenly the lights go out. Laura can't see a thing.

1 d **2** c **3** b **4** c

Week 19, Day 2
Pg 103

> Surely, before leaving, they will check to make sure that no one is locked in the theater? Of course they will check!
> Shona wouldn't leave without her! Shona will look for Laura and ask if anyone has seen her. Shona's parents are supposed to be driving Laura home.
> Suddenly, Laura thinks of her own parents. When she doesn't come home, her parents will worry. They will wonder where she is. They'll ring Shona. They'll come to the theater. They won't rest until they find her.
> A balloon of happiness swells in Laura's chest. She won't have to spend all night in this spooky place after all. The balloon bursts. Will her parents think to look for her in the toilet?

1 she is locked in the theater and is afraid she will have to spend all night there
2 Shona and her parents will realise she is missing and will come looking for her
3 she doesn't think her parents will expect her to be in the toilet

209

ANSWERS • Weeks 19–21

Week 19, Day 3
Pg 104

1 Check for correct spelling of each word.
2 a ambitious, courteous, devious, envious, ferocious, glorious, gracious, hazardous, hilarious, indigenous, marvelous, meticulous, monstrous, numerous, ominous, outrageous, religious, tedious, vicious, victorious
3 a marvelous b ominous c ferocious
  d monstrous e tedious f vicious
4 a envyous envious b ferrocious ferocious
  c hilerious hilarious d deevius devious
  e hazerdus hazardous f glorias glorious
  g teedious tedious

Week 19, Day 4
Pg 105

1 a victorious b marvelous c hilarious
  d indigenous e courteous f tedious
  g numerous h devious i hazardous
  j meticulous k envious l ferocious
2 Check for correct spelling of each word.
3 a surreptitious b miscellaneous
  c suspicious d harmonious
  e righteous
4 a conscious b mischievous
  c superstitious d conscientious
5 a conscientious b superstitious
  c suspicious d advantageous
  e conscious f miscellaneous
  g harmonious h mischievous

Week 19, Day 5
Pg 106

1 Commas after:
  a Labradors, cat b sister, event
  c carnival, week d floats, costumes
  e Tom, friend
2 Commas after:
  a jacket, lost, shoes b Olivia, sister, pianist
  c phones, hundreds, thousands
  d Kipling, 1907, Rikki-Tikki-Tavi
  e speech, conjunctions, prepositions
3 When I scored the winning goal, my grandparents, who had come all the way from Houston to watch me, applauded loudly.

Week 20, Day 1
Pg 107

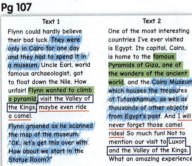

1 a both b both c Text 2 d both
  e both f Text 2 g both h Text 2

Week 20, Day 2
Pg 108

1 both texts tell us that Queen Hatshepsut's husband died and she ruled as regent for Thutmose III before she became pharaoh
2 both texts tell us that she was a strong ruler and a good politician—clever and powerful
3 she dressed like a king and wore a false beard

Week 20, Day 3
Pg 109

1 Check for correct spelling of each word.
2 a quantities b rallies c energies
  d assemblies e highways f essays
  g allies h difficulties i salaries
  j decoys k companies l deputies
  m identities n discoveries o abilities
  p policies q volleys r penalties
  s journeys t countries
3 Missing letters are underlined
  a rallies b identities c allies
  d policies e casualties f energies
  g journeys h deputies i volleys
  j assemblies k decoys l penalties
  m countries n companies o highways
  p discoveries
4 a salaries b journeys c quantities
  d countries e companies f penalties
  g decoys h highways

Week 20, Day 4
Pg 110

1 a energies b rallies c abilities
  d journeys e penalties f allies
  g assemblies h policies i difficulties
  j identities k discoveries l decoys
2 Check for correct spelling of each word.
3 a communities b laboratories
  c possibilities d universities
  e attorneys f casualties
4 a similarities b laboratories
  c possibilities
5 a universities b similarities
  c responsibilities d personalities
  e opportunities f communities

Week 20, Day 5
Pg 111

1 a soon → in a little while
  b immediately → right away
  c afterward → later on
  d before → in the past
  e then → on that occasion
  f sometimes → now and again
  g always → at all times
2 Past: last week, the other day, a while back
  Present: right now, at this time, this instant
  Future: at a later date, in a moment, in time to come
3 a every day b in about an hour
  c at exactly seven o'clock d In the future
  e the day before yesterday
4 a moment b soon c at
  d once e clock

Week 21, Day 1
Pg 112

Mia and Flynn were surprised to find out how many different skills were on board. While almost all the crew were divers, everyone seemed to have another field of expertise as well. There were researchers, oceanographers, shipwreck specialists, artifact conservationists, salvage experts, and a medical team. It seemed that Mel was leaving nothing to chance. He wanted this team to be the best.

1 b 2 b, f, g, h

Week 21, Day 2
Pg 113

"SILENCE!" yelled Bloodbath the Pirate. He was now only a hair's breadth away from Flynn's face. Flynn stood in terror, waiting for the strike of the sword. Then Bloodbath the Pirate began to speak slowly. "You come from The Atocha, eh? The Spanish ship we are after? Hmm. How very interesting. Tell me of its cargo."

"Why, it's a pirate's dream," cried Mia, diverting Bloodbath the Pirate's attention. "It's packed to the rafters with gold, silver, and gemstones! The booty on that ship will make rich pirates of us all, a thousand times over."

"All of us, hey?" He eyed her with his one good eye.

"Why of course! Spare us, and I will lead you to hidden treasures that only we know about."

1 Answers will vary. Talk through responses.

Week 21, Day 3
Pg 114

1 Check for correct spelling of each word.
2 a offering inferring conferring
  b differed preferred transferred deferred suffered
  c different d referee
3 Missing letters are underlined
  a offering b transferred c refer
  d transfer e confer f inferring
  g differed
4 a prefer b different c difference
  d referee e transfer f offer

210

ANSWERS • Weeks 21–23

Week 21, Day 4
Pg 115

1 **a** infers, inferred, inferring
  b differs, differed, differing
  c prefers, preferred, preferring
  d suffers, suffered, suffering
  e offers, offered, offering
  f transfers, transferred, transferring
  g confers, conferred, conferring
  h defers, deferred, deferring
2 Check for correct spelling of each word.
3 **a** reference   **b** inference
  c transference   **d** conference
  e preferential   **f** preference
4 **a** inferential   **b** deference
  c referred   **d** referral
5 **a** preference   **b** preferential
  c conference   **d** inferential

Week 21, Day 5
Pg 116

1 **a** will have realized   **b** will have milked
  c will have repaired   **d** will have labeled
2 **a** will have found   **b** will have tested
  c will have warmed up   **d** will have played
  e will have rested   **f** will have left
  g will have seen
3 Answers will vary. Suggested answers:
  a They will have returned by the time we get back.
  b The shops will have closed by the time you get there.
  c They will have removed the dead leaves by tomorrow morning.
  d The play will have started by the time they arrive.

Week 22, Day 1
Pg 117

> There once was a student who was as poor as a church mouse. He lived in an attic above a grocer's shop. A goblin lived with the grocer downstairs, happy that every year he was given a big bowl of oatmeal with a large lump of butter. One evening the student was very hungry. To stop his stomach rumbling, he went downstairs to the grocer's shop to buy some cheese. The student noticed that the cheese was wrapped in pages from a book of poetry.

1 b   2 b, d   3 a   4 c

Week 22, Day 2
Pg 118

> The goblin listened as the student read from the book of poetry. He was entranced. A tree was a beam of light. The leaves were emeralds, and a flower was the face of a lovely girl. Fruits were shining stars and the air was filled with beautiful music. The goblin had never known such wonders. Great feelings swept over him.
> "Such beauty! Maybe I should move into the attic," thought the goblin. "But the student is poor, and he doesn't have any porridge for me."

1 Answers will vary. Talk through responses.

Week 22, Day 3
Pg 119

1 Check for correct spelling of each word.
2 **a age:** heritage, vintage, damage, bandage, hostage, storage, manage, package, leakage, drainage, coverage, savage, voyage, postage, wastage, stoppage, marriage, dosage
  b idge: bridge, ridge
3 **a** bondage   **b** damage   **c** ridge   **d** dosage
  e heritage **f** savage   **g** bridge
4 **a** covrage coverage   **b** hostege hostage
  c postege postage   **d** leekage leakage
  e voyege voyage   **f** mariege marriage

Week 22, Day 4
Pg 120

1 **a** hostage   **b** dosage   **c** vintage   **d** savage
  e manage   **f** ridge
2 Check for correct spelling of each word.
3 **a** garbage   **b** sewerage **c** luggage
  d orphanage **e** rummage   **f** pilgrimage
4 **a** plumage   **b** garbage   **c** rummage
  d sewerage **e** luggage
5 **a** luggage   **b** garbage   **c** sewerage
  d orphanage **e** plumage   **f** beverage
  g advantage **h** cartilage

Week 22, Day 5
Pg 121

1 Commas after:
  a eat   **b** coat   **c** silver *or* gold
  d Suddenly **e** road, man **f** thief
  g players, coach **h** fast **i** honest
  j Jack *or* Jack, teacher
2 **a** As the shadows grew long, creatures emerged from their burrows.
  b After cleaning the dish, carefully place it back on the shelf.
  c If the patient's condition changes, quickly call the doctor.

Week 23, Day 1
Pg 122

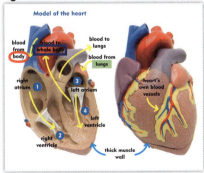

1 **a** right atrium   **b** right ventricle
  c lungs   **d** left atrium
  e left ventricle   **f** the whole body
  g muscle

Week 23, Day 2
Pg 123

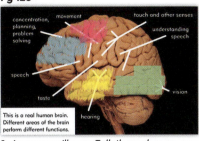

1 Answers will vary. Talk through responses.

Week 23, Day 3
Pg 124

1 Check for correct spelling of each word.
2 **a** settlement, assessment, replacement, attachment, engagement, achievement, management, assignment, abandonment, measurement
  b hardship, citizenship
  c motherhood, priesthood, likelihood, knighthood
  d stardom, chiefdom, wisdom, kingdom
3 **a** replacement   **b** likelihood
  c achievement   **d** chiefdom
  e knighthood   **f** engagement
  g measurement   **h** motherhood
4 **a** achievement   **b** chiefdom
  c hardship   **d** measurement
  e assessment   **f** replacement

Week 23, Day 4
Pg 125

1 **a** citizenship   **b** likelihood
  c wisdom   **d** attachment
  e abandonment   **f** assignment
  g management   **h** stardom
2 Check for correct spelling of each word.
3 **a** imprisonment   **b** recruitment
  c announcement   **d** embarrassment
  e advertisement
4 **a** environment   **b** companionship
  c disappointment **d** apprenticeship
5 **a** embarrassment **b** recruitment
  c encouragement **d** disappointment

Week 23, Day 5
Pg 126

1 Answers will vary. Suggested answers:
  a First   **b** Then/Next/After that
  c Next/Then, After that
  d After that/Next, Then
  e Finally, Lastly, Last of all
2 **a** finally   **b** First, then   **c** eventually
  d next   **e** afterward
3 Answers will vary. Talk through responses with students.

211

ANSWERS • Weeks 24–26

Week 24, Day 1
Pg 127

> Zoos and wildlife sanctuaries are working to save endangered animals from extinction. Some people think animals shouldn't be kept in zoos and that sanctuaries take up valuable land.
>
> Zoos are places where people can see wild animals in captivity. Modern zoos educate people about animals, conduct research, and encourage the conservation of endangered animals. Some animals, such as the California condor, have been saved from extinction by breeding programs in zoos.

1 c 2 b
3 it has been saved from extinction by breeding programs in zoos
4 Answers will vary. Talk through responses.

Week 24, Day 2
Pg 128

> Some species don't breed in captivity. Some people object to zoos because they believe it is wrong to hold animals captive. They say that zoos keep animals in poor, cramped conditions. Zoo supporters say that animals are now kept in habitats as close as possible to their natural habitat.
>
> You can see animals in their natural habitats in wildlife sanctuaries and national parks. Sanctuaries keep animals safe from poachers. African wildlife sanctuaries have increased the population of African elephants.

1 Some people are against zoos. They believe it is "wrong to hold animals captive" and that zoos keep animals in "poor conditions". Other people are in favor of zoos. They say animals are now kept in "habitats as close as possible to their natural habitat".
2 Sanctuaries keep animals safe from poachers. Sanctuaries have increased the population of African elephants.

Week 24, Day 3
Pg 129

1 Check for correct spelling of each word.
2 Missing letters are underlined
  a cos**tu**me   b app**e**tite   c stamp**ed**e
  d cro**co**dile   e **a**thlete   f vol**u**me
  g conc**lu**de   h bri**ga**de
3 Missing letters are underlined
  a **i**ndicate   b **a**ccuse   c **a**bsolute
  d c**o**mmute   e **o**perate   f **c**asserole
  g br**ig**ade   h r**e**cognize
4 a hurricane   b crocodile   c cascade
  d costume

Week 24, Day 4
Pg 130

1 a stampede   b volume   c cascade
  d crocodile   e costume   f control
  g casserole   h calculate   i athlete
2 Check for correct spelling of each word.
3 a demonstrate   b insecticide
  c balustrade   d scrutinize
  e pantomime   f pronounce
  g palindrome   h electrocute
  i cellophane   j diagnose
4 a balustrade   b demonstrate   c diagnose

Week 24, Day 5
Pg 131

1 a to, with   b of, over   c in, on
  d by, about   e at, through   f in/into, across
  g along/on, by/along
2 Across: 2 beneath 3 inside 5 down
  7 around 8 near 9 along
  Down: 1 beside 3 into 4 during 6 on

Week 25, Day 1
Pg 132

> Most earthquakes are caused by the movement of tectonic plates. This movement can create enormous pressure. Earthquakes occur when this pressure is released.
>
> As tectonic plates move, rock is pulled apart and pushed together. This creates stress in the rock. Rock is brittle and with enough force, will eventually break, slip, or shift. When this occurs, all the stored energy is released. This release of energy causes the surrounding rock to vibrate.

1 b   2 d   3 c   4 a

Week 25, Day 2
Pg 133

> Although it is impossible to predict when an earthquake will happen, there are instruments such as seismometers that measure vibrations in the ground. As they record the tiniest of movements, seismometers can detect the minor vibrations that often occur just before a big quake. The digital information recorded by seismometers is turned into a visual record on a seismograph. Seismographs display the vibrations caused by an earthquake as a series of lines.
> The total energy released by an earthquake is measured on the Richter scale.

1 seismometers, seismograph, Richter scale
2 to inform about earthquakes and tools that can help measure vibrations in the ground
3 Answers will vary. Talk through responses.

Week 25, Day 3
Pg 134

1 Check for correct spelling of each word.
2 a action, protection, election, direction, connection, collection, relation, operation, situation, population, attention, application, celebration, introduction
  b discussion, television, conclusion, expansion, admission
  c physician
3 Missing letters are underlined
  a direc**tion**   b popula**tion**
  c celebra**tion**   d protec**tion**
  e expan**sion**   f discus**sion**
  g physi**cian**   h conclu**sion**
4 a acshun action
  b introduccian introduction
  c conection connection
  d situashion situation

Week 25, Day 4
Pg 135

1 a expansion   b physician   c celebration
  d election   e conclusion   f population
  g direction   h collection
2 Check for correct spelling of each word.
3 a opposition   b concession   c institution
  d tactician   e communication   f association
4 a contribution   b mathematician
  c competition   d organization
  e tactician   f opposition

Week 25, Day 5
Pg 136

1 Colons after: a basket   b animal
  c stones   d wanted   e says
  f books   g envelope
2 Answers will vary. Suggested answers:
  a I love all kinds of Italian food: pasta, prosciutto, and best of all, pizza.
  b There is one main reason why I like to read books: I learn so much from them.
  c I can name a few breeds of cat: Siamese, Burmese, and Persian.
  d We were given a list of items to add to our first aid kits: plasters, gauze dressings, and a variety of bandages.
  e There are many chores my little sister helps me with: feeding the dog, folding the laundry, tidying the closets.

Week 26, Day 1
Pg 137

1 c   2 d   3 d   4 a

Week 26, Day 2
Pg 138

212

ANSWERS • Weeks 26–28

1 It has wheels to help it move across the planet. It has a place for a camera, which will allow it to photograph the planet.
2 the illustration suggests that the terrain is much like a desert, with flat areas, rocks and hills

Week 26, Day 3
Pg 139
1 Check for correct spelling of each word.
2 a aching, choral, chrome, chemical, echidna, arachnid, chameleon
b attached, detach, chutney, charcoal, anchovy, chimpanzee, brooch, cockroach, bachelor, check, chariot
c cache, chiffon
3 a detach   b bachelor   c charcoal
d chariot   e cache   f chimpanzee
g cockroach
4 a brooch   b chimpanzee   c chameleon
d chariot

Week 26, Day 4
Pg 140
1 a chutney b brooch c echidna d check
e choral f aching g anchovy h chrome
i arachnid j chiffon
2 Check for correct spelling of each word.
3 a epoch   b crochet   c charisma
d chauffeur   e avalanche   f archaic
4 a chiropractor   b choreograph
c cholesterol
5 a chamomile   b chauffeur   c choreograph
d chiropractor   e epoch

Week 26, Day 5
Pg 141
1 *Commas after:*
a Billy, door   b bears, country
c everything, everything
d spectators, late   e players, squad
2 a There were hordes of people—old and young—at the concert.
b The buildings—many made of granite—were impressive.
c The novel— her first—is about a brother and sister who solve a great mystery.
d Alex—his head held high—walked up to the stage to receive his prize.
e All of the houses—from the smallest to the largest — were painted blue.

Week 27, Day 1
Pg 142

> A solar power station uses either solar cells or concentrating solar power dishes.
> Solar cells are also known as photovoltaic cells. They convert light directly into electricity.
> Concentrating solar power dishes use hundreds of mirrors to focus the sun's energy into heat. It can concentrate the sun's rays thousands of times to produce temperatures more than 1,800°F. This heats a chemical, which in turn produces steam to power a generator, just like a fossil fuel-burning power station.

1 c   2 d   3 a   4 b

Week 27, Day 2
Pg 143

> **How a solar cell works**
> Solar cells convert light from the sun into electricity. They have no moving parts, consume no fuel, and create no pollution.
> **From light to electricity**
> 1 Light is made up of particles known as photons. Photons enter the cell.
> 2 Photons collide with electrons inside the cell.
> 3 Electrons pass from one semiconductor to the other, and then onto the metal-conductor strips. The flow of electrons produces electricity.

1 to explain how a solar cell works
2 photons
3 photons collide with electrons
4 electrons, semiconductors, metal-conductor
5 Answers will vary. Talk through responses.

Week 27, Day 3
Pg 144
1 Check for correct spelling of each word.
2 a yacht   b calendar   c twelfth
d government
3 a neither   b government   c nervous
d naturally   e recommend   f definite
g beginning
4 a government   b beginning   c nervous
d original   e recommend   f people
g neither   h definite   i harass
j persuade   k courage   l similar

Week 27, Day 4
Pg 145
1 a width   b naturally   c twelfth
d beginning   e people   f variety
g recommend   h similar
2 Check for correct spelling of each word.
3 a parallel   b unanimous
c pronunciation   d temporary
e enough   f ceremony
4 a enough   b temporary
c unanimous   d occurred
5 a restaurant   b parallel
c ceremony   d guarantee

Week 27, Day 5
Pg 146
1 a either, or   b not, but   c whether, or
d neither, nor/either, or/not only, but also
e both, and/not only, but also/either, or
f not only, but also/both, and
2 a neither → either *or* → nor
b and → but
c but → or
d and also → but also
e both → neither *or* nor → and
f nor → or
3 a I like neither snakes nor lizards.
b She has not only longer hair, but also curlier hair.

REVIEW 3
Spelling
Pg 147
1 a bridge   b voyage   c courage
d nuisance
2 b   3 hazardous
4 Missing letters are underlined
a attach**ment**   b knight**hood**
c citizen**ship**   d engage**ment**
5 a casserole   b celebrations   c referee
6 chariot

Grammar
Pg 148–149
1 *Commas after:*
a enclosure, giraffes   b competitors, eighty
2 a immediately   b soon   c before
d annually
3 a will have started   b will have gone
4 *Commas after:*
a movie, child   b us   c bakes   d street
5 a then   b eventually   c after   d finally
6 a in   b under   c behind   d above
7 a of, from   b with, for   c past, to   d in, on
8 *Replace comma with colon after:*
a pets   b areas
9 *Dashes after:*
a boat, dinghy   b fruits, oranges
c morning, actually
10 a and   b or   c but   d or

Comprehension
Pg 150
1 b   2 d   3 a   4 c   5 b   6 d   7 a   8 c
9 The wizard has the power to turn humans into animals. Only he can turn the dog back into a human.
10 The dog could talk because he had once been a human.

Week 28, Day 1
Pg 152

> "Alex, this job is very important," he whispered. "It's undercover, so don't tell anyone. I'll leave your assignments near the compost bin out in the back."
> Mr. Piper looked up and down the street. "First I need you to get me some soil samples from Old Man Oliver's garden and spare block. You can leave them by the trash can. Make sure no one sees you. Top-secret," he said as he tapped the side of his nose.

1 b   2 c, d, f   3 b

ANSWERS • Weeks 28–30

Week 28, Day 2
Pg 153

Alex knew how she was going to measure Mr. Piper's spare block. In her sports class she had been told that each of her marching steps was about two feet. As the block was rectangular, Alex was going to march around two of the sides. She'd count how many steps were on each side, and then convert the steps into feet.

If Mr. Piper caught her, Alex was going to say she was practicing her marching.

1 measuring Mr Piper's spare block
2 a Alex was going to "measure Mr Piper's spare block"
  b Alex was going to "count how many steps were on each side"
  c Alex was going to "march around two of the sides"
3 Answers will vary. Talk through responses.

Week 28, Day 3
Pg 154

1 Check for correct spelling of each word.
2 a oo: igloo, baboon, lagoon, snooze, loosen, hooray, shampoo, cocoon, groove, noodle, oozing, cuckoo, ballooned, boomerang
  b ou: wound, should, through, troupe, coupon, routine
3 Missing letters are underlined
  a igloo   b cocoon   c baboon   d groove
  e lagoon   f troupe   g snooze   h noodle
  i loosen   j oozing   k wound   l coupon
  m mousse   n ballooned
4 a troupe   b groove   c oozing
  d routine e wound   f ballooned
  g shampoo h baboon   i lagoon
  j boomerang k noodle   l hooray
  m snooze   n cocoon

Week 28, Day 4
Pg 155

1 a thru through   b cuckou cuckoo
  c snoze snooze   d babone baboon
  e noudle noodle
2 Check for correct spelling of each word.
3 a typhoon   b hooligan   c tattoo
  d mongoose   e schooner   f souvenir
4 a acoustics b typhoon   c cockatoo
  d schooner
5 a cockatoo   b harpoon   c acoustics
  d souvenir   e schooner   f bassoon
  g tattoo   h mongoose

Week 28, Day 5
Pg 156

1 a that   b who   c whom   d which   e whose
2 a who   b whose c that   d which
3 a I will give the apple to the boy who left his post-game snack at home.
  b The pirates are looking for a chest that contains treasure.
  c I went to the doctor whose consulting rooms are close by.
  d Last night I watched a movie which has won several awards.
  e I have had a reply from the people whom I invited.

Week 29, Day 1
Pg 157

Sweat poured from Mia's brow as she lifted the heavy machete to clear the jungle ahead. As they struggled on, the jungle became more treacherous. At times they could barely get a foothold in the soft mud of the rainforest floor. Mia stopped to catch her breath. "This humidity is too much. I'm melting. The jungle is so thick I don't think we'll ever get there!"

Flynn glanced at his watch. It was already 3 p.m. At this rate they'd be lucky to make it to the cliffs by sunset!

Mia stopped for some water and found a chocolate bar. She broke off pieces of chocolate for Flynn and Professor Drake.

1 c
2 b, d, f
3 c

Week 29, Day 2
Pg 158

The Mayan cities survived until 1697 when the last city, Tayasal, was overtaken by Spanish invaders. The king of Tayasal, King Can Ek, and his people vanished into the forest and were never found. They took with them the treasures of the city, including a huge library of Mayan scrolls. These scrolls apparently recorded ancient Mayan medicines, astrology, and the secrets of eternal life. It is believed that King Can Ek took his people and library to caves deep within the Mayan mountains.

In 1994 an American archaeologist stumbled upon a clue to the whereabouts of King Can Ek's library—an ancient glowing stone. Finding the library of the Maya would unravel the mystery surrounding South America's oldest civilization and answer some of our most puzzling questions.

1 their city was overtaken by Spanish invaders
2 their treasures were important to them and they didn't want them falling into the hands of the invaders
3 modern humans would learn the secrets of the Mayans

Week 29, Day 3
Pg 159

1 Check for correct spelling of each word.
2 a wh: awhile, wharf, whiten, whistles, everywhere, whereby, whisker, whirlpool, whine, cartwheel, wheedle, somewhat, somewhere
  b gh: aghast, ghetto
  c ph: graphic, pheasant, phantom, headphones, geography
3 Missing letters are underlined
  a somewhat   b wheedle   c geography
  d headphones e ghetto   f whiten
  g cartwheel   h phantom
4 a headphones b whisker   c wharf
  d everywhere e cartwheel f awhile

Week 29, Day 4
Pg 160

1 a pheasant   b wheedle   c phantom
  d whirlpool e geography f graphic
  g aghast   h ghetto
2 Check for correct spelling of each word.
3 a emphasize b hieroglyphics c decipher
  d metaphor   e cenotaph   f asphalt
4 a lymph   b homophone   c emphasize
5 a lymph   b emphasize
  c hieroglyphics d decipher
  e periphery f asphalt

Week 29, Day 5
Pg 161

1 Circle a doctor b trooper c vice, president
  d president e professor f sergeant g chief
2 a The pilot introduced himself to the passengers as Captain Edwards.
  b The city of Houston in Texas was named after Governor Sam Houston.
  c My grandmother saw Pope John Paul II when he visited the United States.
  d My uncle, Colonel Cooper, is stationed at Scot Air Force Base in Illinois.
  e In 2016 Queen Elizabeth II celebrated her 90th birthday.

Week 30, Day 1
Pg 162

Heavy thumps and loud crashes filled the darkness. The strange noises jolted Flynn awake. Mia was already up looking for a flashlight. She grabbed a carved spear from the wall as she and Flynn crept down the hallway to Uncle Earl's study.

Mia raised her spear. "OK, Flynn, on the count of three, you fling open the door. Ready?"

Mia mouthed, "One... two... three!" and Flynn threw the door wide open.

Uncle Earl was standing at the top of a ladder leaning against a bookshelf. As he turned, startled, he dropped a small box. Mia and Flynn stared at the floor of the study. It was a gigantic mess of books, papers, folders, videos, cassettes, and overflowing boxes.

1 a   2 c   3 b   4 c

Week 30, Day 2
Pg 163

"Why do you need this photo right now?" asked Flynn. "It's 5 a.m.! Can't it wait?"

Mia held up a faded photograph of two men eating pizza. She had found it sticking out of the top of a book. "Is this it?" she asked.

"Yes, that's it!" Uncle Earl took the photograph and held it in the light. "Well done, Mia. I must have used it as a bookmark the other day when I was reading."

Mia and Flynn looked at the photograph to see what all the fuss was about. Uncle Earl looked very young and had a full head of curly hair. The other man was thin and wore a beaming smile. They were sitting at a café table with a glass raised in one hand and a slice of pizza in the other.

1 It was faded. Uncle Earl looked "very young". He [Earl] "had a full head of hair".
2 "I must have used it as a bookmark the other day when I was reading."

ANSWERS • Weeks 30–32

Week 30, Day 3
Pg 164
1 Check for correct spelling of each word.
2 a ance: distance, entrance, elegance, allowance, appearance, arrogance, brilliance, importance, resistance
  b ence: absence, existence, persistence, silence, evidence, violence, difference, obedience, patience, audience, excellence
3 Missing letters are underlined
  a obedi**ence** b allow**ance** c persist**ence**
  d evid**ence** e import**ance** f excell**ence**
  g brilli**ance** h sil**ence**
4 a entrance b audience c elegance
  d absence e persistence f patience
  g resistance h difference

Week 30, Day 4
Pg 165
1 a brilliance b appearance c silence
  d audience e violence f difference
  g obedience h excellence i distance
  j existence k resistance l persistence
2 Check for correct spelling of each word.
3 a endurance b ignorance c magnificence
  d innocence e annoyance f intelligence
4 a inheritance b intelligence c acceptance
5 a interference b annoyance
  c endurance d fragrance
  e magnificence f inheritance

Week 30, Day 5
Pg 166
1 a complex b complex c complex
  d complex e compound f complex
  g compound
2 a I've had lunch, but I'm still hungry.
  b I will visit them if they are at home.
  c I made an appointment before I went to see him.
  d I will feed the dog while you unpack the dishwasher.

Week 31, Day 1
Pg 167

> I remember fallen trunks
> and the rings of growth revealed in death
> Fallen yellow sorbet-colored leaves
> over dusty paths just quelled by a storm
> The blue-green firs, dusted with gray
> in staggered rows, silent choristers* in stalls.
> *choir members

1 c 2 a 3 d 4 c

Week 31, Day 2
Pg 168

> The blue-green firs, dusted with gray
> in staggered rows, silent choristers in stalls.
>
> I remember a sprinting squirrel
> stopping mid-tree to eye my ride
> and the patient inspection of rocks by my horse
> as he picked our way across the stream.

1 sprinting squirrel stopping

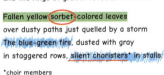

2 a sprinting, stopping
  b they help use visualise how the squirrel suddenly stopped in the middle of its run up the tree
3 patience
4 Answers will vary. Talk through responses.

Week 31, Day 3
Pg 169
1 Check for correct spelling of each word.
2 Missing syllables are underlined
  a Satur**day** b sand**wich** c mar**ma**lade
  d **at**las e vol**ca**no f Tues**day**
3 a volcano b saxophone c python d atlas
4 a marmalade b mentor c America
  d watt e cannibal f diesel
  g volt h Wednesday i vandal
  j python k boycott l Tuesday

Week 31, Day 4
Pg 170
1 a <u>volcanoe</u> volcano b <u>cardigen</u> cardigan
  c <u>pithon</u> python
  d <u>marmalaid</u> marmalade
  e <u>sandwicth</u> sandwich f <u>Janury</u> January
  g <u>atlass</u> atlas h <u>Saterday</u> Saturday
2 Check for correct spelling of each word.
3 a Jacuzzi b guillotine c pasteurize
  d Cartesian e silhouette f mesmerize
4 a Fahrenheit b Braille c silhouette
5 a algorithm b pasteurize c Fahrenheit
  d Braille e Herculean

Week 31, Day 5
Pg 171
1 a the tallest of the triplets
  b like her two older siblings
  c it only came out last week
  d the one with the widest brim
  e see page 32
2 a Danny Lopez (last year's winner) will probably win the event again this year.
  b The last time we saw them was on our visit to Los Angeles (in California).
  c My little brother is crying because he can't find Bootsy (his teddy bear).
  d George and Cassie (the twins next door) invited me to their birthday party.
  e We're spending the summer at Land's End (my grandparent's farm).

Week 32, Day 1
Pg 172

> There was once an Emperor who liked fine clothes more than anything. One day, two traders arrived in the kingdom. They said they could make beautiful cloth, invisible to anyone who was stupid or unfit for his job.
> The traders set up looms and set about pretending to weave the invisible cloth. After a while, the Emperor sent his Chief Minister to check on their progress.
> When the Chief Minister saw the looms, they looked empty. "I mustn't let anyone know I see nothing," he thought. So he said to the traders, "Wonderful patterns! Wonderful colors! I shall inform the Emperor."

1 Answers will vary. Talk through responses.

Week 32, Day 2
Pg 173

> The Great Procession began and the Emperor strode through the streets. No-one would dare admit that they couldn't see his fine set of robes, until a child called out, "He's got nothing on! The Emperor has nothing on!" "Shhhh!" said the child's father.
> The child's words moved through the crowd. The Emperor realized he had been tricked, but he held his head even higher and strode on, not wanting to spoil the procession, while his officials carried a long train that wasn't there at all!

1 Answers will vary. Talk through responses.

Week 32, Day 3
Pg 174
1 Check for correct spelling of each word.
2 basically, beautifully, clearly, completely, daily, enormously, formerly, hastily, hurriedly, ideally, largely, legally, loosely, possibly, primarily, privately, quietly, simply, thoroughly, totally
3 Missing syllables are underlined
  a thor**ough**ly b e**nor**mously c i**dea**lly
  d hurri**ed**ly e le**gal**ly f primari**ly**
  g basi**cally** h to**tal**ly i loose**ly**
  j quick**ly** k possi**bly** l priv**ate**ly
4 a loosely b quietly/privately
  c largely/totally/completely/basically
  d daily e formerly
  f beautifully g hastily/hurriedly

Week 32, Day 4
Pg 175
1 a ideally b legally c hastily
  d daily e beautifully f simply
2 Check for correct spelling of each word.
3 a automatically b occasionally
  c deliberately d temporarily
  e surprisingly f approximately
4 a especially b deliberately
  c occasionally d approximately
5 a particularly/especially b automatically
  c especially/particularly d approximately
  e temporarily f occasionally
  g surprisingly

Week 32, Day 5
Pg 176
1 a preposition b adverb c adverb
  d preposition e preposition f preposition
2 a around b underneath c above
  d inside e aboard f after
3 a around b above c aboard
  d down e under/underneath
  f beyond

215

ANSWERS • Weeks 33–35

Week 33, Day 1
Pg 177

> The Polar Auroras are a (spectacular) natural phenomena near the North and South Poles. They are colored lights that form ribbons and spirals in the sky.
>
> The Polar Auroras are caused by solar winds flowing past the Earth. Solar wind is made up of particles from the Sun's atmosphere. These particles are very high in energy. When solar wind enters the Earth's atmosphere, it mixes with gases which then release light.
>
> The Polar Auroras can only be seen at the most northern and southern parts of the Earth.

1 c   2 b

3 *Answers will vary. Suggested answer:* Solar wind is made up of particles from the Sun's atmosphere.

Week 33, Day 2
Pg 178

> Deforestation: (pros) and (cons)
>
> Some people argue that deforestation in the Amazon destroys animal habitats. They want other countries to stop buying timber from the Amazon. Then, there would be no incentive for people to cut down the forest.
>
> Deforestation is also bad for the environment. During heavy rains, pesticides from crops flow off the land and into rivers. This damages river wildlife.
>
> Other people argue that deforestation helps the economy in South America. Farmers clear land to grow crops, such as coconuts, oranges, coffee, and soybeans. Agriculture and the timber industry provide jobs for people. The country also makes money from selling timber.

1 some people think that deforestation in the Amazon is a bad thing, while others believe it is a good thing

2 **Pros**: Farmers can grow crops on the cleared land. This provides jobs for people and is good for the economy. Selling the timber from trees that have been cut down makes money for the country. **Cons**: Destroys animal habitats. Pesticides from crops run into rivers and destroy river wildlife.

Week 33, Day 3
Pg 179

1 Check for correct spelling of each word.
2 a mosque   b unique   c brusque
  d conquer e baroque f physique
  g grotesque h opaque i plaque
  j pique   k lacquer
3 a mosque   b macaque c bouquet
  d oblique e unique   f grotesque
4 a boutique b technique c mystique
  d lacquer e unique   f plaque
  g opaque

Week 33, Day 4
Pg 180

1 a Barocque Baroque   b racket racquet
  c boucket bouquet   d opaike opaque
  e techniqe technique f lacker lacquer
  g placqe plaque

2 Check for correct spelling of each word.
3 a etiquette b marquee   c masquerade
  d croquette e marquetry
4 a discotheque b clique   c tourniquet
  d croquette e statuesque
5 a croquette b marquee   c masquerade
  d etiquette e critique f tourniquet

Week 33, Day 5
Pg 181

1 a verb   b subject   c subject   d object
  e verb   f subject   g object
2 **Across:** 1 battles 3 scarves 6 goals 9 meat
  10 songs 11 trips
  Down: 2 teams 3 snow 4 eggs 5 patients
  7 tigers 8 steaks
3 *Answers may vary. Suggested answers:*
  a Sean is wearing the new baseball uniform.
  b Ella and Jack are making decorations for the party.

Week 34, Day 1
Pg 182

> **Text 1**
> The respiratory system brings oxygen into the body and removes carbon dioxide from it.
> The body's cells need oxygen to survive, and carbon dioxide is one of their waste products.
> The air you breathe in moves down the trachea into the soft, spongy lungs. It flows through narrower and narrower tubes in the lungs. At the ends of the tubes are alveoli, which look like very small balloons.
>
> **Text 2**
> Air travels through your nose to your lungs via the trachea (windpipe). It divides into two branches, one for each lung. The branches divide into narrower and narrower branches until they reach air sacs called alveoli. Alveoli look like tiny bunches of grapes.
> When you breathe in, the lungs take up oxygen from the air. When you breathe out, carbon dioxide is released from your body.

1 a both texts b both texts c Text 2
  d Text 2   e Text 1   f Text 2
  g both texts h both texts

Week 34, Day 2
Pg 183

> **Text 1**
> The digestive system breaks food down into nutrients that the body absorbs. It expels whatever is left over.
> Digestion starts in the mouth. Chewing breaks food into small pieces. Saliva contains an enzyme, which also helps to break food down. After swallowing, food moves down the esophagus to the stomach.
> The stomach uses acids, enzymes and its own movements to turn the pieces of food into a thick liquid. It then squeezes small amounts of the liquid into the small intestine.
>
> **Text 2**
> The main function of your digestive system is to break down food, extract nutrients and water from that food, and to excrete waste. Digestion breaks food into tiny parts called molecules. Your body uses these molecules as fuel to keep you healthy and active.
> Chewing breaks up the food. When you chew, you produce a digestive juice called saliva. Saliva helps to break down the food into tiny parts.
> When you swallow, your esophagus moves the food to your stomach.

1 the digestive system breaks down food, extracts the nutrients and gets rid of waste
2 the food is broken into small pieces, then saliva helps to break down the food
3 it moves down the oesophagus into the stomach

Week 34, Day 3
Pg 184

1 Check for correct spelling of each word.
2 horrible, horrified, horrify, horrifying, horror, flat, flatten, flattened, flatter, flattest, reside, resided, resident, residential, residing, simple, simplest, simplification, simplify, simply
3 Missing letters are underlined
  a s**i**mplif**i**cat**i**on b fl**a**ttest c s**i**mplest
  d res**i**ding   e s**i**mply   f res**i**ded
  g h**o**rrify   h re**s**ide
4 a simple   b horror   c simplify
  d resident   e flattened f horrify
  g residential

Week 34, Day 4
Pg 185

1 a flatter, flattest, flatten, flattened
  b simply, simplify, simplest, simplification
  c residing, resided, resident, residential
  d horrible, horrify, horrifying, horrified
2 Check for correct spelling of each word.
3 a benefiting b reception   c benefited
  d receive   e beneficiary f receiving
4 a receipt   b receive   c beneficial
  d reception
5 a received   b benefit   c receipt   d receiving

Week 34, Day 5
Pg 186

1 Check b, c, f, h
2 a An egg has been added to the mixture.
  b Their empire is being expanded.
  c A hissing sound could be heard.
  d Lots of cars are being produced.
  e The valuable painting has been stolen.

Week 35, Day 1
Pg 187

> 18 Main Street, Los Angeles, CA 90012
> Belinda Tochner
> Consumer Relations Manager
> SuperSafe Insurance Ltd
> Dear Ms. Tochner,
> COMPLAINT
> Policy No: 98765432
> I am writing to complain about my car insurance claim being rejected.
> On November 22nd, 2009, I arranged car insurance with your company by telephone. On November 25th, I telephoned again to ask that my insurance also cover my 20-year-old daughter, as she would also be driving the car.

1 b   2 c   3 a

Week 35, Day 2
Pg 188

> I am most (upset) that when I telephoned on January 14th this year to make a claim for an accident that my daughter had had in my car, I was informed that my claim was rejected. The reason provided was the policy did not cover my daughter. Furthermore, the claims consultant said there was no record that my policy had been extended, to my daughter or to anyone else.
> However, as I noted earlier, I did call SuperSafe Insurance to extend the insurance. To prove this, I have included with this letter a copy of my telephone bill, which shows that the call was made to your company. I have underlined the call on the bill. The claims consultant I spoke to was Ben Wilkinson.
> I believe you made a mistake in not changing my insurance policy, and I would like you to fix this and pay the claim I have made. I look forward to hearing from you and to having this matter resolved as quickly as possible.

1 upset

216

ANSWERS • Weeks 35–36

2 she includes a copy of her telephone bill, showing that the call was made to the company and also provides the name of the claims consultant
3 Answers will vary. Talk through responses.

Week 35, Day 3
Pg 189
1 Check for correct spelling of each word.
2 Missing syllables have been underlined
  a croiss<u>ant</u>   **b** <u>ge</u>lato   **c** bru<u>nette</u>
  d <u>o</u>pera   **e** <u>bal</u>let   **f** <u>rap</u>port
  g so<u>pra</u>no   **h** <u>gen</u>re
3 a ballet   **b** macaroni   **c** baguette
  d pizza
4 a macaroni   **b** dossier   **c** sauté
  d gelato   **e** studio   **f** pizza
  g soprano   **h** rapport   **i** pasta
  j sabotage   **k** baguette   **l** scenario

Week 35, Day 4
Pg 190
1 a brunette   **b** genre   **c** opera
  d pizza   **e** cliché   **f** ballet
  g sauté   **h** cafe   **i** baguette
  j studio   **k** gelato
2 Check for correct spelling of each word.
3 **Italian:** spaghetti, lasagne, staccato, extravaganza
  French: saboteur, entree, chauffeur, entrepreneur, restaurateur, reconnaissance
4 a extravaganza   **b** entree   **c** chauffeur

Week 35, Day 5
Pg 191
1 a sentence   **b** sentence
  c sentence fragment   **d** sentence fragment
  e sentence fragment   **f** sentence
  g sentence
2 Answers will vary. Suggested answers:
  a On Sunday we're going to the beach with our neighbors.
  b I had to ride the train to practice because I missed the bus.
3 Underline: Scared, Not really, You, A bit nervous, Not long now

Week 36, Day 1
Pg 192

> We know that the thylacine once lived in New Guinea and mainland Australia because fossils have been found in these places. But these populations died out—killed by the introduced dingoes, or wild dogs, of the Aboriginal peoples. The island of Tasmania then became the thylacine's last refuge. When European farmers arrived in Tasmania, they believed the thylacines were responsible for killing sheep. In 1888, a bounty was put on the thylacine's head. Killing them was now a profitable business encouraged by the government.

1 c   **2** b   **3** d   **4** a

Week 36, Day 2
Pg 193

> More tigers lurked in the Siberian woods than anyone thought. Finding 600 instead of an expected 300 has increased the chance that the magnificent Siberian tiger will survive. Conservationists were thrilled to find out that the Siberian tiger population was twice as big as believed. Siberian tigers live in the dense forests of Siberia. This cold and wild area is called the taiga (TIE-ga) and is vast enough to help the tigers hide from us. Poachers kill some, and forestry and mining have an impact on their habitat. But for now, the tiger seems safe.

1 a hid   **b** thick   **c** very big
2 conservationists

Week 36, Day 3
Pg 194
1 Check for correct spelling of each word.
2 a anti: antismoking, antidote, antifreeze, antihero, antisocial, anticlimax, antislavery, antiseptic, antibiotic
  b circum: circumvent, circumscribe
  c extra: extramural
  d semi: semifinal, semicircle, semiformal, semidarkness, semicolon, semiskilled, semiprecious, semidetached
3 Missing syllables are underlined
  a semi<u>dark</u>ness   **b** ex<u>tra</u>mural
  c semi<u>circle</u>   **d** semi<u>co</u>lon
  e semi<u>de</u>tached   **f** semi<u>fi</u>nal
  g <u>an</u>tihero   **h** antis<u>mok</u>ing
4 a antidote   **b** semicircle   **c** circumvent
  d antifreeze   **e** antislavery   **f** anticlimax

Week 36, Day 4
Pg 195
1 a antedote antidote
  b semefinal semifinal
  c antebiotic antibiotic
  d anteseptik antiseptic
  e antislavary antislavery
  f semiformale semiformal
  g antisocel antisocial
2 Check for correct spelling of each word.
3 a circumnavigate   **b** extracurricular
  c circumference   **d** antihistamine
  e extraordinary   **f** antibacterial
  g extraterrestrial
4 a extracurricular   **b** semipermanent
  c antibacterial   **d** semiconscious

Week 36, Day 5
Pg 196
1 a Mandy, why are you wearing your best shoes?
  b When we drove through the forest, we saw maple, pine, and fir trees.
  c You have completed all your chores, haven't you?
  d I ordered him a hamburger, but he refused to eat it.
  e Yes, I've been to New York, and so has Ruby.
2 a "How good was that!" exclaimed Alex, as he stepped off the ride.
  b When she saw the creature, Jemma asked, "What is it?"
  c "The clouds are gathering," said the man, "and I think it might rain."
  d "I'd like some roast potatoes," said Aunt Lydia, "and a spoonful of mashed pumpkin."
  e "Is this your wallet?" asked the girl, "or does it belong to someone else?"
3 a My cousins, Max and Sophie Harris, are coming to visit us on Saturday.
  b They have been to Yosemite National Park in California's Sierra Nevada Mountains.
  c Did you see the Statue of Liberty when you went to New York?

REVIEW 4
Spelling
Pg 197
1 a semifinal   **b** dossier   **c** antibiotic
  d rapport
2 c   **3** gelato
4 Missing letters are underlined
  a c<u>u</u>ckoo   **b** <u>i</u>gloo   **c** w<u>o</u>und   **d** n<u>oo</u>dle
5 a simplest   **b** ideally
6 martial   **7** headphones

Grammar
Pg 198–199
1 a who had helped her once before
  b which was large and fierce
2 a mrs. jones Mrs. Jones
  b captain reynolds Captain Reynolds
3 a complex   **b** compound   **c** compound
  d complex
4 a (the one with the leather cover)
  b (a very old one)
5 a Circle: outside   Underline: past
  b Circle: nearby   Underline: to
6 a The little girl is singing
  b The police have arrested
7 a the grass   **b** the roofs
8 a The lightning rod
  b by the fire fighters
  c have been spotted
  d attended the conference
9 On my bed I put it on my bed.
10 a "When is their train due to arrive?" asked Ryan.
  b There was so much food on the table: platters of meat, salads, fruit, and little cakes.

Comprehension
Pg 200–201
1 b   **2** d   **3** a   **4** b   **5** a   **6** b   **7** d
8 c   **9** c
10 Responses will differ. Talk through answers together.

Reading Eggs *Reading for Fifth Grade*
ISBN: 978-1-74215-351-3
Copyright Blake eLearning USA 2018

Published by:
Blake eLearning USA
37 West 26th Street,
Suite 201
New York, NY 10010

www.readingeggspress.com

Publisher: Katy Pike
Series writer: Laura Anderson
Series editor: Amy Russo
Editor: Sara Leman

Designed and typeset by The Modern Art Production Group
Printed by 1010 Printing International LTD

The following extracts are reproduced with permission from the publisher, Blake Publishing and Blake Education.

Week 1 *Above and Below,* Christopher Stitt, Blake Education, 2001. **Week 2** *Just Call Me Jungle Boy*, Christopher Stitt, Blake Education, 2001. **Week 3** *Book Review,* Mark Stafford, Blake Education, 2011. **Week 4** *The Wolf and Seven Little Kids,* retold by Mark Stafford, Blake Education, 2011. **Week 5** *A Journal of a Tour of Discovery Across the Blue Mountains,* Gregory Blaxland, 1813. **Week 6** *Gold,* Nicholas Brasch, Blake Education, 2009. **Week 7** *Fitness,* Susan Mansfield, Blake Education, 2007. **Week 8** *Press Release,* Liz Flaherty, Blake Education, 2009. **Week 9** *Modern Wonders,* Nicholas Brasch and Mark Stafford, Blake Education, 2009. **Week 10** *Runaway,* Chris Bell, Blake Education, 2002. **Week 11** *Chatroom Trap,* Damian Morgan, Blake Education, 2002. **Week 12** *Racing for the Birdman,* Katrina O'Neil, Blake Education, 2002. **Week 13** *The Village Blacksmith,* Henry Wadsworth Longfellow, 1840. **Week 14** *The Four Musicians,* retold by Mark Stafford, Blake Education, 2011. **Week 15** *Volcano,* Ian Rohr, Blake Education, 2006. **Week 16** *Wild Weather,* Ian Rohr, Blake Education, 2006. **Week 17** *Technological Wonders,* Nicholas Brasch and Mark Stafford, Blake Education, 2009. **Week 18** *Renewable Resources,* Nicholas Brasch, Blake Education, 2009. **Week 19** *Back-stage Betrayal,* Robyn Opie, Blake Education, 2002. **Week 20** *Egyptian Queen,* Katrina O'Neil and Lisa Thompson, Blake Education, 2002. **Week 21** *Diving for the Ghost Galleon,* Lisa Thompson, Blake Education, 2002. **Week 2** *The Goblin and the Grocer,* retold by Mark Stafford, Blake Education, 2011. **Week 23** *Body Systems,* Mark Stafford, Blake Education, 2007. **Week 24** *Endangered Animals,* Katy Pike, Blake Education, 2006. **Week 25** *Earthquake,* Ian Rohr, Blake Education, 2006. **Week 26** *Technological Wonders,* Nicholas Brasch and Mark Stafford, Blake Education, 2009. **Wee 27** *Renewable Resources,* Nicholas Brasch, Blake Education, 2009. **Week 28** *Operation Green Thumbs,* Lisa Thompson, Blake Education, 2002. **Week 29** *Decoding the Mayan Marvels,* Katrina O'Neil, Blake Education, 2002. **Week 30** *Quest for the Cup,* Katrina O'Neil and Lisa Thompson, Blake Education, 2002. **Week 31** *Coffee Creek,* Mark Stafford, Blake Education, 2011. **Week 32** *The Emperor's New Clothes,* retold by Mark Stafford, Blake Education, 2011. **Week 33** *Natural Wonders,* Nicholas Brasch and Mark Stafford, Blake Education, 2009. **Week 34** *Body Systems,* Mark Stafford, Blake Education, 2007. **Week 35** *Letter of Complaint,* Mark Stafford, Blake Education, 2011. **Week 36** *On the Edge of Extinction,* Claire Craig, Sharon Dagleish and Ian Rohr, Blake Education, 2003.